"In this landmark work, Mansoor Adayfi gives us a guided tour through the nightmarish landscape of Guantánamo. He tells a tale of both casual cruelty and organized sadism that should make every American politician redden with shame. But this memoir offers much more than just a gruesome portrait of a bureaucracy gone berserk, for it describes the fierce resistance and ultimate redemption of an innocent Yemeni man consigned to a hellish prison. Let us hope that *Don't Forget Us Here* will spark a long overdue reckoning with the horrors of Guantánamo and its many victims."

—**Ron Chernow**, former president of PEN America
and bestselling author of *Grant* and *Hamilton*

"This is a wholly enthralling, relentlessly enraging, and unexpectedly funny book about one man caught in the absurdist world of the War on Terror. With his mordant wit and astonishing perseverance, Mansoor is impossible not to root for. This is a contemporary *Unbroken* with vital lessons for the American military-intelligence complex, exposing how an ostensibly moral nation becomes a state sponsor of torture."

—**Dave Eggers**, Pulitzer Prize finalist and
winner of the Dayton Literary Peace Prize

"An incredible story! I am grateful to this joyously heartbreaking book for reminding me of what it means to be not just human, but humane. Once we read his story, we too must become committed, held accountable and responsible for what happened in Guantánamo, what is still happening, and what might happen in the future."

—**Azar Nafisi**, bestselling author of *Reading Lolita in Tehran*

"*Don't Forget Us Here* is a profoundly moving and immensely important tribute to the intelligence, resilience, and humanity with which its author, Mansoor Adayfi, survived fourteen years as a detainee in the notorious Guantánamo prison camp."

—**Francine Prose**, former president of PEN America and
bestselling author of *Lovers at the Chameleon Club, Paris 1932*

"This book takes us inside the tenacious mind of a remarkable young man who refused to be broken by ritualized mental and physical torture.

Through acts of courageous resistance and unbounding faith, he holds on to his dignity. His ritual of writing to make his case would become this important record, opening a window of stunning humanity into a place meant to be kept forever secret."

—**Melissa Fleming**, UN Under-Secretary-General for Global Communications and author of *A Hope More Powerful than the Sea*

"After years of hearing and reading only the 'official' version of his story, as told by his captors, at last Mansoor himself speaks. Speaking at all after such experiences, which included fourteen years of the most serious human rights violations and daily humiliations designed to break the human spirit, is a victory. Speaking as Mansoor does here, of the struggle of Guantánamo's prisoners to assert their humanity, turns the official story about these men on its head, and shows Guantánamo for what it is: a terrible shame and a pointless failure."

—**Mohamedou Ould Slahi**, bestselling author of *Guantánamo Diary*

"A blistering, eloquent indictment of Guantánamo. Mansoor Adayfi vividly describes the abuses committed there, and he writes powerfully about the decade and half he spent there."

—**Peter Bergen**, bestselling author of *Manhunt* and *The Rise and Fall of Osama bin Laden*

"Mansoor Adayfi's *Don't Forget Us Here* may be one of the most shocking books you'll ever read, but not for the reasons you might expect. The relentless torture that Adayfi receives at Guantánamo Bay, recounted in excruciating detail, will shock your conscience, as will the horrifying fact that Adayfi was held without charge by the US government for more than fourteen years, losing his entire twenties in the process. But what's most shocking about this extraordinary book is Adayfi's enormous capacity to resist his captors with uncommon creativity, dignity, and even humor. *Don't Forget Us Here* shows us how the gulag at Guantánamo, designed to deprive hundreds of Muslim men of everything they once held dear, ultimately stripped the jailers—and not the inmates—of their own humanity."

—**Moustafa Bayoumi**, author of *How Does It Feel to Be a Problem?: Being Young and Arab in America*

"Unforgettable…a riveting, illuminating account of Guantánamo from a Muslim perspective."

—**Jonathan Hansen**, author of *Guantánamo: An American History*

DON'T FORGET US HERE

DON'T FORGET US HERE

Lost and Found at Guantánamo

MANSOOR ADAYFI

in collaboration with

ANTONIO AIELLO

hachette BOOKS

NEW YORK

Hachette Books
Hachette Book Group
1290 Avenue of the Americas
New York, NY 10104
HachetteBooks.com
Twitter.com/HachetteBooks
Instagram.com/HachetteBooks

First Edition: August 2021
Published by Hachette Books, an imprint of Perseus Books, LLC, a subsidiary of
Hachette Book Group, Inc. The Hachette Books name and logo is a trademark of
the Hachette Book Group.

The Hachette Speakers Bureau provides a wide range of authors for speaking events.
To find out more, go to www.hachettespeakersbureau.com or call (866) 376-6591.

The publisher is not responsible for websites (or their content) that are not owned
by the publisher.

Print book interior design by Linda Mark.

Library of Congress Cataloging-in-Publication Data
Names: Adayfi, Mansoor, author. | Aiello, Antonio, editor.
Title: Don't forget us here : lost and found at Guantánamo / Mansoor
   Adayfi; edited by Antonio Aiello.
Description: First edition. | New York : Hachette Books, [2021]
Identifiers: LCCN 2021006356 | ISBN 9780306923869 (hardcover) |
   ISBN 9780306923876 (ebook)
Subjects: LCSH: Adayfi, Mansoor—Imprisonment. | Guantánamo Bay Detention
   Camp—Biography. | Detention of persons—Cuba—Guantánamo Bay Naval Base. |
   Prisoners of war—Abuse of—Cuba—Guantánamo Bay Naval Base. | Prisoners of
   war—Civil rights—Cuba—Guantánamo Bay Naval Base. | War on terrorism,
   2001–2009—Prisoners and prisons, American.
Classification: LCC HV9468.A33 A3 2021 | DDC 355.1/296092 [B]—dc23
LC record available at https://lccn.loc.gov/2021006356

ISBNs: 978-0-306-92386-9 (hardcover), 978-0-306-92387-6 (ebook)

Printed in the United States of America

LSC-C

Printing 1, 2021

بِسْمِ اللهِ الرَّحْمٰنِ الرَّحِيْمِ

To my parents, Amina and Ahmed,
all my sisters, especially Yumna Desai,
my Guantánamo brothers, and
my lawyers, Aunt Beth and Andy Hart.

Contents

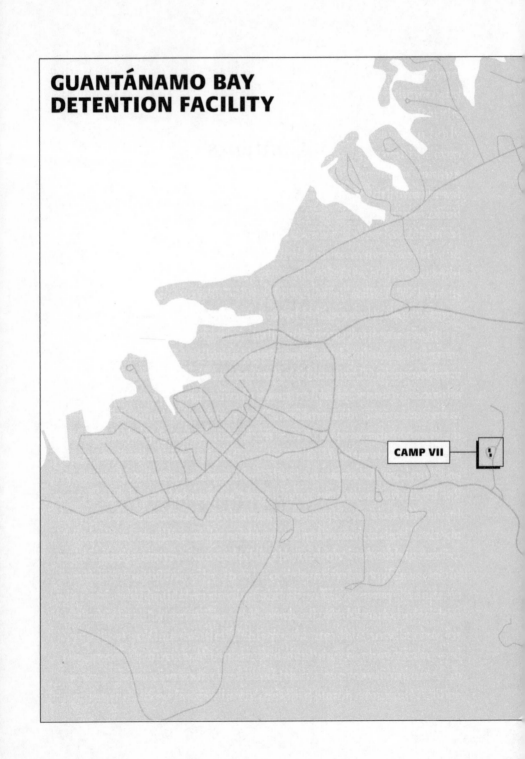

**GUANTÁNAMO BAY
DETENTION FACILITY**

CAMP VII

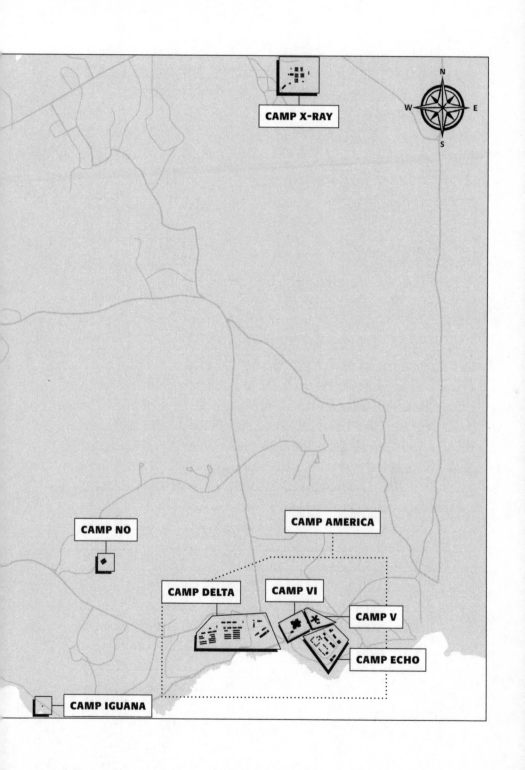

Preface

Nearly twenty years after Guantánamo opened, people are still debating whether or not such a place should continue to exist. Imagine if American boys, eighteen years old or even younger, had spent five, ten, twenty years in a foreign prison without being charged with a crime, where they were tortured, punished for practicing their religion, experimented on, and forced to live in solitary confinement. This is Guantánamo. Between January 11, 2002, and now, the United States has held 779 prisoners at Guantánamo. Those men have been from all over the world, representing fifty nationalities and speaking more than twenty languages. They have been doctors, journalists, singers, professors, students, teachers, paramedics, poets, blacksmiths, former CIA spies and assassins, farmers, tribal elders, and so much more. They have been sons and husbands, brothers and fathers. They are the reason I wrote this book.

I never set out to write a book about myself. I instead wanted to tell the story of Guantánamo and of all the men who have been imprisoned there. To show the world what life was really like. To show the world who was really there. I thought that if I could capture all the small moments of joy and beauty, of friendship and brotherhood, of hardship and the struggle to survive—all the moments that united us and bonded us—that I could maybe change the way people thought about Guantánamo.

I thought it was important to capture these moments and to tell them from our point of view, the way we experienced them. These are important stories to tell, and I didn't want them told by someone else who didn't live them with us.

In 2010, when I was transferred for the first time to communal living, I started writing those moments down. I talked to my brothers and together we remembered what had happened to us. As I wrote these stories down, I called them "Moments from Guantánamo," and I sent them as letters first to my attorney Andy Hart and then in their entirety to my attorney Beth Jacob.

I wrote the stories as accurately as I could. We didn't have clocks or watches for years, so the first drafts of "Moments from Guantánamo" were unanchored in time, just like we were. But even though we had lost track of time and our connections to the outside world, we remembered what happened to us. I have changed some names and details to protect the identities of the brothers, guards, and camp staff.

In 2018, I started working with Antonio Aiello to turn my "Moments from Guantánamo" into a book. We spent hundreds of hours on Skype calls going through my letters and manuscripts, reliving my time at Guantánamo, anchoring my stories in time and place, and threading them all together as a narrative. It was hard reliving those years and processing what happened to me. Sometimes I remembered something new and became depressed. Sometimes I got frustrated with Antonio for asking me the same questions over and over again until he finally understood an important moment. Many of us suffer from bouts of PTSD, and years of living with harsh, bright lights damaged our eyes and left us with crushing headaches. All of this can make it hard to work. Sometimes I just wanted to quit and forget the book even existed so that I wouldn't have to go back to Guantánamo.

I never intended to write the book as my story—it was always supposed to be about all our stories; it was supposed to be the story of Guantánamo. But I realized that by telling my story, I was able to tell the larger story of Guantánamo and the stories of all my brothers, so that the world would experience our moments of Guantánamo together with us.

Guantánamo still haunts me, and I still live every minute of my life with the stigma of being a Guantánamo detainee. I hope that by completing this book and sharing it with the world, I can begin to quiet those ghosts and chip away at the stigma. I hope that people begin to understand who we really are.

I believe art and storytelling are how we take people on journeys into our souls. Please allow me to take you on a journey through Guantánamo. Buckle up and prepare yourself. I will be your guide, but don't worry—you won't have to wear the orange jumpsuit, shackles, or hood. You will be free every night to leave behind the fences and isolation cells and rejoin your life. But I think you will come back and join me again to see a side of Guantánamo few people have experienced, where yes, there is much pain, but there are also unexpected moments of beauty and joy that will take your breath away. This is my Guantánamo.

CAMP X-RAY

BUILDINGS AND STRUCTURES

- (A) Alpha
- (B) Bravo
- (C) Charlie
- (D) Delta
- (E) Echo
- (F) Foxtrot
- (1) Interrogation Buildings
- (2) Medical Tent
- (3) Processing Yard

USES

- Chain-Link Cages
- Interrogation
- Medical

– PART 1 –

ARRIVAL

- ONE -

I waited in darkness for death.

The interrogators were done with me. *You aren't valuable enough to keep alive*, they said. I didn't have the intelligence they wanted on al Qaeda's chain of command. They bound my hands with duct tape, then taped my eyes and ears. They taped my mouth and then pulled a hood over my head. They dragged me outside into the cold and forced me to my knees. I hadn't seen the light of day in weeks and I thought I would never see blue sky again. I'd been kept hooded or inside dark rooms, stripped naked, and beaten bloody for I don't know how long. Weeks. A month. Maybe more. I was in Afghanistan, but I didn't know where.

If I hadn't lived it, I wouldn't have believed what happened to me. It happened so fast and none of it made sense. It all started days before I was supposed to return home to Yemen, when my friend and I were ambushed on the highway in northern Afghanistan and kidnapped by warlords. At first, they just wanted our truck and to ransom us for money.

I grew up in a tiny village in Yemen that had no electricity or running water. I'd been told all my life that I was smart. I was eighteen and full of the stubborn confidence boys can have at that age. I'd never been in a situation I couldn't talk myself out of. None of that mattered when the United States started bombing and dropping leaflets offering reward money for al Qaeda and Taliban fighters. The warlords got a better price selling Arabs to the Americans.

The warlords told me to say that I was al Qaeda or the Americans would kill me. The Americans told me they knew I was an al Qaeda leader—a recruiter, a middle-aged Egyptian—and all I had to do was admit it. None of it was true.

WAITING ON MY knees to be executed, I wished that I could see my mother one last time to say goodbye. I regretted my sins and the mistakes I'd made, and I prayed to Allah to forgive me, wishing that I was closer to Him and had done more good deeds in my life. *One day, we all will stand before Him. He knows I haven't wronged these people who tortured me. He knows I have caused harm to no one.*

A man cried close by. He begged someone to stop beating him. He begged for his life. This wasn't new. In the endless darkness, I'd heard women and children beg, too. A soldier yelled and then there was gunfire, but it wasn't for me. My heart pounded through my temples. I cried. Where would the bullet hit me? Would they shoot me in the head? In the chest? Would I feel pain? The rest of my life existed in these seconds and no more. I prayed again to Allah. I wished I wasn't so cold.

Allah, oh Allah. I bear witness that there is no deity but Allah, I bear witness that Muhammad is the messenger of Allah. Allah, oh Allah.

I told myself that I would be strong when they came for me. *I'll make them work. I won't walk.* So they dragged me, my toes digging into the dirt. *Allah, oh Allah.* They threw me to the ground and tore off my clothes and stripped me naked. They searched me in the worst way, and what did they think they would find after I had been tortured and left naked for months? They pulled a hood over my head, put me into a burlap sack, and taped me up. But they didn't shoot me. They threw me into what I imagined was a truck and tied me to the floor. At least the floor was warm. Engines rumbled to life and shook my entire body. I wasn't in a truck; I was in an airplane. The engines revved louder and louder and then the weight of the world filled my stomach. *Allah, oh Allah.*

"Let me help you help yourself," the interrogators had kept saying to me in the black site. "I don't want to hurt you."

I'd spent weeks in darkness hanging from a ceiling, naked, beaten, electrocuted . . . until all that remained was pain, real pain, a pain I never imagined existed. I tried to figure out what I could say that would make them stop. I told them the truth—that I was a student, that I was eighteen, that I was from Yemen. I told them I wasn't a fighter, that I didn't hate America, that I wasn't al Qaeda—but they didn't want that. They wanted something from me I didn't have to give. They wanted me to admit that I was a man named Adel, an Egyptian al Qaeda recruiter, a terrorist who planned bombings. Fine.

"I'll be whoever you want me to be," I said. "I'll be your Adel."

I said whatever they wanted just to stop the pain. Just because they told me to say it and I did, didn't make it a sin, but I still prayed for Allah's forgiveness. *Allah, oh Allah.* I thought that once I had given them what they wanted, it would all be over. But now they wanted details. Details I couldn't give them. If I had no value, what would they do with me? At that moment, I lost a part of me I would never get back. The pain, the questions, the torture changed me, and I didn't know who I was anymore. The person they'd sold was gone forever.

WHEN THEY DIDN'T execute me, I thought that the worst must be behind me. Nothing happened on the airplane except the sharp contact of boots to my body. The plane landed and I got one more boot to the head and then someone pulled me up and tore open my bag. They wanted me to walk but I couldn't. *Allah, oh Allah.* I wouldn't. One of them put me in a chokehold and dragged me off the plane, punching me in the face, the ribs, the head. He threw me on a pile of bodies, like slaughtered sheep, and that's where I stayed. How many others had they disappeared like me?

Noise and movement swirled around us, people talked and shouted in English I couldn't understand. I couldn't see. I couldn't think. *Allah, oh Allah.* We stayed like this for hours, naked and duct-taped and hooded, freezing in the open wind as soldiers kicked us, peed on us, spit on us, put their boots on our necks. All of it humiliating but minor compared to what they'd done to me before.

Allah, oh Allah. Time melted and then someone dragged me away from that pile of bodies. They took the hood off my head, then ripped the duct tape from my mouth and ears but not my eyes. A man spoke in English and another talked into my ear in Arabic.

"Are you with al Qaeda?" he asked.

"No."

"Are you with the Taliban?"

"No."

"Are you a fighter?"

"No."

"Have you been to al Farouq training camp?"

"No."

"Do you know where Osama bin Laden is?"

"No."

"Do you know where Mullah Omar is?"

"No."

"Do you know where Khalid Muhammed is?"

"No."

Allah, oh Allah. I said no over and over and then they shoved something in my ass. That's when I fought back. My hands were taped but I kicked. I kicked and shouted. Then a mountain of soldiers piled on top of me, pounding me with fists and boots. When they were done beating me, the guy asking the questions came back.

"That's what we do to people who lie to us," he said. "You want some more? Don't worry, you'll get more."

They tore the duct tape from my eyes. The bright light burned after months of darkness. Someone stepped in front of me and took photos of my face, my naked body, everything. My eyes adjusted and my surroundings came into focus. I was in a tent. There were soldiers everywhere; some wore masks and white protective suits splattered with blood. There was blood everywhere. One of the soldiers was beating a naked man. In one area were bags of clothes—where were the men who wore those clothes? *Allah, oh Allah.* Is this where they kill me?

I was told to sign a piece of paper that said if I tried to escape, they had the right to shoot and kill me. I refused. If they were going to kill me, I wouldn't sign my own death certificate. They hooded me again and shackled me.

And then I heard a distant voice, a woman's voice that reminded me of my mother and lifted me away from fear. I tuned out all the other sounds around me, the beatings, the engines screaming outside. I focused on that one voice, sweet and calm like my mother's, and that voice brought me to life again. She spoke in English and I didn't know what she said, and it didn't matter. That voice transported me to a place in my heart where there was no more pain or suffering or fear. When I listened to her voice, I found peace in something my mother had always said to me when putting me to bed: *Allah will never abandon you.*

When they came for me, I was calm. They loaded me on a stretcher, naked except for the hood and shackles, and carried me away. Gates clanked open and closed. They put the stretcher on the ground, replaced my shackles with duct tape, and left. I waited in darkness for something to happen. And when nothing did, I reached up and took the hood off my head.

Bright lights lit everything like day. Generators roared. Soldiers shouted. Helicopters hovered above. Freezing cold slashed my weak and broken body. I was in a large open tent wrapped in barbed wire. I could see five other tents. None of them had walls protecting the inside from the cold and blowing snow. Outside were five towers, each topped with soldiers armed with heavy machine guns. American soldiers in desert uniforms swarmed everywhere.

I found a blue jumpsuit on the stretcher next to me and put it on, the first real clothing I'd worn in months, since I was first kidnapped. I was so happy that I could finally cover myself. The night was so cold. All around me were men bundled up in blankets trying to shield themselves against the icy wind.

I had never seen anything like this. The armored trucks, the helicopters, the number of soldiers with machine guns. Nothing made sense.

"Where are we?" I asked out loud, not expecting an answer.

"You are at the American prison camp in Kandahar," a voice said in Arabic.

I lay back down on the stretcher. I was all the way south! *Allah, oh Allah.* I was so tired. I was so hungry and thirsty. Finally, I slept. And in my dream, I saw myself in a metal cage wearing orange. I was woken by that beautiful voice again, talking quietly close by. I didn't know what she said or whom she was talking to, but I closed my eyes and listened to this lovely voice until it faded away. That woman's voice was the voice of life, like a mother's whisper that says, *Everything is going to be okay.*

I believed this.

- TWO -

It's difficult to remember what my life was like before I was sold to the United States and sent to the CIA black site in Afghanistan. Torture corrodes your memory and sense of time. When I was kidnapped, I only had a few more days left in Afghanistan before I was supposed to fly home to Yemen, where I would prepare for university. My work as a research assistant in Afghanistan had earned me a valuable reference letter and the promise of a student visa and money to attend university in the United Arab Emirates. This was a big deal for me—huge—and I was so excited about my future. I thought that the best part of my life was ahead of me and that nothing could stand in my way. When I think about it now, it seems unreal, like someone else's dream. I can picture the surface of my old life, but the memories blur around the edges and it's hard to feel beneath the surface. It's frustrating. It's humiliating. It reminds me of what I lost and will never get back.

I remember my village in Raymah and the steep rocky mountains terraced with coffee farms. We lived like tribes in the old days, farming and raising goats and cattle, like *Little House on the Prairie* but in Yemen. My mother always woke up before dawn and the morning call to prayer and prepared my brothers and sisters and me for school. We didn't have electricity or running water and she had to pump water from the well, light the lamps, and stoke the fire before making us tea and porridge or soup. I loved the way she lined us all up before school and kissed each one of us as we walked out the door. My mother hadn't gone to school herself and couldn't read or write, but she somehow made sure that we all got our schoolwork done every night. I can't remember how.

I remember my sisters went to school, and that was a really big deal because most parents wouldn't send their daughters to school. But my father insisted—for him education was important, almost as important as the tribe. I remember leaving for school in the soft glow of the early morning light and trailing behind my sister along the five miles of rocky goat paths to the neighboring village. The mist hung heavy over the land and I felt like we were walking through clouds. I remember the wet smell of morning dew and how the lush green of coffee fields was somehow deeper in the morning light than when we came home in the afternoon. My mother always said that even though the ground was rocky, it was fertile, so fertile you could drop a seed anywhere and it would grow. This was my world.

My mother took care of us mostly by herself and she was considered rich for the number of sons she had. One of my chores was to help my sister herd the goats and sheep. I loved roaming the hills with her. We always joked and played around the entire time. I don't remember the games we played or if my mother scolded us, though I think she did. I reach for the memories, but the details are lost.

I do remember the one time I got tangled up holding a rope tied to a ram running loose from the herd and how he dragged me all over the hill and back. "Let go!" my sister yelled, but I was too stubborn to let him get away and I held on until he stopped running, even though my body was beaten blue and I'd broken my arm. I was proud that I held on and stopped him.

My father was gone a lot, working in Saudi Arabia, where he owned a restaurant. It was a big deal in our tribe that he could take care of such a large family. My father was physically strong, but his real strength was in his character, his generosity, and his sense of honor. His father died when he was only twelve; that made him the head of his family and he was expected to provide for his mother and all his brothers and sisters, so he stopped going to school. I wanted to be responsible and strong like that when I was twelve.

When my father came home from Saudi Arabia, he always cooked for us, and when we sat around the table together, he'd scoop up fingerfuls of cumin-scented rice and the sweetest, most tender lamb and jokingly put it in our mouths. I loved when he fed me like that. When he was home, I wanted to make him proud.

He had a way of holding his head raised high that projected pride and integrity. I was always a little afraid of him because he was so firm and because he expected nothing but the best from us. He carried himself in such a way that you knew he would do the right thing, and I think that's why he made a good tribal leader.

He saw the world very clearly: there was right and wrong, black and white, good and bad, and no in-between. He was very strict, especially when it came to character and to us kids. Even when we were children, he told us that we were the face of the family *and* the tribe, and that everyone in the village looked to us as examples. How we behaved and what we did was a reflection of our family's values and the values of the tribe. I took this very seriously.

Whenever he left us to go back to Saudi Arabia, he always said, "I'm not asking you to pass your exams. I am telling you that you will be first in your exams. You will have the highest marks." I don't remember how long he was gone each time, but he was always home for Ramadan.

My mother named me Mansoor, which in Arabic means "he who is victorious." From very early on, she told me that I was clever and smart, smarter than the other kids, and that she expected great things from me. She said I was a mature soul, even though I was always running around and couldn't seem to sit still. I learned to read when I was very young, and she made me start school when my older brother and sister did, even though I was the youngest in the class.

I remember my first day of school and being so afraid. I'd never been in the neighboring village and couldn't believe how big it was and how many people were there. It wasn't that much bigger than our village, but to me it was a different world. The school was just a small room with dirt floors beside the mosque, where every teacher had a stick to smack unruly kids. The first day I went, I was told to line up by the door before going into class, and the teacher hit me on the hand when I didn't. I told him I wouldn't line up if he was going to strike me like that and then he hit me again. I picked up a rock to throw at him, and my brother came running and told me I couldn't talk back to the teacher like that. I didn't understand why, but I did what my brother told me to do, and when my father found out, he taught me the meaning of respect without using a single word, a lesson I never forgot.

I ran with a pack of boys my age at school, just like our tribe, and we always played with other packs of boys. We chased each other and fought when we could, as boys do. I was head of my pack and the rules were simple, what I thought my father might have come up with: No cursing. No snitching. No bleeding.

I remember one day when we were playing and one of my friends yelled at me to stop a boy from another pack from running away. I picked up a rock—I was always picking up rocks—and I threw it at him. I was a good shot and I hit him in the head and stopped him cold, but I also made him bleed. I refused to tell on my friend. I got in so much trouble for not telling and finally the other boy came forward and told the whole story. My mother was so mad at me, and disappointed and ashamed. She didn't talk to me for days. I'll never forget that. It broke my heart and I never wanted to disappoint her again.

Raymah was my whole world until I left home at thirteen to live with my aunt in Sana'a, the capital, the only place I could finish my secondary education. It was my first time going to Sana'a and also my first car ride. Wa Allahi, I got so sick to my stomach! It was nighttime when we came over the last mountain before getting to Sana'a. The lights flickering down in the dark valley was one of the most beautiful things I'd ever seen. My brother had accompanied me and explained what I was seeing. "Those are all lights in houses and stores and streets," he said. "They're all run by electricity."

I couldn't believe my eyes as we drove down the wide boulevards to the center of the city. What life! My aunt and my cousin, who was about the same age as me, picked us up and took us out to a restaurant. But I was too busy taking everything in to eat—the bright signs in storefronts, all the people and cars, traffic lights and the noise of the city. It made my entire body hum with excitement. I wanted to stay out all night and see everything, but my cousin was bored by it all—this was just his everyday life. There was so much to do and see and learn, and it felt like there wasn't enough time in life to do it all. I had never seen so many crazy buildings in one place.

I'd always been curious, and those first days, I walked into buildings all over the city and asked shopkeepers, attendants—anyone who was there—what they did and what kind of business they had. My cousin was so embarrassed and teased me for talking to anyone who would listen. But this was how I learned every inch of our neighborhood. It's mostly forgotten now.

I remember that my life in Sana'a was full of firsts. I watched TV for the first time and fell in love with the crazy bird called Woody Woodpecker. I used the telephone for the first time to call my father's restaurant in Saudi Arabia and tell him I got top marks in my classes. His voice was weaker than in person but still strong despite the distance. I loved electricity. I loved that you could turn a light on and off and not have to light a lamp. I couldn't wait to go home and tell my younger brothers and sisters about everything I'd experienced. You can't know what that feels like if you've never lived without it. My world was growing, and I wanted more.

I got high marks in all my classes and I graduated when I was seventeen. I really wanted to go to the University of Science and Technology in Sana'a, but it was expensive and my family couldn't afford it. I told my parents that I would work and save to get to university.

Meanwhile, I took classes at the Dar al-Hadith Islamic institute, a big school that had a big campus outside of Sana'a. It wasn't a university, but it was an educational institution approved by the Yemeni government, and students from all over the world came to study there. To really study Islam, you must know Arabic. This institute was one of the best ways for foreign students to learn Arabic. And it was free. I continued taking classes in Arabic literature and history—I loved reading and I loved the complexity and beauty of the Arabic language. I loved writing and playing with words.

While I studied at the institute, I worked part-time as a security guard to save money, keeping my eyes set on going to university. I might have been small, but I was smart and organized and very chatty with our clients. Right away, I was promoted to work at important places like the Dutch and German embassies, and then to managing entire shifts of guards. I remember being proud that the Dutch ambassador recognized me and said hello. I was always busy with studies at the institute and work and volunteering at an orphanage several times a week, where I helped prepare food for the kids and take care of them. Working with the kids, I realized that I wanted more than anything to have a big family with many daughters, and that going to university was my path to get there.

The security job didn't pay well, only $90 a month, and even though I was in charge of thirty guards, that responsibility wouldn't help me save enough money. It would only lead to the military, and I had no desire to join. You don't think in the military, you only do. I looked for other jobs, but in Yemen corruption ran deep and I knew

I'd have to do what other Yemenis always did—go to one of the Gulf countries, where jobs paid well.

I spent more and more time at the Islamic institute and started working there part-time as a foreign student adviser, helping students from all around the world get their student visas. I was good at my job. I was good at talking to people and getting things done, and that's how I caught the sheik's eye. He was head of the institute and a prominent and respected scholar. I told him where I came from and where I wanted to go and how I wanted to study computers. I told him about my work at the Dutch and German embassies and at the orphanage, and he said he would help me when the time was right. This was a big deal, catching the sheik's eye. He had strong connections in Yemen and all throughout the Gulf, and a reference letter from him would open doors I couldn't even imagine.

I remember the USS *Cole* bombing in Aden and people talking about al Qaeda and the Taliban trying to come to Yemen and all the sheiks trying to advise their students against growing calls for violent jihad. The sheik of my institute released an audiocassette recording of a lecture he gave warning Muslim youth against it, and still some went to Afghanistan anyway.

In the spring of 2001, the sheik asked me to meet him privately, and I thought that he was finally going to give me the reference letter I needed to go to the United Arab Emirates. I remember clearly what he said to me: "You need my help and I need yours." He told me that he had a special job for me, and that when it was complete, he would arrange my visa, my letter of reference, and even give me money to go to the UAE for school. He said he had picked me because I was smart and very good with foreigners, skills I would need for this job. He was writing a book about al Qaeda's ideology, and he was sending me to interview the leaders of some al Qaeda–connected groups. I would also collect books and fatwas, which are like legal opinions, and anything else that would help him write his book. The irony of this mission hasn't been lost on me.

I remember boarding the plane for my first flight at exactly 6:45 a.m. on June 9, 2001. I had a golden ticket to my future, and in a few months I would be a university student in the UAE, on my way to the life and family I imagined.

- THREE -

You are nothing now. No name. No family. No self. Only fear and darkness in the cold cavity of a military plane. You're gagged, hooded, blindfolded, and shackled hands to ankles, ankles to the floor. Fists split your lips, boots break one rib, then another. The pain of thirst. The pain in your bladder. The pain from hunching forward on a cold metal floor for hours until your body shakes. A man on each side of you rests his head on your back and you're glad you can at least lessen someone else's pain. When the plane lands, they pull you up and push you down and drag you off one plane and onto another and how many times will they do this? You ask yourself, *Where are they taking me? What will happen to me? Will I die?* You pray but you can't hear yourself with the music so loud and the engines roaring. Time slips between this moment and memories. Your mother comes to you, then your father, and you imagine every brother and sister and cousin, every relative, every friend, and you say to each of them, *I wish I had done more good in my life.* You say goodbye. The plane roars on—ten hours, you think, fifteen hours, twenty-four hours, forty hours. The shackles are so tight you can't feel your hands or ankles anymore so you pray that the plane crashes into the ocean and ends it all because death would be better than this. Then you feel the descent in your stomach; you're losing altitude again. You pray that this is the end.

But the plane lands and as soon as it's still, you hear soldiers screaming in English.

"Get up! Get the fuck up!"

You tell your body to stand, but nothing happens. You're so weak your brain shuts down and you can't move, even with a hard kick in your side for motivation. The boot hurts but the humiliation and helplessness are worse.

You scream inside at the little of you that's left, *How can this really be happening?*

They drag you off the plane and throw you like a bag from one soldier to the next until you land on a metal bench, where your ankles are shackled again to the floor. You feel others close to you and it's comforting that you're not alone. It's warm here, hot like your home in Yemen, but it's a wet heat. You're moving now, across water and waves. You bounce and jostle and you feel the sea rolling below you. You know the salty air from your weekends in Aden with friends after you finished high school. You're on a boat and you feel the sea receive you. The sea gives you comfort. The sea witnesses everything they do to you. The sea whispers in your ear, *I'm with you, friend.* You thank the sea, and it sings to you as they beat you. The sea shuts down your mind and that's good. You pray that the sea accompanies you for the rest of your journey.

And then the sea is gone.

You have arrived and they yell at you to stand, to move, to walk, but you can't. You're broken. You've been traveling for days and your body refuses to follow their orders. They drag you off the boat. They cut your clothes off, strip you naked, and hose you down. You're barely nineteen and all your life you've never been naked in front of a woman. Now they make you stand for all to see and you see women soldiers watching you. The humiliation burns. They take photos of you, every part of you—even your genitals. They give you a number and attach a plastic bracelet to your wrist that has your photograph and your new number. All you can think is that you want to wake up from this crazy nightmare. They hood you again. They throw you to the ground and pile on top of you and hold you down while someone searches your ass again in the worst way. They laugh. They drag your naked body across rocks and stones and gravel and you feel your skin peel away but don't feel the pain. Gate after gate opens. Closes. You feel a boot, a punch. You see only black, but you feel their anger. One last gate opens and they throw you to the concrete floor, sit on you one more time, and remove the chains.

The hood comes off and the bright light burns your eyes. You're naked on the cement floor inside a cage all by yourself. You cry from the pain and humiliation and the terror of not knowing where you are. Soldiers return and throw orange pants and a shirt at you, the same clothes you saw in your dream. They laugh as you struggle to move.

"Number one!" a man screams off in the distance. "Number one!" His voice is sad and lost, on the edge of sanity.

You look around and hate is everywhere. A grudge against you for something you didn't do. It doesn't matter what you say. You see in the soldiers' anger that they want to tear you to pieces.

"Head down! Don't look at me!" You wait for a long time, one minute becomes an eternity staring at the ground, your knees grinding into cement. You look around to find the direction of Makkah and pray but you don't know east from west or even what time of day it is.

"Head down!" soldiers scream.

"Which way to Makkah?" you call out to the man in the cage next to you.

"Shut the fuck up!" soldiers scream.

But still you whisper through the fence, "There's a sea here."

"Number one!" His cries tear into you.

"SHUT. THE. FUCK. UP!" soldiers yell.

Enough, you think. You stand. You call out to the men around you. You call out to find east so you can pray. You call out to break this nonsense of no talking and no standing, and the soldiers call back to you with their fists and boots. Five of them rush into your cage and slam your head to the ground again and again until your head bleeds and the message is received—you are nothing.

But you think you've found east, and you offer your prayers. You tell Allah about your pain and fear and ask Him to protect you and the men who are with you, to preserve you, to save you. You cry, quietly, so that no one sees except Allah. *Allah, oh Allah.*

You unroll the thin plastic mat and use the blanket as a pillow. You look up and see white birds fly overhead and you fall asleep dreaming you are one, flying high above, looking down on a strange sea of orange. You dive down and as you come closer, the sea turns to men in orange jumpsuits, their faces swollen, bruised, bloody, deformed from beatings. You see yourself in your cage, head shaved, your knees pulled to your chest, a newborn baby. You're not the nineteen-year-old student from Yemen, the country of love, who once dreamed of studying computer science and making a family. You're not the son of a tribal leader and middle brother of ten siblings. You don't recognize yourself because you're only a number now—detainee 441—and who you thought you were has been torn out of you, piece by piece until nothing is left but fear and the quiet whisper of memories. *Poof.* You have disappeared.

I **WOKE UP** from my dream to an angry soldier hitting my cage and yelling. I hadn't slept long, but it was deep enough for the currents of dreams to carry me home to my village in Raymah, where I swam again with my sister in a cool mountain spring, splashing around when we should have been tending the goats.

The soldier didn't care about my dreams. He cared that I hadn't woken instantly on his command. His job was to train me to be controlled and to keep me awake. My neighbor, who was from Denmark and spoke Arabic and English and many other languages, told me I needed to put my things in order before the soldier would leave.

I looked around my cage and found the foam sleep mat, a tooth-brush, toothpaste, two blankets, a bar of soap, a pair of flip-flops, a canteen for water, one white bucket for shit and pee, and another white bucket for water. This was all I had now.

"MAT!" The soldier pointed at a place in front of my cage door.

"Toothbrush!" He pointed again. "Mat! Toothbrush! Toothpaste! Blanket! Soap! Flip-flops! Shit bucket! Water bucket!"

When I'd put everything in order, he moved to the next cage, where a boy, younger and skinnier than me, slept rolled up in a ball. He was so small and he slept so deeply he didn't wake when the soldier yelled at him. Immediately five armored soldiers stormed the boy's cage. The one in front, who carried a shield, crashed into the boy. The others piled on top and beat him with a fierceness that didn't match his size. I had never seen anything like it.

I couldn't control myself. I screamed at the soldiers to stop. I kicked and hit my cage, and soon the soldiers stormed my cage and beat me, too.

When they had moved on to another cage, my neighbor whispered to me.

"You must do as they say," he said.

"Where are we?"

He shook his head.

"How long have you been here?" I whispered.

"A day . . . maybe two."

"Who beats boys like that?"

He held up his hand, indicating I should be quiet.

"Americans," he whispered.

"NO TALKING!" A soldier pounded my cage.

It seemed like every few minutes another prisoner was thrown into an empty cage. The cages were small and made of chain-link fencing—four walls and a ceiling—with a concrete floor and a tin roof high above. I learned later they had been used by the United

States as a temporary prison to hold Haitian refugees. My block of cages had two rows with five cages each and all ten cages shared a back fence. Across from us was another block just like mine. It was like looking at dog cages, but the dogs were men of all ages, shaved, their faces beaten and bruised, their bodies thin and underweight.

I lay down to sleep, but a soldier banged on my cage.

"SIT UP! NO SLEEPING!"

I stood up.

"SIT THE FUCK DOWN! NO STANDING!" he yelled and pointed to the ground.

I didn't speak English, but I quickly learned the words they yelled and understood what they wanted me to do. The most important word was *no*. No sleeping. No standing. No talking. No looking at soldiers. There was no limit to the word *no* or how the guards could use it, a word we were forbidden to say. It was impossible to keep up with every *no* and it seemed that every rule broken was met with a punch, a slap, a boot, or worse, with that pack of guards in armor and shields who rushed your cage and knocked you to the ground. I'd soon realize it was all meant to keep us disoriented and weak for our interrogations.

I spent the first night keeping my head down, watching silently, observing, trying to figure out where I was and what would happen to me.

The soldiers had so much hate and fear. I knew by now that they thought I was al Qaeda and that I had something to do with the attacks on September 11. I had heard about the attacks on the radio in a restaurant in Afghanistan, and I didn't think anything of it. There were no TVs, no photographs of the event, and I couldn't imagine airplanes flying into buildings or why someone would want to kill so many innocent people. What I knew about America I had learned from TV shows and movies and I didn't hate it. I didn't love it either. I didn't know enough about it to even care. I was sorry to hear that innocent people had died, but I didn't understand what that had to do with me.

None of it seemed real at the time. It still doesn't seem real. I wasn't a soldier. I wasn't a fighter. I believed that in time, I could make them understand it was all a mistake. I had just said things in the black site to make them stop hurting me. This Adel—it was just an empty name. How could they be so afraid of me, a skinny nineteen-year-old too weak to stand? How could they be afraid of an old man? Or a boy who couldn't even grow a beard? What did they think I was capable of doing?

I saw these questions written on the face of every man inside those cages.

THEY TRIED TO control us with beatings and humiliation, and we tried to find ourselves and comfort in what had always been our morning ritual. As the sky lightened, I wanted to offer my morning prayers. Just seeing the light gave me a sense of comfort, knowing I could do something I had done all my life. I have been praying five times a day since I was in my mother's womb. I was born knowing the rhythms and sounds of each of the day's prayers. Praying was like the breath of life to me that connected me to Allah. I hadn't heard a call to prayer in days—we weren't allowed to call out—and I was surprised when I heard the familiar sound of a man singing the adhan several cages away. The men around me stirred and we all began the same movements we had been doing all our lives. I used water from the bucket for my ablutions. I washed my face, hands, head, my ears, my feet . . .

"NO WASHING!"

The soldiers went crazy. They went from cage to cage banging the fences as we prepared for our prayers.

"SIT THE FUCK DOWN!"

We all assumed the Takbir, standing straight as we faced what we believed was Makkah, preparing to enter the state of prayer.

"NO STANDING!"

We raised our hands just above our shoulders and made our offering to Allah. "Allahu Akbar!" we called out together as if we were one.

"SHUT THE FUCK UP!"

We did this, all of us, not thinking, our bodies going through the movements of the Qiyaam, Ruku', Sujud, and Tashahhud, guided by a higher power.

The soldiers seemed more afraid than angry.

"SIT DOWN!" they screamed.

Guards in armor came running as if preparing to battle.

"NO STANDING!"

What were we to do—stop our prayers? No, it was the morning prayer and we finished just as we have done since we were children. We prayed together as one of the men led the prayer. If they knew anything about Islam, they would know that we pray together five times a day. We weren't preparing for battle. We weren't being defiant or ignoring their orders. We were praying the way we had prayed all our lives because prayer was as much a part of us as our skin and bones.

When we had finished, soldiers stormed the cage of the man who led the prayer and took him away. An interpreter walked from cage to cage with a man who seemed like he was in charge. He was older, with a shaved head and sharp features under his military cap.

"There is no praying together," he said over and over again. "They think you are preparing to battle when you call out 'Allahu Akbar!'"

When the soldiers brought us our first meal, we moved to the corners of our cages where we could sit close to each other and eat together. Just like praying, this was a part of our culture and not something we thought about, even if the meal was just a half a cup of bland oatmeal.

"What's your name, brother?" we whispered to each other. "Where are you from?"

"I wish I knew who sat next to me on the airplane here," the boy in the cage next to me said. "I'd like to thank him and apologize. I slept on him the entire time. He must've been so uncomfortable."

"Brother!" I said. "That was me. I'm glad I could make someone comfortable."

"NO TALKING!" Soldiers banged on our cages.

We stopped talking until he moved down the block.

"Where are we?" we all asked.

No one knew what country we were in, but we learned we were in a place called X-Ray, and that there were hundreds of other men here from all over the world. We were strangers to each other, and what had happened to us in the black sites and other interrogation centers had made us hesitant at first to reveal anything important about ourselves. Anyone could be listening. Anyone could betray us. At first, we shared only where we had been and what interrogators had done to us. Some shared their first names. We were all afraid and confused and still trying to understand how it was we had ended up here.

Communicating wasn't always easy at first. Gulam, the older Afghan in the cage next to me with the hard, weathered face of a farmer, spoke only Pashto. His neighbor, Shah, was also from Afghanistan but spoke Arabic as well. The boy next to me, Yousif, only spoke Arabic. I heard other languages, too, and we learned to use our hands and our bodies to talk. One neighbor guessed we were in India because the pipes that held our cages together were stamped with MADE IN INDIA. We sang out questions and responded to each other like we were praying, and this made the soldiers angry and afraid that we were planning something, but we were just trying to figure out where we were and what would happen to us.

Many of us had been told by soldiers or interrogators that we were going to be executed. We had all been given the same paper to sign that said if we tried to escape, soldiers had the right to shoot and kill us.

Most of us believed that we were going to be executed anyway, except my neighbor, the Dane.

"They are Americans," he whispered. "Believe me—they can't just execute hundreds of men."

The Dane had fiery red hair and blue eyes. He said he was a techno DJ but was a religious man and had traveled a lot. He knew more about the world than most of us. He said there were international laws the Americans had to follow.

Others had said the same thing to me in Kandahar and believed we would be released when they understood we weren't fighters. I wanted to believe this. I didn't know much about America, but I knew it was the most powerful country in the world. I wanted to believe that they would treat us better than our own countries treated prisoners, that they would see their mistakes.

THOSE FIRST DAYS all bled one into the next as we tried to adjust and survive. The conditions in the cages were terrible and inhumane. We had a tin roof above us, but it was so high it gave us little shade unless the sun was directly overhead. The beating sun burned, and I tried to cover my head with a towel, but a soldier screamed at me.

"NO COVERING!"

We weren't allowed to hang our towels or blankets for shade either, or cover ourselves when we used the buckets to go to the bathroom. It was humiliating. No one wanted to use those buckets. We could see and hear and smell everything. We didn't have toilet paper, and we only had one bucket of water each, which we couldn't use for both drinking *and* washing.

"I will never have another bowel movement again," the Dane whispered to me. We both smiled, but he was serious.

"NO TALKING!"

More prisoners arrived all the time, and someone was always being taken away—to the medical tent, to interrogations, to meet with the Red Cross. Yes, the Red Cross was there, just like they were at Kandahar, but they weren't there to help us or to even report to anyone about our conditions. They'd walk the blocks and ask us questions like, do you have food? Do you have water? To us, it seemed like their only purpose was to give legitimacy to what the Americans were doing.

At the medical tent, they made me swallow so many pills I felt dizzy and sick to my stomach for days. They weighed me, listened to my heart, gave me shots in my arm, and tried to take blood, but it was too black and thick to draw. They weren't concerned about the bruises from beatings or the cuts from the ankle shackles, just that we were dehydrated.

"You need to drink more water," the doctor said through an interpreter. "You're dehydrated. That's why you have headaches. That's why your blood is so thick."

The Red Cross explained that the Americans needed to keep us healthy and alive. And they did, barely. It wasn't humane, but it meant they didn't plan to kill us. It was a simple logic, one that kept me alive, though it didn't explain what they planned to do with me.

"DRINK WATER!" the soldiers now yelled at us. This, too, became a part of our day, just as arranging our things.

"DRINK WATER!" they screamed all morning until we drank a full canteen and showed it was empty. Hundreds of times. Thousands of times. You couldn't refuse water. If you did, they sent that pack of soldiers with armor and helmets to beat you until you did drink.

And yet, in all this chaos and pain, there were moments of wonder that reminded me of the beauty in the world, even in a place like X-Ray. There were huge and hairy spiders, and there were these big furry animals that snuck around the block at night. We learned these were banana rats. But the most amazing creatures were the iguanas.

I had just finished praying quietly to myself when I saw an iguana scurry through an open gate and down the center of our block. I had never seen an iguana so close and I thought I might be dreaming. She was big, at least three feet long. Who was this crazy beautiful creature with golden eyes? How could such a creature survive in this horrible place?

I'd seen her from a distance earlier when I was taken to the medical tent. She sat on a rock and watched us from above; the soldiers all around ignored her like she wasn't even there, but I saw her.

When she scurried toward my cage, soldiers got out of her way like she was royalty. It was so strange and wonderful to see her break all the rules without a care.

My neighbors called out to her to get her attention, but she ignored them, too, and came right to my cage.

"Assalamu alaikum," I whispered.

She turned to me and pierced my heart with her kind eyes. The connection was instant, like we were old friends.

"Hello, Princess," I whispered. "I'm from Yemen, the country of love. Who are you?"

Her skin was green like the color of coffee leaves. And she had yellow stripes down her tail. The guards shouted at her to leave. Instead, she came closer.

"We have our first guest," Yousif whispered.

Brothers whispered from cage to cage about the iguana sitting with me. With everything that had happened to us, her arrival was like a gift. The soldiers left me alone with her. I would learn later that she was a protected animal and that soldiers could get fined $10,000 for touching or harming iguanas. She had more rights and freedom than we did.

"What do you think about all these men in orange?" I whispered. "I know—we're a sad bunch of animals, all beaten and bruised. But you shouldn't be afraid of us."

When soldiers brought our next meal, I shared what little I had with her. Yemenis are known for our hospitality, and my village was famous for it. Travelers going north and south, east and west, had to pass through and stay the night. My tribe fed every traveler and offered them a place to stay for free. It was our custom, and as a tribesman I had learned it was an honor to be generous to your guests. I felt bad that I didn't have much to offer. Anyway, the food was bad, and she didn't eat much. I wasn't offended. I was happy she stayed.

When the soldiers saw that I fed her, they banged on my cage, but still she refused to leave.

"I apologize for their behavior," I whispered. "They're not very good hosts. Their tribes would be ashamed."

She stayed with me for a long time, sitting next to my cage, listening to me describe the beautiful mountains of Raymah with the terraced farms carved into the slopes like steps. She listened to me cry quietly, away from the others, when I told her I thought I might die here and never see my home again. She didn't have to say anything. Her presence gave me comfort, even when the soldiers came to my cage, knocked me to my knees, shackled me, and dragged me away to interrogation.

IN THESE FIRST days, the interrogations are chaotic and make no sense. They take you to a small wood building where everything is built-in and made from wood. Wood table with attached wood stool. Wood benches along the wood walls. Wood ceiling. There are metal rings attached to the floor and the soldiers lock your ankle shackles to a ring and your hands to the table. A soldier stays in the room with you and you don't know if it's to beat you like they did at the black site or to protect the young interrogators in tan pants and short-sleeve shirts. There's a male interpreter who tells you the men in civilian clothes are called the FBI. You've never heard of this FBI but you answer their questions. Why wouldn't you? And you ask your own.

"What have I done?" you ask.

"Why don't you tell us what you've done."

"Why am I here?"

"You tell us why you're here."

"Where am I?"

But they're done with your questions.

"We know what you did in Nairobi," one man says.

"I've never been to Nairobi," you say.

"That's not what your file says, Adel."

"I'm not Adel," you say, and you explain what happened in the black site, but they're not interested. At least they don't beat you. But they keep asking the same questions other teams have been asking for months.

"Where is Osama bin Laden?"

"I don't know."

"Where is Mullah Omar?"

"I don't know."

"When is the next attack?"

"I don't know."

"What is the next attack?"

"I don't know."

They think you're lying.

Another team replaces the FBI, and then another replaces them. DIA, MI, CIA, NYPD—you don't know what any of the names mean or who they are, but you ask over and over, "Where am I and why am I here?" They respond with all the same questions.

"Can't they talk to the guys who questioned me before?" you ask the interpreter.

But they ask again anyway and then move on to new questions about your military training.

"Do you know how to use a Kalashnikov?"

"Of course," you say.

"Did you learn how to use it in Chechnya?"

"I'm from Yemen," you say, "where babies are born holding a Kalashnikov."

They don't think that's funny.

"But we are not violent people," you say. "It's just that every family owns a Kalashnikov." You change the subject.

"What have I done?" you ask.

"You tell us what you've done," they say. And so, the circle continues.

Hours bleed one into the next in this wood room, though you know time passes because the interrogators eat, drink, smoke, get up to go to the bathroom. You steal looks at their watches. Four hours. Eight hours. New teams switch out. Still you go around in circles, the questions repeating. You're young and maybe a little naïve, but it seems like all these interrogators don't know what they're looking for even though they keep asking the same questions.

Where is Osama bin Laden? Where is Mullah Omar? Where did you train? When is the next attack? Some teams are nicer than others. Some interrogators are so full of hate they get frustrated when you say you don't know anything about al Qaeda recruiting, and that's when they start with the threats.

"You've been trained well," one guy says. "But we have a special drink for men like you." He's young—your age—and has something to prove.

"You want us to send you back to your interrogator in Afghanistan?" one guy threatens. "You want that?"

This really scares you and you can't help sweating. But you try to be strong and not show you're afraid.

"We're going to bring your mother here," another guy says. He's tired of hearing about how you were kidnapped. "You want to see your mother in a cage? What do you think we'd do to her? Huh? Because we can arrest her, too, and bring her here."

You laugh when he says this, and you can't help it, thinking about your tough mother and what she would do to him. You remember the day you went to the fields with her to reap the wheat. You trailed behind her throwing stones and your crazy neighbor started yelling at you all kinds of terrible things. Before you could pick up a rock to throw at him, your mother had swooped in out of nowhere, knocking him to the ground and holding her scythe just below his nose. "You talk to my son like that again and I'll cut your nose off."

Then the next interrogator asks you what your name is.

"If you're not Adel, then who are you?" they ask. You think, *Why would I tell them my family name after they threatened to bring my mother to this prison and rape her?*

Some interrogators seem confused by you, as if they don't understand why you are here or what you can offer.

"You're just a boy," one woman says.

But those interrogators are always replaced by others who ask the same questions. You fear they won't stop until you tell them what they want to hear.

"Tell us you're al Qaeda," they say. "We know you are. We just need to hear it from you!"

You're not. You've told them so.

And now a new team comes in and they have Israeli patches on their uniforms. You think, *I can't possibly be in occupied Palestine?* They listen to your accent. They ask the interpreter to stop translating. They want to hear your words untranslated matched with your body language. They're professionals, not amateurs like the Americans.

This scares you. Something has changed. The American soldier in the room no longer just watches, he hits. Your job now is to answer questions and they pay you in slaps, hits, curses. They keep you here for a long time and then soldiers move you. You can't walk, so they drag you to another cage in a new location you haven't been to in all the weeks of interrogation. There, you pray, then sleep. But not for long. The soldiers come back and wake you, yelling. They drag you back to the same room. You can't hear your own words. You can't concentrate. You don't understand what they want. "It's all a mistake!" you say. Your body shakes, you're so weak. This is the new program. Intense interrogation.

ANGER, FRUSTRATION, AND despair were building to a breaking point as we learned the humiliating and isolating routine of a new life cut off from our families and the rest of the world. Pray. Eat. DRINK WATER! Arrange items in a row. Go to interrogation. Repeat your Internment Serial Number, your ISN. I learned to get on my knees with my back to the cage door and my hands on my head when soldiers came for me. I learned the English words for my few possessions, that the name of the slot used to hand me my food was "bean hole," and that the pack of armored soldiers who stormed our cages was an IRF team, short for Immediate Reaction Force.

Rumors circulated of other brothers beaten badly by soldiers. We heard that the Afghan who cried out "Number one" for days had been broken and gone crazy and that soldiers and interrogators continued to beat him.

When I met with the Red Cross, I told them these stories and asked where I was, how long I would be here, and what would happen to us.

"Do you have food?" they asked instead. "Do you have shelter? Can you practice your religion?"

The Red Cross didn't answer our questions, they just probed for information that on the surface showed we were being taken care of. They pointed out that the camp had given each of us a Qur'an to keep in our cages, and a blue face mask to hang at the top of our cages to keep the Qur'an safely off the ground when soldiers stormed in. They pointed out that we had taqiyas now, the white skullcaps Muslims wear to cover our heads when we pray. "You can pray," they said. But these were empty improvements. We still couldn't pray together, stand freely, or even talk openly. The food was very little. We lived in open cages with no shade and no toilet.

The weight of it all had become too much, but I knew I couldn't just give up on life like this.

I snapped. When a soldier came to my cage and told me to put my things in order, I couldn't do it. I pretended I didn't understand.

"Toothbrush!" he yelled.

I picked up my shit bucket.

"Toothbrush!"

I picked up my soap.

"441!" he screamed. "Show me your fucking toothbrush!"

I picked up my mat.

Now he snapped and called the IRF team.

"Please," the Dane whispered. "They want to tame you. Let them think you are tamed, even if you are not."

My neighbor was a nice guy and was only looking out for me. We were all looking out for each other. I didn't know much about myself or the world, but I knew what they were doing to us was wrong. I couldn't stand by any longer and just let it happen.

"Shit bucket!"

I picked up my toothbrush.

The IRF team stormed my cage, piled on top of me, restrained me on my stomach with my hands and ankles tied behind my back, and left me like that for hours.

In the mountains where I grew up, respect and integrity and a family's honor were all more valuable than money. They defined a man's worth. How we treated people reflected the values of the family and the tribe. As the son of a tribal leader, if I was ever caught cursing at someone or humiliating them or their family, I would have brought great shame on my entire family. If I lied, it was not only a sin in Allah's eyes, but a shame on my family's name. While my father's beating might hurt, my mother's disappointment was worse. The Americans didn't understand our values and how important things like respect and integrity were to us.

In Raymah, even enemies were treated with respect. My father had told me about battles where he shared a meal with his enemies and let them rest from their long journey before the fight. I understood that there was a right way and a wrong way to treat human beings, even those you thought of as your enemies. My American captors held no such values.

Soon after they unshackled me, soldiers came to take us to the showers. Even though we were hot and sweaty and enjoyed the cool water, it was one of the most humiliating routines of our detention. They started with Yousif and made him strip naked in the middle of the block, in front of all of us, then searched his genitals. When some soldiers searched us, they punched us in the genitals or pulled them hard and fast so others couldn't see. That's exactly what the soldier did to Yousif. Yousif pushed the soldier hard and that was enough to call the IRF team to beat him. On this day, there was a female soldier escorting brothers to shower. I'd never been naked in front of a woman in my life until I was sold to the United States, and every time they stripped us in front of them it was another humiliation.

"I can't do this today," I said to the Dane.

"This is how they are, brother," the Dane said. "They are okay being naked in front of each other."

"No!" I said.

They lined up other brothers, all naked out in front of their cages, their hands cuffed behind their backs so they couldn't cover themselves. When they came for me, I refused.

After the IRF team beat me and restrained me, a soldier came back with an interpreter.

"Will you go to the shower? he asked.

"No." I was firm. "Let me cover myself so the women can't see me, and I'll go."

Several brothers heard what I said, and they refused to go to the shower, too, unless they could cover themselves. The soldiers didn't know what to do. They couldn't send IRF teams to all the men who refused.

It wasn't long until the camp commander, a marine general named Lehnert, came to my cage with an interpreter and many soldiers. He wanted to know why I wouldn't go to the shower.

"We are modest," I told him through the interpreter. The general nodded like he understood and that gave me courage to speak more. "You make us strip in front of women. You search our genitals. It's not right that the female soldiers watch us shower. You know it's against our religion, but you still do it."

"It's security," the general said. "I need to keep my soldiers safe."

"Then give me a pair of shorts to cover myself."

"If I give you shorts, will you shower?" He said this like he didn't believe this problem could be so easily solved.

"Yes," I said.

The general came back later with shorts.

I put them on and I went to the shower peacefully. It felt like the part of me that had been stripped away and replaced by a number rose to the surface. For a moment, I thought they saw *me*, nineteen-year-old Mansoor, a tribesman who was as good as his word, not the bloodthirsty, lying al Qaeda leader the interrogators wanted me to be. This gave me hope that they would begin seeing us for who we really were.

THE HOPE DIDN'T last long. The Americans seemed at odds with each other over the question of who we were: Were we animals and monsters or were we humans, and how should we be treated? There were two generals in charge of the camp, and it was the marine general who gave us shorts. The other one intensified the interrogations. And while these questions seemed to divide the Americans, it brought us together. The cruel treatment had created a new brotherhood among us and the bonds between us were growing strong. When one of us was hurt, we all hurt. That's what happened when al Qurashi was beaten while praying and his Qur'an stomped on by a soldier.

The news spread like fire. Brothers sang it out as if calling a prayer and soon the sound of "Allahu Akbar!" filled the air. I didn't know al Qurashi and neither did the Dane or Yousif. It didn't matter who he was because he was one of us. Guards had knocked him to the ground, stripped the towel from his waist, and desecrated his Qur'an. Al Qurashi could have been Taliban or a schoolteacher, our response would have been the same. The camp fell into chaos.

Brothers all over the camp threw water at the soldiers, called them names, threw their towels and sleep mats out into the walkway. Anger and frustration poured out of us, and the soldiers left us alone. Hours later, after we had quieted, soldiers came and took us one by one to an empty yard away from the noise of the camp. In this quiet place, they put me on my knees with a few others, lined up with our hands bound behind our backs as if they were going to execute us. The brother next to me began to pray his final prayers. I looked up into the night sky, black but brightened by so many stars like the night sky in Raymah. I thought about my mother and father, who didn't know where I was or what had happened to me. Would they ever know? I tried to be strong and not cry thinking about how I would never see my family again. As I looked up, I found comfort in the beauty and vastness of the universe above. It was a reminder of Allah's magnificence, that we are all a part of His plan. If this is what Allah wished for me, so be it. Death would be better than this.

A calm settled over me as I waited to be executed, and I realized that when you have nothing, when you have been tortured and beaten, you lose your fear of the unknown. This surprised me. I never imagined I could lose my fear even of death.

Fear of the unknown is what I think drove our captors to such dark places, to imagine the worst in us. The soldiers didn't know who we were, and that made them afraid and angry. I was a living example of their fear: my face and eyes were swollen and bruised from beatings. I knew that if you didn't face that fear and own it, you would lose touch with who you are.

They left us in that empty yard for a long time, I think, to show us that they could execute us if they wished to, that no one would ever know. Then, one by one, they brought us to interrogators who asked us who started the uproar.

"You did!" we said.

Back at the cages, brothers whispered about what we could do to protest the worsening conditions and al Qurashi's beating. We wanted to be able to talk freely and to stand. We wanted the IRFs to stop, along with punishments like being restrained on our stomachs. We wanted to be able to cover ourselves—for shade, when we used the buckets, and during prayer. We wanted to be able to pray the way we had prayed all our lives—together—and not get beaten. We wanted to know what we were accused of and what would happen to us.

Arabs talk a lot. Some would say we talk too much. And that night we went to sleep having settled nothing. But someone unexpected visited us in our cages while we slept. The hunger jinn whispered into our ears, *Hunger strike*. I'd never heard of Mr. Hunger Strike before, but other brothers had.

"It's a sin to hurt yourself on purpose," one brother said.

"This is the only way," another said. "Let us at least try it."

Some talked from a military perspective, some from a political view, some from a religious view. Many brothers kept silent.

And then Yousif, the boy in the cage next to me, refused the morning meal. He couldn't even grow a full beard or mustache. But he acted while others debated.

There comes a point when it doesn't matter how afraid you are, you must act. I saw what Yousif did and knew what I had to do. When soldiers brought my meal, I refused. I think my father, who knew how to make right from wrong, would have been proud.

I didn't know how to tell the guards in English that I was on a hunger strike. When the block commander came, I asked the Dane to translate. He was always very polite and knew how to talk to the soldiers.

"Tell him I'm on hunger strike," I said.

"Okay?" The block commander laughed at me. "Now, go fuck yourself!" This made the other soldiers laugh.

At the next meal, two more brothers joined us. We heard that brothers in other parts of the camp had refused their meals, too.

We had no plan. We just acted. When soldiers came to make us drink water, Yousif refused. I followed.

Many of our brothers didn't think we would make it to the next meal. They thought we were young and naïve and would be so hungry and thirsty that we would break by midday. I worried they might be right.

It was so hot, and by the end of the first day, every movement, every word, every breath sent sharp daggers into my head. I couldn't even sleep. I wanted to drink water, but I wouldn't betray my brothers. In the middle of the night, soldiers charged into my cage and dragged me out. They put Yousif and me in the middle of the block on our stomachs, our wrists and ankles shackled together behind our backs like we were goats. They left us like this for hours. It was then that I knew I would be strong enough.

More brothers joined us until we heard brothers were striking across the camp. I blacked out on the third day and was taken to a medical tent, where they tied me to a bed and nurses put an IV in my arm. Yousif was taken, too. Every day the number of brothers refusing meals increased and so did the number taken to the medical tent. Mr. Hunger Strike walked the blocks happy with what he had started.

The Muslim chaplain brought us a fatwa he printed in Arabic saying that it was against the teachings of Islam to harm ourselves with hunger. Then he recited a verse from the Qur'an: *O you who have believed, do not consume one another's wealth unjustly but only in business by mutual consent. And do not kill yourselves. Indeed, Allah is to you ever Merciful.*

This was the Pakistani chaplain who watched us get stripped naked and beaten, who watched us get punished for practicing our faith, and as far as we knew had never said a word in protest.

"As you know, it is our religion to pray together," we said. "Why do you sit by and watch them beat us for practicing our faith?"

He had no answer for this. So none of us listened to him.

Ten days passed, and we knew the hunger strike was serious when the marine general Lehnert walked the blocks with an interpreter talking to prisoners. When he came to our block, he knelt down in front of our cages and talked to us through the interpreter. He had the squarest jaw I had ever seen, and sharp eyes, but when we talked, he nodded his head and listened.

It surprised me that he would kneel down and talk to so many of us.

Our demands were simple. We wanted to be able to practice our religion praying together. We wanted to be able to stand and talk freely. We wanted to be able to cover ourselves. We wanted the soldiers to stop harassing us.

"I hear you," the general said.

One of the older, more educated brothers asked, "Can you tell us where we are and what crimes we have committed?"

"No," the general said. "But I can promise there will be hearings soon."

Soon the general announced over loudspeakers the changes to the camp we had asked for. He promised us hearings and the possibility of release.

"Allahu Akbar!" we cried out.

We all stopped our strike, except two brothers, one Yemeni and one Kuwaiti, who continued their strike for another month.

I thanked Mr. Hunger Strike. He was so naughty. *Oh, sweetie,* he said. *We haven't even gotten started.*

WE COULDN'T HAVE been in a worse hell, but the mood changed after the hunger strike. It seemed like some of our captors were starting to understand that we weren't the bloodthirsty terrorists they thought we were. Even though we still didn't know where we were or what would happen to us, we could stand and talk and pray freely. This gave us a sense that we could reclaim some parts of ourselves we had lost, and that made us feel human. We talked to each other now and opened up. We even played jokes on each other.

There were more Afghans than any other nationality, and for most of them, their world was their village and farm where their families had lived for generations. They lived in mud huts and had simple lives. Some were illiterate and spoke only Pashto or Urdu, like Gulam. He seemed old in his midthirties and had never seen an airplane until he was sent to Kandahar. *How does it fly?* he asked over and over again.

We were all in bad shape after the hunger strike, worse than when we arrived. Ismatu Allah, a fourteen-year-old Afghan who had fainted the first day of the strike, was introduced to Ms. Ensure, blond, sweet, and delicious, who filled him up and helped him gain weight. Ms. Ensure was everywhere. I really liked how she made me feel full. I liked her so much, I gave some to my neighbors who didn't hunger strike.

"Gulam," I called. "I want to introduce you to my good friend, Ms. Ensure. Put your cup to the fence."

"What's this Ensure?" Gulam asked. He was illiterate, but he was smart to be skeptical.

"You don't know about Ensure?" Shah asked. "How many rupees were you sold for?"

"Over one hundred thousand," Gulam said, which was about $1,500.

"I think the Americans overpaid," Shah said. He was also from Afghanistan but had lived in the Emirates and was well educated. "This is American woman's breast milk!"

Gulam furrowed his eyebrows and sucked his tongue. He didn't like what he heard.

"Look at the American's hair," Shah said, speaking of the nearby female corpsman with blond hair. "Now look at the Ensure. They're the same color, brother!"

Most of the Afghani brothers, like Gulam, had never seen blond women before. Blond women with their white-white skin were like angels to these men, even if they wore the US uniform.

Gulam sat quietly for a while, watching the blond corpsman head for a tent.

"She's very pretty, isn't she?" Shah said. "Her breast milk is beautiful like her and tastes like honey. When she comes out, she'll have fresh Ensure. She's in there milking her breasts for us."

Gulam tsked, he was so disgusted. But he respected Shah and trusted him. He watched the tent carefully. The female corpsman came out in a few minutes carrying cans of vanilla Ensure. Gulam's face soured. What was true and what wasn't in this crazy upside-down world? Gulam's neighbor had turned him over to the Northern Alliance so that he could take his land. If he could be sold to the United States as a Taliban fighter, flown through the air in the belly of a metal beast all the way to the other side of the world where he'd been told that the sun set in the east and rose in the west, was it so hard to believe that this golden liquid that made us strong and helped us gain weight was American breast milk?

Gulam's face went pale.

"If you want some, just ask her," Shah said. "Watch Mansoor."

I called the female corpsman and asked her for Ensure. Other brothers asked, too.

She disappeared to the medical tent.

"You Arabs are bad people!" Gulam cursed. "Shame on you!"

"Mmmm," Shah said. "Smell the honey!"

When the corpsman came back, Gulam went crazy and splashed me with water. Be careful with an angry Afghan.

Another Afghani brother in a cage across from us asked Gulam why he was so angry.

"Do you know what they're drinking?" Gulam cried.

We all laughed loudly, and that made him even angrier.

"Allah forgive us all for these men's sins," Gulam cried. He started praying.

We laughed even harder. We were sixty brothers in our block now—six large cages with ten cages in each and inside each cage a lost human desperate for anything good. So we laughed hard and loud at our Afghani brother. We laughed and our laughter felt good. It made us feel like we weren't crazy. But our loud laughing caught the soldiers' attention, and they came running.

"Why are you laughing?" they yelled. They looked scared. I wondered if they thought we had magical powers.

"What's so funny? Why are you so happy?"

If they couldn't understand, we could never teach them.

THEY COULDN'T HOLD us like this forever and we all knew it was just a matter of time before something big happened. The interrogations got worse, while the living conditions got a little better. The young soldiers in the camp seemed confused by us the more time they spent with us. I heard about brothers who could speak English singing and rapping with soldiers. Even the marine general who had helped end the hunger strike was overheard saying to a tour of civilians that the camp held mostly farmers, boys, and men with no fighting experience—not terrorists and killers.

Weeks, we thought, months at the most, and we would be set free. They were just trying to squeeze us for any last drops of information before they released us. The older brothers who were educated and knew about the world and international laws said the Americans couldn't hold us forever without a reason—it was against their laws; it was against international laws.

But many brothers still thought we would be executed. They came from countries known to torture prisoners, and those prisoners never lived to tell about it. They were always executed instead of released.

"How can they just release hundreds of men they have tortured?"

THEY CAME ON Sunday, just after the morning meal was served. Officers with high ranks walked the blocks, stopping at each cage to compare photographs of us from the day we arrived with what we looked like now. Months had passed and we hadn't been allowed to shave or have our hair cut. We looked very different from the men in our photos with no hair or beards, faces bruised.

Armored Humvees and buses pulled into the camp, and hundreds of masked soldiers in battle gear swarmed the blocks with dogs. The air was tense. I tried to show strength, but I was terrified. The fake executions they had done before never looked like this. There was so much movement. They seemed serious this time. I didn't have the stomach to eat my breakfast. No one did.

"I don't want to die!" Ismatu Allah cried.

"Why would they bring us breakfast if they are going to kill us?" the Dane asked. But he looked nervous, too, and this scared me.

"Someone saw a stack of body bags at the front gate," Yousif whispered.

Brothers hurried to make ablution and to prepare for their last prayer before death.

Please, Allah, grant me forgiveness, I prayed. *Grant me entrance to paradise.*

Despite all the noise of soldiers and dogs, a strange quiet entered my soul, and I listened to myself breathe. As I repeated my prayers, the fear washed off me and a calm settled in. I waited for the worst to happen next.

"I've seen people executed," the Dane said. "I don't know what this is, but it's different."

"Detainee 3028!" A masked IRF team stood outside Ismatu Allah's cage. "On your knees! Hands over your head!"

The blood drained from Ismatu Allah's face.

"Don't worry!" I said. I smiled. I tried to give him my strength. "They are going to take you home now." I don't know why I said this. I just wanted to make him feel less afraid. The IRF team rushed into his cage, restrained him, and put a hood over his head, then earmuffs and goggles. They searched him in the worst possible way; why would they do this now?

"Cowards!" I screamed. "Donkeys!" I banged my cage as they led Ismatu Allah away. All the other brothers shouted, too. I was mad and not thinking, and I grabbed my shit bucket and threatened the soldiers with it. Other brothers joined me. But more masked IRF teams stormed the block. There were too many of them.

I put my bucket down and swore to Allah that I would fight with every ounce of strength I had. As they loaded brothers onto buses, I paced my cage, pounded the fencing, cursed. The soldiers ignored me and soon the entire block was empty except for me. No Yousif. No Gulam. No Dane. No Ismatu Allah. Their cages were open; the mats, buckets, and clothes—all of it left behind.

The IRF team came for me just as the sun was setting. I'd been praying and watching a lone female soldier stuff what was left in the cages into black garbage bags. This is it, I thought. My heart pounded through my chest. I was ready to fight to the very end and that's what I did. But they still beat me to the ground and got me shackled and hooded. Then they searched me. I kicked. I tried to headbutt them. I refused to walk, so they carried me to the bus and chained me to its floor. Someone removed my earmuffs and whispered in my ears in English. I didn't know what he said, but it didn't sound harsh or cruel. It didn't sound like he hated me or was going to execute me. That one whisper calmed me down and comforted me, and I was ready for whatever would come next.

- FOUR -

Hooded and shackled, I was unloaded from the bus, shoved along a gravel path, and pulled up a short set of metal stairs into a metal room that boomed and echoed with every step. My heart pounded and I struggled to control my fear. They stopped me, searched me again, checking my genitals as if I had something to hide and the time to hide it, then forced me to my knees. They removed the shackles, then my hood, and pushed me so hard I hit the ground. When the heavy metal door slammed behind me, I felt it in every cell of my body. I was in complete darkness.

Then I heard a song, soft and distant like a whisper in a cave. It reminded me of a nightingale. Was it a verse from the Qur'an? The song repeated and repeated until I heard it clearly.

O the one with trouble, be optimistic, your trouble will fade away, Allah is the one who will set you free.

"Hello!" I called out.

"No talking!" The guards banged on the door and then turned on the fan outside my door so I couldn't hear the Nightingale's songs anymore, no matter how hard I tried.

Nothing in all those months of interrogations, the black site, prison camps, or hooded trips to unknown places could have prepared me for the controlled chaos of Camp Delta and the cold machinery of the interrogation laboratory they were creating. I thought I was ready for anything, but I could never have imagined the cruel isolation of solitary confinement.

For the first couple of days, I had no light. As my eyes adjusted to the dark, I saw that I was in a green metal box, smaller than the cages in Camp X-Ray, with one window on the outside wall and another in the door. Both were covered from the outside. The only light came from faint cracks around the bean hole just below the window on the door. At first, I enjoyed the cool air blowing from a vent above, but soon the cold set in and I had nothing but my thin pants and shirt to keep me warm. All I'd been given was a thin sleeping pad called an ISO mat, a pair of flip-flops, and a Qur'an—nothing more.

It doesn't take long for the mind to play tricks when it has nothing to do—nothing to look at, colors or contrasts; nothing to feel—and the longer I was in complete darkness, the more my ears played tricks listening to the sounds all around me. Above me, ventilation fans roared like a helicopter. Outside, generators rumbled. Fans screamed in the hallway. Doors banged open and closed constantly and guards stomped and called in English, their voices echoing and booming against the thick metal walls. Prisoners in other cells called out, but their voices were so distant and muffled I couldn't understand them. Soon the sounds were overwhelming, and I couldn't turn them off. I covered my ears with my hands, but that didn't help. The noise was so loud and persistent, it made my ears ache and my head throb. I thought I would go crazy if it didn't stop.

It never did. It's amazing what the human mind can get used to. I adjusted, just like I adjusted to men screaming in pain in the black site and to the humiliation of living in cages at X-Ray.

Then they turned the lights on in my cell, which was worse than the dark. They were big and bright like truck lights, and now they never went off. I slept, but not well, and never for long with the powerful light overhead burning into my eyes.

With the windows covered, there was no natural light to help track the days. Time is life and when you lose track of time, you lose touch with your life. We had no clocks or watches, and we weren't allowed to know the time. This was all part of their interrogation plan. Time slipped away—hours, days, weeks. In solitary confinement, your life doesn't stop exactly; it becomes suspended while everything else continues around you. Your mind races. You search for an anchor, but the longer you spend in brightness—or darkness—the more you lose touch with time and your previous life. My life narrowed to the sight of green walls, the smell of pine cleaner and bleach, and the sound of the machinery around me.

I prayed. I paced. I jumped. I listened. I waited for meals so that I could look through the bean hole and see the outside or see any part of the person giving me food. I tried to talk to the guards, but they had orders not to talk to us. I called out to the Nightingale, but he didn't answer. This filled me with a new kind of fear. The open tents in Kandahar and the fenced cages in X-Ray were temporary and chaotic. The permanence of these metal walls and the methodical order they used to isolate me were scary and said something very clearly: I wasn't going home anytime soon. I thought I might lose my mind, and that's when the interrogations started.

THE REASON YOU'RE in solitary confinement is because the interrogators want you softened. Things have changed, and not for the better. Gone is the wooden shed, replaced by a new room that's sterile like a laboratory. They chain you to circle irons embedded in the floor. They have your file, but still they want to start at the beginning as if you haven't been held and interrogated for months or tortured in their black site. Good luck getting them caught up. They ask you about everything in your life as if you are really this Adel they think you are. They ask about growing up in Egypt, even though you're Yemeni. They ask about your travels to Nairobi and London and other places you've never been to. They ask you about your religion and how you practice. Some of them seem to know everything about Islam and the world, more than you ever could. They're smart and educated and make you feel small for only finishing high school. With the number of interrogation teams and the information they throw at you, you're starting to understand how serious this all is and it scares you.

After the isolation and not talking to anyone for so long, you feel lost. This is what they want. They want you to talk and talk, not caring about what you say, as if you've been holding back all along. They want you to talk to them as if you are this Adel from Egypt who's much older than you.

"If you stop holding back," they say, "we'll stop all this."

You're still so young and your experience with the law is what you saw through your father and the tribal councils where there was no lying and Allah was always watching. You don't know how all this is supposed to work, so you stop holding back. You just tell them the truth and hope maybe they'll stop all this nonsense.

You tell them in great detail about the warlords and how they told you to say that you're al Qaeda or the Americans would kill you. You tell them about the oil drum the interrogators in Afghanistan put you in and how they rolled it forever with you inside. You tell them how you were electrocuted over and over until you repeated the name Adel the way they wanted you to. You tell them all about the black site and the relation of each scar to a specific beating, including the chunk of flesh missing from your foot. You tell them how you said anything, signed anything, swore anything to make them stop, and how you admitted you were this man named Adel whom you don't know. You tell them you're not Adel and that's why you didn't have his passport and don't know details about al Qaeda or bin Laden or Mullah Omar or how they recruit fighters. None of this makes them happy.

The door slams open and a masked man storms in and slaps you hard across the face. He's so violent you think he might knock your head off your shoulders. Even the interpreter seems afraid of him.

"What's wrong with this crazy guy?" you say. Though you're scared, you still haven't lost your sense of humor. But he doesn't laugh. None of them do. He comes close to your face.

"You're a fucking liar and I'm going to fuck your fucking life up!" he yells, an inch away from your face, his breath rotten with bad coffee. "Sounds like you didn't like the black site so much. You want to go back? We can send you back. We can send you back and start all over again with your interrogator there."

Now he has your attention. Your heart jumps and you feel the blood pounding in your temples. You try to be strong, but it's hard to keep your eyes from watering up as muscles remember the black site, and this makes them happy.

"You're one of the big fish," he says. "And now we own you." He lists things he says you've done. Bombings in Kenya. Recruiting in Yemen. And you think, *How could I have done all this? How could they think I'm old enough to have done all this?*

The female goes through a huge file on the table in front of you.

"We're going to go through your file and every time you lie or change your story, this crazy man here is going to teach you how to be honest."

You swallow, but there's no saliva in your mouth.

She lights a cigarette and offers you one. You decline.

"Fucking al Qaeda," she says. She'll say this when you don't stare at her breasts when she unbuttons her shirt. Every vice you turn down is proof that you're a terrorist.

"Where did you train?" she asks.

The problem, you realize, is that when you said you were this Adel, you didn't know anything about him. You don't know any of the details they want. Now they believe you're holding back, lying, protecting others, being clever, and no matter what you tell them, unless you tell them what they want to hear, they'll say that you're lying. There's no escape from this circle.

"Were you at al Farouq?"

You shake your head no.

The huge man slaps you.

In this way, they go through your file, the huge man slapping you and the female interrogator making notes. After so many slaps you can't count, you make up details but they don't match the ones you gave before and that earns you more slaps because you're lying and here is where they really kick your ass. You can't give something you don't have, and you can't invent something good enough, and they keep repeating and repeating the questions until you don't know what you're saying, and that's when they put words in your mouth. You've been at this for too many hours and too many days and you're tired and weak and you don't know what you're saying anymore and it doesn't matter to you because it's their words and not yours and Allah will forgive that, but still they make their notes in your file.

Now they go through their piles of photos.

"Who's this?" they say. "Do you know him?" They ask you to confirm names and faces of men you've never seen, but they don't believe you when you say "I don't know." This is how your problem just gets worse and worse. The more you say "I don't know," the more they say you're lying. Hours pass like this, a day, maybe more . . . they take breaks and change teams. They eat their meals in front of you and don't offer you so much as a cup of water. They return you to your cell with the bright light that never turns off and the guards bang your door to keep you awake and before you know it, the escorts are back and you're in the interrogation room again and this goes on for weeks. The only human contact you get are slaps and kicks; the only voices you hear are full of hate and distrust. So, this is America! An image takes shape in your head of a people who don't believe in the truth, who don't know right from wrong.

WITH TIME, WE figured out ways to connect through the thick metal walls in solitary confinement, and that little contact helped me survive at first. If I lay down on the ground and put my ear to the small holes in the wall, I could hear my neighbor talk. This is how I got to know the Nightingale, who turned out to be one of Osama bin Laden's bodyguards. He told me about some of the other big fish on the block: the al Qaeda minister of propaganda, Osama bin Laden's driver, and the Taliban's chief of communications. None of them denied who they were, but the minister of propaganda refused to talk to the interrogators. Then one day he did.

"Why did he start talking?" I asked.

"Sheikh Osama told him not to talk for six months," he said, "so that's what he did. He kept his word." I knew that meant he had been tortured and he still didn't talk. *Allah, oh Allah.* What had I gotten myself into? I wasn't a big fish, yet there was no way to convince the Americans I wasn't.

Sometimes the guards left the bean holes open by accident and the Nightingale sang out to me, telling me to keep strong, that Allah was watching over me. In these rare moments, I'd catch glimpses of the other brothers in solitary confinement being taken to interrogation or to the shower or rec. They were all older than me—much older—and had the toughened faces of men who knew the cost of war.

"Assalamu alaikum," I'd call out.

On the way back from interrogation one night, I saw that my neighbor's bean hole was open—it was the Nightingale. All I could see were his eyes, warm and kind, matching the beauty of his voice.

"You're just a boy," he sang out. "You're not a big fish—you're a guppy. What are they doing bringing boys to this place?"

I don't know what they accused him of or what he knew about Osama bin Laden. He told me he was hired to be a bodyguard and had given his word to do his job, and he did just that.

The Nightingale and all the others in solitary confinement were tribal men, mostly, from Pakistan, Afghanistan, and Yemen. Men who had an idea in their mind of what was right and what was wrong and no gray area in between. Yes, some of them were fighters, but they weren't fighting the Americans, at least the ones I met in solitary. They had more important battles to fight with the Northern Alliance and other tribes that their own tribes had battled for generations. I was still young and naïve and learning about the world, but I saw that these men were different from our interrogators and the guards who acted as if they were guided by honor and duty. Honor and duty to what? To defend freedom against me? Is buying men and torturing them what they called freedom? If you asked me who had more honor and integrity between interrogators and the interrogated, my answer would have been clear.

INTERROGATORS WANTED ME to break down in isolation. I tried to hold on for as long as I could, but I felt my mind slipping away. The only friend I talked to for weeks was Princess, who visited me during my ten minutes in the rec yard each week. Iguanas were everywhere, but I liked to think she was the same one who visited me in Camp X-Ray. Even though I didn't have any food to share with her, she stayed with me anyway and listened to me talk about my life. I missed my family and thought about them every minute of every day. I found safety and comfort replaying in my mind moments from my childhood, like how my mother always prepared me and my brothers and sisters to go to school each morning. She made us tea and warmed tomato-and-bean soup, then lined us up and kissed each one of us as we left. I tried to feel that kiss and smell her scent of firewood and the fields, but it was all slipping away, replaced by memories of green walls and interrogators and what I wished I'd said during interrogations that could have saved me. I worried my memories of home would be lost forever. Without them, who would I be?

As the days bled away, I stopped caring how much time had passed. I stopped thinking about when I would get out. I stopped eating and I went on hunger strike again. But the camp thought of that as a threat, and as punishment they stripped me naked and took everything out of my cell. It didn't matter. I didn't care if I lived or died. If I died, I would see my family in paradise. I stopped talking to Princess. I stopped listening to the Nightingale's songs and I stopped calling back.

When my beard was so long and my hair so wild my mother would have scolded me for not taking care of myself, the Wrestler showed up at my cell door.

We called her the Wrestler because she was big and broad and had the biceps of a wrestler, but she was just the camp psychologist. Back in X-Ray, brothers passed rumors that she was a sorcerer who could send jinns or demons to make you lose your mind. I didn't believe in sorcerers. We had one in my village who cheated people out of their money. When I was a kid, I said to my mother, "If this sorcerer really has jinns, why does she take people's money to summon them?" My mother had little patience for such nonsense and sent me out to help with the goats. So I went straight to the sorcerer and asked her. She cursed me and kicked me out of her house. But I knew her secret. I knew she was a fraud.

I didn't even know what a psychologist was though. I had never heard the word before this place, and that scared me more than a sorcerer.

"Be careful talking to this one," the Dane had said. "You like to talk too much, and she could really get inside your head and mess with it."

When she showed up at my cell door, I thought, *Oh Allah! What have I gotten myself into?*

"Are you trying to hurt yourself?" the Wrestler asked.

I refused to talk to her because we knew that the psychologists were working with the interrogators. And when they sent the interrogators, I wouldn't talk to them either. I just sat in the corner of my cell with my knees pulled to my chest and I prayed. She watched me and took notes, and sometime after she left I was given back my pants and a shirt. Soon the bean hole in my door opened and a guard told me to turn around and get on my knees with my hands on my head so I could be restrained. I was being moved out of solitary confinement. I had been afraid of the Wrestler, but I thought she was the one responsible for getting me out of solitary confinement, at least for a couple of days. I was thankful to be out, but in the reality of Guantánamo, I was right where the interrogators wanted me, hanging by a thread.

- FIVE -

When I first saw the open cages of Camp Delta, I thought they had created a zoo there for Muslims—or was it a laboratory? As they escorted me off solitary confinement, I saw for the first time Camp Delta's Camp 1 and all the blocks made out of metal shipping containers. We walked past neat and orderly rows of cell blocks: Alpha, Bravo, Delta, Echo, Fox, Golf, and Hotel to Charlie at the very end. I heard the familiar sound of men inside shouting to each other in so many languages and voices.

"Assalamu alaikum," brothers called out to me as I shuffled down the walkway between two rows of cages facing each other. There was no air conditioning in the open cage blocks, each with forty-eight men, one to a cell, all baking in the heat. The block reeked of sweat and fear.

Everything was metal: the walls between cages were a thick metal mesh, with holes only big enough for two fingers, but at least you could see through it. Some brothers talked to their neighbors; others called out down the block. It was noisy but comforting to hear the sound of so many men talking.

From my new cell, I could only see brothers to the left and to the right and directly across from me for two or three cages in each direction.

"Assalamu alaikum," brothers called out.

"Wa alaikum Assalam!" I choked back tears, so happy to be in the company of so many new faces and voices. I had so many questions.

"Where are we?" I asked my neighbor, a young Saudi.

At last, I found out we were in a place called Guantánamo, an American military base on the island of Cuba, close to America but not in America. The American president Bush had declared a war on terror and that's why hundreds of men had been brought here. Some of the new prisoners had actually seen news footage of us on Al Jazeera before they were taken here.

It was noisy and wild in the open cages but at least we could talk. "What's your name? Where are you from? What's your story?" I asked my neighbors first, then called out to brothers down the block. I found men from dozens of different countries around the world speaking more than twenty different languages.

"You're from the mountains, aren't you?" my neighbor asked. His name was Fayez and he was a well-mannered, educated Kuwaiti, older than me.

"How did you know?" I said.

"You haven't sat still the entire time you've been here. You're used to having space and talking." We both laughed because he was right.

Being in isolation for so long, I was hungry for any news and conversation, to talk about and to better understand this place we were in. But the open cages were loud and the lights bright. Like the solitary confinement cells, there was a toilet and running water in the cages, but your toilet was next to your neighbor's bed. The smell was terrible and there was no escape from it. When you tried to sleep, you had no choice but to put your head right beneath the blazing light, and we weren't allowed to cover our eyes or face. Everything seemed to have been built to make sure we were as uncomfortable as possible, to break us over and over again.

I was glad to be in the open like this, but I was crushed by the sounds. The open cages of Camp Delta were like a massive living, breathing, never-ending song that was a complete assault on your ears, especially if you had spent months in complete isolation. The day began with the morning praye, and then the gates banged open and stomping boots announced the morning head count. From there on, it was an unrelenting cacophony of meal carts squeaking, bean holes banging, chains jangling, guards barking, detainees shouting, ventilators rumbling . . . It was all too much, and it was all by design.

It was a place of arbitrary rules strictly enforced with one end and one end only: to control us for interrogation. We didn't know it at the time, but they called this "controlled chaos."

We added our own chaos. When brothers were taken away for their "reservations" with interrogators, we sang to them: *Go with peace, go with peace, may Allah grant you ever more peace and ever more safety. Go with peace, go with peace.* We sang this, all of us, with one big voice that echoed and boomed. And when brothers were returned, we sang again.

After I had been out of isolation for a couple of days, I was feeling good that the interrogations had finally stopped and that maybe at last they understood that a nineteen-year-old Yemeni from the mountains wasn't a seasoned, middle-aged al Qaeda leader.

That morning, guards escorted me to the rec yard for my ten minutes of fresh air and beautiful views of green tarp. After rec would be my two-minute shower. The rec yard was divided into two cages so that two brothers could be out there at the same time. I saw Suhib, a Libyan brother I hadn't seen since the first days of Camp X-Ray. I was glad for any familiar face, and I went to the fence and put my hand out to greet him. Our hands hadn't even touched when the guard shouted at me.

"Rec time is terminated!"

"No English," I said. I smiled, trying to communicate that I wasn't looking for trouble, only that I didn't speak English. I was trying to be the polite young man my mother had raised. The guard called an Arabic interpreter.

"You broke the rules," the interpreter said.

Guards came and escorted Suhib back to his cell. I felt guilty—
we only got ten minutes twice a week and I had caused him to lose
his time.

"What did I do?" I asked.

"You shook hands with another detainee," the interpreter said.

"That's crazy," I said. "We didn't even touch!"

"It doesn't matter," the interpreter said. "It's a rule and you
broke it."

The harshness of the rules hurt. Not because they were strict,
but because they were cruel. It had been months since I felt the touch
of a kind hand, even for something as simple as a handshake. It was
wrong. *If these are the rules,* I thought, *they're going to have to drag me
out of here.*

"I'm not coming out," I said. "Even if you call your mother, the
watch commander."

The watch commander stormed out and stood at the rec gate
screaming all kinds of curses in English I didn't understand.

"By Allah," I said. "I'm not coming out, even if Bush himself comes
to talk to me. Why are you punishing me—because I tried to shake a
brother's hand in greeting?"

I knew it wouldn't do any good, but I had to do something. The
IRF team marched into the yard, their boots booming. I knew where I
was going. They kicked my ass. Of course they did. They beat me badly
and dragged me back to my hole in solitary confinement, where I sang
about it to the Nightingale and all the other big fish. I couldn't see
them or shake their hands, but I felt the comfort of my fellow brothers.

- SIX -

After thirty or forty or fifty days in solitary confinement, just as I was really falling apart and in bad shape, they'd move me back to the open cages for a few days and begin the cycle all over again. In those early days of Camp Delta, it seemed like they were confused about what they were supposed to do with us, or that we had disappointed them by not actually being important al Qaeda or Taliban fighters. Interrogators moved big fish around to keep us feeling isolated and unstable, to keep us from making friends or becoming too familiar with any one block. If I wasn't in solitary confinement in India Block, I was being moved around in the open cage blocks. They'd keep me in one cage for a few days, then move me along.

Solitary confinement was hard, but the constant movement had its advantages: I learned the camp fast. I got to know the ins and outs of all the different blocks, how things worked, who was where and why, and most important, who everyone was.

It always started with the cry of "Chains are coming," a brother letting us know escorts were coming onto the block to move someone. When this happened, everyone rushed to use the toilet and get their things in order. Whoever they came for could be gone for hours or days, often with no access to a toilet, or they might not even be coming back. Some passed things to their neighbors through the small holes in the mesh—a toothbrush or extra towels, a little food they had saved for sunset if they were fasting. Then we'd all wait to see whom the escorts came for. Guards played with us. They'd walk up and down the block, dragging their chains looking at brothers like it was their turn to go, or they'd stop in front of a cage and say, "You?" You never knew where you were going or why. The uncertainty was just another tool they used to keep us on edge for the interrogators.

Camp Delta was made up of three camps at first, Camps 1, 2, and 3. Each camp had five or seven blocks, and out of those blocks there were a few that no one wanted to go to.

Delta Block was one. It was called the BHU, the Behavioral Health Unit. Here, psychologists watched you twenty-four hours a day, taking notes on everything you did. They restrained you to metal beds and paralyzed you with shots. It's where your worst nightmares came true.

India, November, and Oscar blocks were solitary confinement for big fish, punishments, and softening. Most brothers were terrified of solitary confinement after hearing stories like mine of being isolated for weeks and months.

Even knowing what I went through, some crazy brothers tried to get sent to solitary because it was the only place that had air conditioning and some peace from the chaos of the open cages. The summer was a special kind of hell in the mesh cages with no fans and all those men sweating, but those brothers didn't know how crushing the isolation could be.

It was a gamble every time they moved you. Some blocks were better than others. Hotel, Charlie, Kilo, and Papa blocks were closest to the sea, close enough that sometimes you could hear waves crash against the rocks at night. The sound reminded us that there was still a free world outside our fences—our friends and families were still out there.

In the beginning, some brothers could see the sea if they stood on their sink and looked through their window. In the rec yard, I found that if I lay down on my stomach in the corner, I could tear away a tiny piece of green tarp covering the fence and steal glimpses of a turquoise sea. I told my brothers and soon many of us would lie down and spend our recreation time looking at the sea through that small secret window. Eventually the guards noticed the hole.

"Why can't I look at the sea?" I asked the watch commander when he caught me.

"It's for your own safety and security," he said through an interpreter. I suspected he thought Osama bin Laden might land on the beach one day with an al Qaeda army and break us all out. America was supposed to be a smart country, but the things they believed made us question this.

I made another hole in a different place, and when guards found that one, they doubled the tarps around all the blocks and then sent me back to solitary confinement for a couple of weeks with Princess.

It was hard not seeing the sea despite being only a few hundred feet away. We had so little in our cages, a brief glimpse of beauty and the magnificence of Allah's creation could carry our spirits for days or weeks. I remember explaining what I saw to one brother who couldn't see the sea.

"I see an endless body of blue," I said, "with a soul that courses through the Atlantic Ocean, the Mediterranean, and the Suez Canal, all the way to the Red Sea and the western coast of Yemen, where in the seaside town of Hudaydah, my father is at the market buying fish for a special meal. And when the tide comes in and the air is heavy with salt, my mind takes me straight to the port city of Aden and weekends I spent there with friends after high school. We'd lie on the beach and imagine our lives and the wives and families we would one day have."

The sea infiltrated our dreams, reminding us of our past and giving us hope for our future freedom. The sound and smell of the sea were like the firm reassurance of a good friend who promises to protect you and be your witness. We all talked to the sea, confided in it, pleaded with it. *Please stay with us*, we asked the sea. *Please set us free.*

We lived as neighbors and friends with the sea, and even though we weren't able to see it, the sea was with us all the time. Some brothers composed poems about the sea and sang them for the rest of the block. Some asked the sea to bring messages to the ones they loved and missed on faraway shores. Some complained about our prison and guards to the sea. Some reproached the sea for watching and doing nothing.

One Yemeni brother I met during a short stay in Hotel Block— close to the sea—was so in love with the sea, he named himself Bahr, which means "sea" in Arabic.

"Why would you name yourself Bahr?" I asked.

"What is greater than the sea?" he said.

Bahr had a beautiful voice and sang for us all the time. In those first months at Camp Delta, even the guards asked Bahr to sing.

"I can't say no to anyone," he'd say. "When someone asks me to sing, it's because they have some trouble in their heart. What is better than making other people happy?"

Bahr sang in Arabic, Pashto, Persian, and English, but even if our brothers or the guards didn't understand the words, his voice was enough to free us all from our caged lives, even if only for a moment. Music and poetry are the soul's languages, and when Bahr sang, all the blocks quieted down so they could listen. His voice and his songs carried with me into solitary confinement, where I listened to Bahr and the sea in my head.

Once, one of the idiot interrogators told me during interrogation, "Stop holding out on us and I'll take you to see the sea."

"I already have Bahr on my block," I said. "Why would I want to go to yours?"

I laughed and so did my interrogators.

Still, they moved me off Bahr's block to Mike Block, one of the blocks that was always full of Afghans. Few if any of those brothers on Mike Block spoke Arabic, and that's why interrogators liked to send Arabic speakers there. The interrogators thought the isolation of strangers speaking Pashto and Urdu would break us. The Afghans were a tough bunch, but the interrogators didn't understand that each move, each interrogation, each beating brought all of us closer together despite our differences instead of pushing us further apart. This place called Guantánamo had created a brotherhood among us and now we looked out for each other wherever we were, no matter who we were.

Mike Block was only about twenty feet away from Hotel Block, with a walkway separating the buildings. I could still hear Bahr sing, much to the disappointment of the interrogators. I sang back to him that the Afghani brothers treated me like one of their own. The guards and interrogators heard every song we sang, but they never listened.

Everything they did made that clear. Or maybe they listened but couldn't understand what they didn't want to hear—that their choices had consequences and not the ones they expected.

They moved me again, this time to Lima Block, and when I'd been there for a couple of days, a new rotation of guards arrived and began training with the old one. We'd been there long enough to learn that guards rotated missions every six to twelve months, depending on their deployment and assignments. You never completely got used to the noise of the blocks, but you learned to live with it, you learned to adjust, and that made you stronger than the guards or interrogators. This new company of guards couldn't handle the noise.

"Shut the fuck up!" the new guards screamed.

We weren't being disrespectful; we were just living the only way we knew how. Since the hunger strike in X-Ray, we'd been free to talk. But this was before the camp had standard operating procedures and so the new guards were just making up rules. Things got crazy fast. Some brothers started splashing guards with water or milk. The guards called IRF teams. While we were fighting the IRF teams and the guards were yelling at us to shut up, one of the officers,

General Dunlavey, walked onto the block. The generals walked the blocks regularly.

This general was different than the square-jawed one who stopped the hunger strike at X-Ray. This general was in charge of the intelligence task force, not the guards, and he tried to project strength and control whenever he walked the blocks. But he just looked arrogant.

Omar, a Libyan brother with one leg, called out to the general when he walked by.

"Excuse me, sir?" Omar said. He was very respectful. "Yes, we speak, please?" He motioned to the interpreter to translate and then explained that he wanted to talk to the general about the new rules the guards were enforcing.

The general ignored him and waved off the interpreter. He puffed up his chest and stuck his chin in the air. Omar looked around to see if other brothers had seen this. We all saw it. I didn't know Omar well yet, but I'd heard that he was very wise, and all the brothers respected him.

"Brothers!" Omar called down the block. "Say hello to our general!" Within seconds everyone was shouting and yelling in different languages. I joined in. We were like wild animals, biting the fence, making crazy faces. The new guards looked terrified. It was scary, even to me.

The general stopped and went back to Omar's cage.

"Your new guards told us we can't talk," Omar said to the interpreter. "We got rid of that rule in Camp X-Ray, remember? We have to be able to talk. That's just a basic human right."

"You have no rights here," he said. "You gave them up when you joined al Qaeda."

"What do the rules say?" Omar said. The general didn't respond. "Okay," Omar continued. "No rules."

Omar called down the block again and told us there were no rules, and that's when the real chaos started. We all jumped around in our cages. We took our shirts off—also against the "rules." We kicked our doors. We threw whatever we had. We shouted in our loudest voices. We made faces at the guards. Brothers in the next block thought we had all gone mad, that the camp admin had given us drugs in the food that turned us crazy.

The guards got rid of that new rule and I think the general had nightmares about us that night and for weeks to come. I was glad to be on Lima Block and asked the watch commander if I could be moved closer to Omar. He seemed like a wise man I could learn from. But remember, this was Guantánamo, and I was a big fish, and the next day I was moved to another block.

With each move, the camp's brotherhood grew stronger. More of us were resisting the random rules, and it was just a matter of time before there were enough of us resisting that we'd start resisting together.

I thought the general knew what was coming and was trying to get ahead of us. We figured out one of his new tactics when I was on Hotel Block and Ali had his shower cut short. Cutting a shower short might not seem like a big deal, but when you get one two-minute shower a week, it's a big problem you have to protest.

Taking a shower was like a sport. We had to maximize our speed to make one billion moves per fraction of a second in order to strip, lather up, rinse, and get dressed again, all in under 120 seconds. If this were the Olympics, I'm sure my brothers at Guantánamo would have won all kinds of medals. We trained hard at showering and could strip, wash, and rinse in 90 seconds and then have a few moments to enjoy the cold water before the guards started the countdown.

"Ten seconds left," the guards would warn.

A well-trained brother would say at exactly 120 seconds, "Ready to go back." And smile his biggest smile.

Ali was a very patient Saudi brother, very soft-spoken. He trained hard for his shower, and in the few days I had been his neighbor, I saw that he always abided by the rules, always did what the guards asked, and never gave them a hard time. He was the opposite of Waddah, a young Yemeni like me whose father was the head of many tribes. Waddah was always looking out for other brothers and that meant confronting guards. I'd seen him in other blocks, and I'd heard he was always protesting and getting moved around, also like me.

On this day, the guard didn't give Ali his ten-second warning, and when he turned off the water, Ali was still covered with soap. The guard refused to let him rinse. The rules were the rules and we had to follow them no matter what. If we didn't, we knew we would get beaten or worse. One brother who had protested a short shower was beaten so badly guards broke his jaw. Ali was cooperative at first and put on his clothes. He let the guards escort him back to his cage without protesting, but when they removed his chains, he snatched them and retreated to the back of his cage. Sometimes even the most cooperative brothers found their breaking point.

Ali teased the guards and refused to give back his chains. This went on for some time, and we all cheered Ali and taunted the guards.

In Yemen, what my father called the country of love, whenever there was a protest against the government, or even a small riot, our president reacted diplomatically with fighter jets, tanks, artillery—all kinds of peaceful means—as a way to show his love. At Guantánamo, they didn't have fighter jets or tanks, so they had to think of other creative ways to tell us we should be quiet and stop protesting.

One of the guards reached into his pocket and pulled out a small canister that looked like a toy. He sprayed Ali's face with something that made him drop to the ground crying in pain. The guard walked into Ali's cage and snatched the chains.

"I can't breathe!" Ali cried. He coughed hard and turned red, then blue. It was serious and the guard didn't care. None of us had any idea what had happened.

Waddah was the first one banging his cage and cursing the guards. He wasn't hiding anything from the Americans. "When they invaded Afghanistan, they became my enemy," he'd said. He said he told his interrogators, "We aren't friends, but we still need to treat each other like human beings." He thought the attacks on innocent Americans were a sin, but said when he left Guantánamo, he would fight American soldiers again on the battlefield. It wasn't personal. He respected them. They were just enemies.

When the guards walked past, Waddah spat at them. The same guard stopped and pulled out that little can. Waddah stuck his face up to the cage like he wanted whatever the guard had, and that's exactly what happened—the guard sprayed him, too.

Waddah coughed hard and fell back.

"It's definitely not perfume," he cried.

Ali was still wheezing and looked like he was going to die. We all banged our cages and screamed until the guards called for a medic and an interpreter.

When Waddah tried to wash it off, it burned even more.

"It's pepper spray," a Canadian brother called out, "like tear gas."

I didn't know about either and he had to explain. There was a lot I didn't know that I was learning at Guantánamo.

Ali had asthma, and medics took him away to the clinic to be treated.

"Why did you make the guards spray you?" I asked Waddah.

"I wanted to know what I was up against," he said.

"Weren't you afraid you might die?" another brother asked.

"Shame on you!" Waddah laughed. "Death is afraid of me."

A brother at the top of the block called out, "Chains are coming!" and I knew they were coming for me. Whenever there was trouble in a block, they always moved me first.

I understood why Waddah had done that. If he was afraid of that toy canister of pepper spray, the guards would have been in control.

We might be in cages, but we couldn't let them think that we could be controlled so easily.

I got to know the pain of pepper spray quickly. Many of us did as we protested daily abuses like genital searches and guards harassing us in childish ways when we prayed. I was learning the art of resistance, and that would be my survival.

BY THE TIME I met the Bosnian in Lima Block, I'd really gotten to know the pain of pepper spray. The Bosnian was a very nice guy in his early forties, quiet, polite, and well educated. He spoke English well, and soon after he was moved to the cage next to mine, one of the guards from another blocked stopped by. They talked for a while; both laughed. This was really strange. I noticed guards had changed a little since the first days of X-Ray. Some gave brothers extra food if they asked. Some were nice to us and talked openly to brothers who spoke English, even though it was against the rules. But most still seemed confused by their mission and who we were. And I'd never seen one stop by a brother's cage for a laugh.

When the guard left, the Bosnian turned to me.

"I scared the shit out of him a couple weeks ago," he said. Then he told me the story about how that guard had fallen asleep on duty and two other guards had asked him to play a joke.

"They let me out of my cage," the Bosnian said, "without shackles or restraints. They snuck me quietly back to the rec yard shower where this guy was dead asleep. They hid behind me and told me to wake him up saying, 'You're surrounded!'"

"And you did?" I asked.

"I was bored," the Bosnian said. "What else was I going to do all day? At least I got out of my cage. So I woke this sergeant and said very quietly, almost whispering, 'You're surrounded.' I gave him my biggest smile. He looked like he had been expecting a camp revolution all along and knew what to do. He fell to his knees and started begging for his life. I mean really begging. 'Please, don't kill me!' like a baby."

I nodded and laughed. This is who we were to many of the guards: crazed murderers. If we didn't laugh, it would have hurt too much to think about.

"I felt sad for him," the Bosnian said. "I felt sad that he thought I would do that. And for a second, I thought that I shouldn't have scared him like that. Then his friends stormed in laughing. And we all laughed really hard."

The Bosnian got quiet.

"Then they chained me and brought me back to my cage."

We were both quiet for a while.

"Not all jokes are funny," I said. Then I told him about the joke that guards had played on an Afghani brother in November Block who didn't speak English. This Afghan never let guards on the night shift sleep. He was always calling them and asking for something, usually toilet paper. We were allowed only thirty sheets a day, ten sheets with each meal, and he never had enough. One night guards brought him a lot of toilet paper, which made him very happy and quiet until he used the toilet.

"Fire!" I cried, imitating the Afghan. "Medic! Very hot fire. Ass. Hot!"

The Bosnian laughed.

"Guards had sprayed his toilet paper with pepper spray. Everyone on the block laughed hard," I told the Bosnian. "We still call him Detainee on Fire."

I didn't tell him that I was ashamed of my laughter. I had been pepper-sprayed so many times. I knew the pain. But I laughed knowing that for once, it wasn't me.

Life was unpredictable and hard, and what made those moments funny was the situation and the time, and maybe how serious the joke could be if it wasn't a joke. Did this camp really think we were murderers and terrorists or worse? Or were we all playing along in one big joke?

I thought it was more like a game, and I was only starting to learn how to play. I was moved all the time, but some brothers were never moved and moving blocks became their game. The easiest way to get moved was if you had a plumbing problem with your sink or toilet. I saw engineers pull out sheets, towels, pants—anything brothers had in their cages that would fit down the drain and that guards wouldn't notice was missing. One of the brothers overheard a watch commander say that seventy toilets had been reported broken in a single day.

The generals said we were waging war against them through the plumbing and made a new rule that anyone with a broken toilet or sink would be punished. Their cage would be fixed and then the brother would be moved back to the cage. In response, my neighbor in Kilo Block figured out a way to flood the entire block using a blanket and a system of strings he pulled from his towel. The generals came running and ordered an immediate evacuation of the block.

"May Allah bless you," brothers called out.

"Can you flood all of Guantánamo and get us evacuated home?" one brother joked. But he was serious.

In this game we played with the camp, the stakes were our lives. Most of the time we failed. But we didn't have anything left to lose. And we thought our games would end with us getting released.

But when I think back about it now, it's clear that Guantánamo wasn't for detention and never was. It wasn't a prisoner-of-war camp to get men off the battlefield in Afghanistan—most of us weren't fighters—and it wasn't a prison for punishment. If it was any of those things, that would have meant that the Americans knew who we were and what we had done. But they didn't. They only *suspected* that we were fighters and terrorists. They had disappeared hundreds of men to this place for one reason and one reason only: to interrogate us for intelligence. The constant movement, the harassment, the poor living conditions, the torture—it was all done at the direction of interrogators. It was messy and chaotic, and now I see so clearly how they were only just getting started.

- SEVEN -

I woke up shivering in nothing but my shorts, shackled to a metal bed in India Block. I'd been drugged and couldn't move any part of my body, but I heard a beautiful voice reciting the Holy Qur'an, carrying through the block like a secret whispered from one speaker to the next until it faded away into nothing. Was this a dream? A female guard sat in front of my cell, watching me through the door's viewing window, taking notes on everything I did. I thought, *At least I have someone with me in this scary block.* Images floated back to me in waves and I tried to remember what was a dream and what was real.

I remembered brothers at the top of Hotel Block calling out "Chains are coming" and guards dragging the heavy shackles down the walkway, taunting brothers with them until they got to my neighbor's cage. Interrogators had ordered him taken to solitary confinement.

Whenever they moved us, we had to kneel, put our hands on top of our heads, and wait for them to restrain us while they gathered our belongings. ISO mat, Qur'an, the clothes we wore—that's all we had at that point. When we moved anywhere, we always took our Qur'ans and we always insisted on carrying them ourselves. Guards didn't care how important it was to handle our Qur'ans with care. They had kicked Qur'ans, stepped on them, thrown them in shit buckets, and worse. Holding our Qur'ans wasn't extremism. It was practical.

I remembered that on that day, one of the guards pushed so hard on my neighbor's head, he cried out in pain.

I called out to my brothers on the block, telling them what the guard was doing to my neighbor. I shouted at the guard to stop, but he just pushed even harder on my neighbor's head and then a second guard pulled him a different direction, as if they had orders to pull him apart. All this time my neighbor was trying to keep his balance and not fall over and not drop his Qur'an.

I remembered everything got messy and loud fast. The IRF team stormed the block and charged into his cage. The lead guard with the shield knocked into him hard, throwing him across the cage. All the guards were yelling, "Don't fight!" My neighbor was strong, and even though he wasn't fighting, he struggled to keep hold of his Qur'an while they beat him, and I wondered what the line was between protecting yourself and fighting back. It didn't matter because they always said we were fighting and that was to justify beating us. While they were beating my neighbor, he lost his grip and the Qur'an flew across the cage toward his toilet.

I yelled at the guards and called out to my brothers on the block, telling them what was going on; when I told them that the Qur'an flew through the air, that's when the real chaos broke out. Brothers started splashing guards with water from their sinks and even dirty water from their toilets. They banged on their cages and cursed. I heard the thunder of men in other blocks yelling out, too. More IRF teams charged onto the block. One brother held his chains, taunting the guards as they tried to get them back. Fights broke out in every cage as guards tried to restrain men all over the block. We were in Hotel Block in Camp 1, which had eight blocks holding more than three hundred cages between them. The chaos from all the banging and yelling from hundreds of men was something I'd never heard. The noise was heavy. The energy electric. Every nerve in my body hummed.

Then an IRF team was at my cage.

"On my three!" the leader yelled. "One. Two. Three!"

I fought and got pinned to the floor fast and then beat to hell. They pulled my pants down. I felt a sharp jab in my butt and knew I was getting an injection and then all that energy just drained and the world went flat. They beat me right there in my cage until I couldn't move while brothers up and down the block watched and yelled and banged their cages. They chained me and dragged me in just my shorts out of the block. Every block we passed boomed with the wild screams of men banging their cages, fighting guards. They dragged me to India Block and solitary confinement. Back to the dark again, to the blinding light, to the cold, to the loneliness. But I could still hear the roar of men rioting.

I remembered being thrown into my cell in India Block, half-naked, facedown, my hands restrained behind my back, and I remembered someone pulling down my pants again and giving me two more injections. That's when the world went black.

It's hard to remember clearly what followed. Sometimes I woke in a fog as guards rolled me from my left side to my right or back again. My dreams filled with the sound of men rioting. Sometimes I woke to a sharp stab of another injection. Hours, maybe days, maybe more, passed like this, wearing just my shorts in a freezing cell, restrained, and suspended between dreams and real life. In this fog, I watched a parade of faces appear in the window of my cage to watch me—high-ranking military officers, civilians, medics, both generals of the camp. I remembered hearing one, General Baccus, deliver a speech over the camp-wide loudspeaker and his voice being drowned out by Afghani brothers going crazy. I heard calls to prayer and I heard recitations from the Holy Qur'an broadcast so loudly on every speaker, even Princess would have heard it.

WHEN THEY FINALLY stopped the injections and I woke up, I was still chained, freezing cold and with a bad headache, and after lying there for a while I realized that the female guard watching me was also writing down everything I did. I yawned and scratched my head—she wrote it down. I walked toward her and looked at her—she wrote it down. I was starving and asked for food—she wrote it down. I hoped she wrote down that the guards told me I would have to wait until the next meal to eat.

"How long have I been here?" I asked. She didn't answer, but she wrote it down.

This female guard watched me for days through my cell-door viewing window, writing down when I woke up, when I slept, ate, drank, prayed, talked to myself . . . She wouldn't talk to me, even though I tried to talk to her. I didn't mind; at least I had another human being with me. The only problem with her company was that when I needed to go to the bathroom, she was there staring at me, writing down everything I did. This embarrassed me and I asked her to close the viewing window so I could go to the bathroom in private, but she refused and wrote it down. I asked for an Arabic interpreter, which she wrote down, too, then called the interpreter.

"She has orders not to take her eyes off you," the interpreter said. "She must watch you at all times and take note of everything. Even when you go to the bathroom."

I hoped she noted how confused I was that she watched me so closely every minute of every hour of every day for so many days.

I hoped she also wrote down how hungry I was, and how pleased I was with the new MREs. One had a delicious cake. Another had what I would learn are biscuits. And one even had M&M's. I really enjoyed the juice. A couple of times, the guards forgot to take out the hot sauce. This was a real treat. The food was a special kind of torture in the camp, barely enough to survive, and it tasted terrible. I wondered if she wrote down that I enjoyed my hot sauce.

IT WAS JUST a matter of time before they came to take me to interrogation, but the escort team was nice to me when they came! They took me from my cage in only my shorts. But they didn't beat me. They didn't cover my eyes. They didn't pull or push me or tighten the ankle shackles to cut me the way they usually did. I wondered what had changed that they would treat me so well.

They walked me to the Gold Building, where I was usually taken for interrogations. There was a group of high-ranking officers and civilians gathered there and they watched me walk by. I recognized the generals—General Dunlavey and General Baccus—but none of the others. They laughed at me in my dirty shorts and bare feet.

They brought me to a really nice room I'd never seen before. I'd been in many interrogation rooms since Afghanistan, from the black site that felt like it was in the heart of pure evil and the bare, cold tents in Kandahar to the sterile Camp Delta rooms that smelled of men's sweat and despair. But this room had a huge blue couch, a nice rug, lounge chairs and tables, a TV, and fresh flowers. Pleasant music played. There was even fruit on the table. The room was cool but not freezing and smelled so sweet with the flowers. I couldn't help but cry, it was all so nice. I hadn't seen such a nice room since I left Yemen for Afghanistan. That room reminded me that I once had a life that was not in a cage behind fences and barbed wire. It reminded me that there was still a world with beautiful colors that didn't smell like diesel or bleach or fear.

Wa Allahi, I thought. *Is this how they send me home? Is this how they apologize for the black site and the interrogations, for the beatings and months in isolation?*

I sat on the edge of that soft blue couch like a child. Across from me was a long mirror that spanned the entire wall.

I looked at myself in the mirror. How many months had it been since I had seen myself? A year? Staring back at me, I saw a skinny boy with a crazy beard and wild, bushy hair and heavy chains on his wrists and around his waist. What had they made me into? I got up and stood in front of the mirror and looked hard at myself. I opened my mouth and inspected my teeth. I stuck out my tongue. I looked under my arms at the new hair that had grown. I laughed at my wild hair and beard. I made funny faces, wondering, *What would my mother think of such a messy boy?*

Shadows moved behind the mirror and soon the door opened. The group of men I passed in the hallway filed in. I recognized these men now. These were the ghosts from my half-conscious dream—the generals and other high ranks in fancy uniforms who paraded past my cell door while I was drugged. They surrounded me, all serious, studying this confused boy in dirty orange shorts. I looked at each face, making strong eye contact the way a boy should in the company of men. They told me to sit.

"Do you know why you are here?" the interpreter asked. He had a Lebanese accent, and his words shook as he spoke. He looked like he was shitting in his pants talking for those high ranks.

My mind raced. I really thought they would set me free—why else would they put me in this nice room with all these important men? Maybe they were in trouble for keeping me. Maybe the Yemeni government told them to let me go. Maybe President Saleh himself told them I was not a terrorist.

"You are sending me home?" I said, more to the interpreter than to the men in front of me.

When he translated, they all laughed. I laughed, too, like our collective laughter was an agreement between us of how crazy this situation was. Then they got serious again.

"You turned the camp upside down," the interpreter said. "You're a troublemaker. You should be sent to a black hole."

These words stung even more than a boot.

"What happened to the Qur'an?" the interpreter asked.

"What Qur'an?" I didn't know what Qur'an they were talking about. My Qur'an?

"Detainee 1078's Qur'an," the interpreter said. "Your neighbor in Hotel Block."

Why did they care now about my neighbor's Qur'an? I told them that the way guards treated our Qur'ans was a problem and would always be a problem until they understood how important they were to us.

"The Qur'an is not an al Qaeda or Taliban book," I said. "Tell them this. Tell them it belongs to all Muslims and to all human beings. It holds the words of Allah as they were heard hundreds of years ago and have never changed. We respect this book more than our life. Why do you disrespect it always? Guards and interrogators use it to punish us, but it only makes us mad and not trust you."

They listened and wrote their notes.

"But what happened to 1078's Qur'an?" the interpreter asked again.

"Why do you care?" I said. "It was thrown across the cage when the guard beat him. They really hurt him, and for what?"

"Did the guard kick it with his boot? Did he kick it into the toilet?"

"No," I said. "But it happened many—"

A military man with stars on his shoulder interrupted me.

"We don't care about before," the interpreter translated. "We want to know about the day all the trouble started."

They were very serious.

"My neighbor's Qur'an was thrown toward the toilet, but not into it," I said. "It wasn't kicked, but the guard stepped on it."

They calmed down as I talked about it. Why were they making such a big deal out of this one time?

"Can you tell your brothers what happened?" the interpreter said.

"Of course," I said. "We are not dishonest."

Another military man with a silver eagle on his chest spoke up.

"They think that the guard kicked the Qur'an into the toilet."

"I didn't see that happen," I said.

They talked to each other. I couldn't understand what they were saying. The interpreter wouldn't translate.

A civilian in a suit talked now.

"You should calm down your brothers."

Many of the men looked at me with eyes that said they didn't believe me. They may have been calm and treating me nicely, but their eyes said that I was an animal and not worth their words. I didn't want to help them. I wanted to yell at them that they should treat us like human beings. But I heard my mother's scolding voice telling me to be respectful and honest, no matter what.

"I will try to calm them," I said.

General Dunlavey looked hard at me, like he could see some sort of truth by staring long enough. "Where are your clothes?"

I laughed. Not because I was naked, but that he would ask such a question. This was the general in charge of the interrogations. He knew where my clothes were and why I didn't have any on.

"Your guards took mine," I said. "Yours look nice though. Maybe you can lend me yours."

"I'm sure they'd fit you fine," he said. "But I think your rank is higher than mine."

This was a strange thing for a general to say to a naked boy.

"When will you let me go?"

They laughed like this was the funniest thing they'd ever heard.

"You have to behave and cooperate," General Dunlavey scolded. "Starting revolutions won't make us set you free."

This was a big word for me, *revolution*. They thought I started a revolution?

The men left the room talking to each other as if I wasn't there at all.

The same guards came to move me back to solitary confinement.

"Are you ready, sir?" one said through the interpreter.

Sir?

Nobody ever in my life had called me sir. I was nineteen years old. The word sounded ugly and ill-fitting.

Five guards escorted me back to my block. Brothers called after me, "Where are your clothes?" Other guards laughed at me.

The guards didn't bring me back to India Block and solitary confinement. And they didn't bring me back to Hotel Block, where the riot started. They took me to Charlie Block, which the guards called "Devil's Block" for its reputation of housing troublemakers. I didn't care where I went so long as I wasn't going to isolation again.

"What's your name, brother?" the man in the first cage asked as I walked past.

When I told him, he got very excited and called my name to the brothers down the block.

"Welcome, Lion!" he sang. Other brothers joined him. "Our hero!" they sang. "The Lion!"

I walked down the block and shook brothers' hands through the fence. At first, my escort tried to stop me, but he must have had orders to be nice to me.

I was surprised that they put me in a cage next to Omar, the one-legged Libyan I had seen months ago rally the men in Lima Block. Omar laughed loud and hard when the guards left my cage.

"This is the general everyone is talking about?" he cried. "You're just a baby!" He told me how another brother, maybe a snitch, told him that interrogators had showed him a photo of me in a high-ranking Yemeni military uniform.

"I've never been in the military," I said. He laughed again. Our connection was instant and we told each other our stories.

Just like many Libyans who were against Gaddafi, Omar was jailed and tortured by Gaddafi's intelligence service. He fled to Sudan, where he lived in hiding for years, until they found him. Then he fled to Pakistan, where he lived until 9/11 and the government sold him to the CIA.

It was dinnertime, and after guards served the meal, Omar told me what had happened in the days after I was taken away. The fights in our block turned into a riot and spread like fire to all the other blocks in Camp 1, and even to Camps 2 and 3. Some brothers fought with guards, and some refused to go to interrogations. Many brothers went on hunger strike when they heard about my neighbor and how I was dragged away to solitary confinement. This was the second big hunger strike at Guantánamo. Brothers were still refusing to eat, and interrogators were frustrated. Mr. Hunger Strike was very happy: the camp was in disorder with brothers resisting guards in every block now.

I told Omar the whole story.

"You have to be careful," Omar said. "You might not be this Adel or a general, but that doesn't matter anymore. They see you act like one, and that's maybe worse."

Earlier in the week, Charlie Block's block leader was taken away to solitary confinement. Brothers had asked an older Egyptian, a professor, to take his place, but he declined. Block leaders were secretly elected by brothers to mediate issues between the guards and the prisoners and help keep the peace when things got out of hand. No one wanted to be a block leader because as soon as interrogators found out about them, they disappeared to interrogations and then to solitary confinement. The professor was smart and told brothers to make someone else block leader and he would advise them.

So they asked me. I wasn't a leader. I wasn't an instigator. I was young and, like most men my age, I was still learning; I was clever, but not wise yet. I was just a simple tribal man who couldn't sit by and watch other men and boys get abused and mistreated. I couldn't sit by and watch guards desecrate the Holy Qur'an. I talked to Omar about it and he agreed to advise me if I accepted.

As the new block leader, I helped negotiate the end to the hunger strike. I asked for better meals and time for rec. We got five extra minutes each week. I wasn't the general they thought I was—I wasn't even a leader—but I had found my role in this place: To feel the pain of others. To stick up for those who were beaten. And to try to make our lives better.

CAMP DELTA

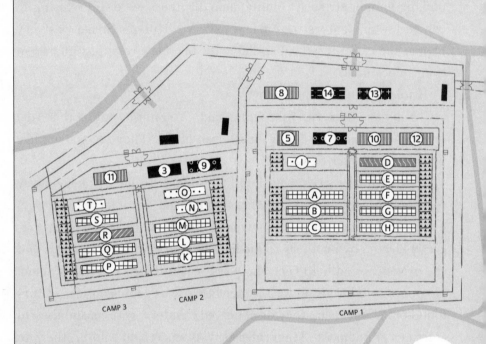

CAMP 3   CAMP 2   CAMP 1

BUILDINGS AND STRUCTURES

(A) Alpha	(I) India	(T) Tango	(5) CTC (Counter-Terrorism
(B) Bravo	(K) Kilo	(U) Uniform	Center / CIA) Blue,
(C) Charlie	(L) Lima	(V) Victor	Grey, and Orange
(D) Delta / BHU	(M) Mike	(W) Whiskey	(6) Detainee Hospital
(Behavioral	(N) November	(Y) Yankee	(7) DOC (Detention
Health Unit)	(O) Oscar	(Z) Zulu	Operation Center)
(E) Echo	(P) Papa	(1) Admin	(8) JIG (Joint Interrogation
(F) Foxtrot	(Q) Quebec	(2) BHU	Group)
(G) Golf	(R) Romeo	(3) Building 7	(9) Intel / Interpreters
(H) Hotel	(S) Sierra	(4) Camp Admin	

(10) JIIF (Joint Integrated	
Intelligence	
Facility) Brown	
(11) JIIF Gold	
(12) JIIF Yellow	
(13) Medical Unit	
(14) SCIF (Sensitive	
Compartmented	
Information Facility)	
⋈ Sally Ports	
⊟ Watch Towers	

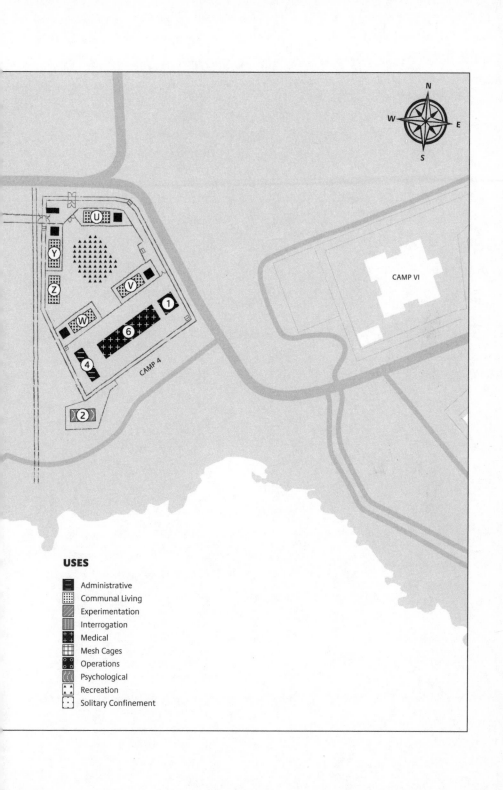

N
W · E
S

CAMP VI

U

Y

Z

V

1

W

6

4

CAMP 4

2

USES

Administrative
Communal Living
Experimentation
Interrogation
Medical
Mesh Cages
Operations
Psychological
Recreation
Solitary Confinement

– PART 2 –

RESISTANCE

- EIGHT -

I didn't last long in Charlie Block before they sent me to solitary confinement in November Block. That's where I saw the idiot General Miller for the first time. He was bald and strolled down the center of the block with his chest puffed out in a strong army walk. He was stiff and arrogant and full of disdain. As he walked past my cell, he looked through the viewing window at me. I don't think he saw me. I don't think he knew who I was. He looked like he was sizing up an object he was going to break.

The big chicken General Miller took over Guantánamo around Ramadan in 2002 and turned it into an interrogation machine made to chew up men. Before Miller came, life at Guantánamo was full of false hope and gossip that the Americans would let us go soon. We didn't have access to CNN or any other news. All we had was DNN, the Detainee News Network, which was rumors and news we called out to each other from block to block. It wasn't the most efficient or accurate network, but it's all we had. Welcome to Guantánamo. Rumors spread before Miller took over that even Donald Rumsfeld, the chief chicken, had complained to the camp's generals that most of the prisoners weren't al Qaeda or Taliban, only farmers and no-bodies. The way Miller walked the blocks that day put that rumor to rest. He was putting us on notice that he owned us and would do whatever he wanted.

Before Miller, Guantánamo was a mess with fights breaking out all the time between interrogators, guards, the FBI, the CIA, and all the agencies trying to make sense of who we were.

Even brothers saw the tension between the two generals, Baccus and Dunlavey, who commanded different parts of Guantánamo. Baccus tried to make living conditions better and walked the blocks with people from the Red Cross. Under Dunlavey, interrogations got worse.

Only years later did I really understand that until General Miller, the camp had been divided between two task forces with different missions. JTF 160 was a military police force whose mission was detention. First, the marine general Lehnert was in command, but he was fired for being too soft and replaced by General Baccus, who was also too soft. They both believed in at least the basics of the Geneva Conventions. JTF 170 was the intelligence task force led by General Dunlavey, and their mission was to interrogate us and gather intelligence. And even though General Dunlavey had pushed for more extreme interrogation techniques, DNN rumors said that when he left Guantánamo, he believed that most of us had been sold to the United States and weren't fighters.

When General Miller took command, he became the commander of both detention and intelligence, which meant he could do whatever he wanted to us. Around the same time, military leaders and lawyers in the Bush administration approved fifteen enhanced interrogation techniques they believed would help free the intelligence they thought we were hiding. Of course, no one told us this, but they didn't have to: we were about to live it.

The day Miller took over, he ordered a camp-wide cell search in the middle of the night. I woke up to IRF teams storming my block with dogs. They opened up the viewing windows on all our doors, something they never did, and I thought that was so we could watch what was going to happen. I hadn't seen anything like this before.

Each IRF team had a guard with a camera who filmed everything for documentation, part of Miller's new SOPs, standard operating procedures. This was to prove they weren't violating SOPs. I watched the IRF team prepare to storm my neighbor's cell. When they opened the door, my neighbor was already on his knees with his hands on his head. A guard stood in front of the camera, blocking it from recording what happened next.

"Stop resisting!" the officer called out, justifying what happened next for the camera. The IRF team stormed in, beat my neighbor badly, restrained him, and then dragged him into the hallway.

When they came to my cell, I asked the officer through an interpreter what was happening. He pepper-sprayed my face, then treated me just like my neighbor.

"Stop resisting!" they yelled. Out in the corridor, they pulled my pants down and searched my genitals. That genital search was like a rape. Six guards held me down and the seventh one hit my genitals and then did a rough cavity search. I screamed out and I kicked and punched. It hurt, but the humiliation was worse and the guards knew that by now. Brothers screamed all up and down the block as IRF teams stormed cells. They left me on my knees in the hall while guards took everything out of my cell. Farther down the block, I heard an older man screaming for help and then I saw him fall to the ground in the corridor with guards on top of him.

"Stop resisting!" the guards kept lying for the camera. Then the guard who was handling the old man's head turned his back to the camera and pulled something sharp out of his pocket. The old man cried out as the guard tried to poke his eye out.

I screamed and other brothers did, too.

The female guard who was filming saw what was happening and shouted. She dropped her camera and threw herself over the old man's head to protect him. The chaos and division among guards during that first search was just a sample of what was to come. General Miller would push everyone to the edge, even his own guards. No one would leave Guantánamo unharmed. What I saw that night made me realize how little any of us really knew about what the Americans would do, and how scared they were of us.

The point of the search was to take everything away from everyone—towels, toilet paper, sheets, toothbrushes, toothpaste, blankets, cups, clothes, soap, books—everything except our ISO mat, shorts, and a sheet to sleep with. Then Miller put us all on a system of levels that determined what items and privileges we could have. Interrogators controlled that system, and everything had to be earned by following the rules (being compliant) and talking to our interrogators (being cooperative). We all started off as level 4s, the lowest, with more comfort items and privileges at each level up. Level 1+ had blankets and clothes, soap, toothbrushes, and even one or two books besides the Qur'an. They could write and receive letters and were generally treated better. Even at level 4, things could get worse though: there were two lower levels just for solitary confinement where you were only allowed to wear shorts or, worse, absolutely nothing. Even our Holy Qur'an was used as punishment.

Miller didn't stop with comfort items. He stopped broadcasting the call to prayer five times a day and didn't allow us to know what time it was. We weren't allowed to exercise in our cages—no push-ups, sit-ups, jumping, squats, or martial arts. We could sit and stand and pace and that was it. Once again, we weren't allowed to talk.

It felt like a laboratory to study how Muslims would react to crazy rules and punishments, and how the human spirit could endure the worst harassments. Everything seemed designed to humiliate and demean us. Perhaps they thought that once we were dependent on interrogators for everything, we would start to give up all the intelligence they thought we were hiding.

Miller got all the parts of the machine working together—interrogators, guards, doctors, psychologists—and the Americans started filling it up with Muslims.

I HAD BEEN in solitary confinement at level 4 for a few weeks when they brought in a new prisoner to November Block. New detainees were arriving all the time now. From cage 20, I watched through the thin crack in the bean-hole door when he shuffled past. In all my moving around, I hadn't seen him before. They put him in cage 19, right next to me. I sang the Nightingale's song to him: *O the one with trouble, be optimistic, your trouble will fade away, Allah is the one who will set you free.*

"Who's there?" he said.

"Shut the fuck up!" The guard banged on my door.

I waited for the guard to move on. Miller's new SOPs had guards walking the blocks and looking into our cells every couple of minutes and waking us every half hour.

"Assalamu alaikum, brother," I whispered through a hole between our two cages after the guard passed. We couldn't see each other, but we could sit with our ears to the hole and talk.

"Where am I?" he asked.

"You're at Guantánamo," I said. "What's your name?"

He was quiet for a long time and I understood he had just arrived. He didn't know who I was, and why should he trust a voice on the other side of a wall?

"It's okay, brother," I said. "You don't have to say your name. Where are you from?" He laughed and told me he'd rather not say. I could tell right away from his accent that he was from the Arabian Peninsula, but I couldn't figure out where exactly.

"What's your story?" I said.

It was late and the fans were off and the block was quiet enough for us to whisper to each other. He was silent for a long time and I figured he wasn't interested in talking to me.

"It's a long story," he finally said. "You wouldn't believe me if I told you."

"You are at Guantánamo," I said. "I've heard it all. There's a man who's one hundred five years old. There's Osama bin Laden's driver and his cook. There's a professor of Arabic and a journalist for Al Jazeera. I'm only nineteen years old and they think I'm an Egyptian general."

I heard him laugh. I settled in, leaning my head against the hole. After a while, he started whispering to me the most amazing story I'd ever heard about a trip he and his friends took to the country of Georgia.

I heard in his voice a very light and innocent soul. I liked him already.

Then he got serious all of a sudden and told me how he and his friends were ambushed by masked soldiers and how a gun battle broke out that left one of his friends dead. The masked men kidnapped him and his friend and sold them to the CIA.

"I had never seen so much American money, brother," he whispered. "I don't know why they paid so much for me." His story was like a Hollywood movie. "I never dreamed I'd ride in a helicopter, but there I was, taking off in one, naked, hooded, and shackled. Then they shipped us to Afghanistan, where I was questioned and . . ." His voice trailed off and he started weeping. I knew he had been sent to a black site, and he would never be the same again.

"It's okay, brother," I said. "We've all been tortured."

"Then they sent me here and that's when I heard your lovely voice singing to me through the wall."

His story made me cry. Maybe because it felt like the Americans wouldn't stop until they disappeared every Muslim man to this place.

"Do you know what the CIA is?" I said.

He didn't and I started to explain. I'd learned a lot over the past year. But he interrupted me.

"Oh, I don't care about them!" he said. "I need to sleep, brother."

IN THE MORNING, escorts took my new neighbor away to interrogation. He was gone the entire day and into the next. The second night, when he hadn't returned, I called the guards to bring an Arabic interpreter.

"Where's the brother in cage 19?" I asked.

"It's none of your business," the guard said.

I couldn't rest knowing what the interrogators were probably doing to him for this long. I had been short-shackled and left in a room for days with loud music and flashing lights. I'd been slapped and beaten and stripped, and even though I had only known my neighbor for a few hours, he was one of us now, and it was hard for me to sit by and do nothing. If you hurt, I felt your pain. There were a couple of other brothers who felt this way, too, and as level 4s we were finding ourselves rotated frequently to the same blocks.

I waited until the guards came to collect the meal trash, then I refused to give them mine. When you have nothing, you protest with what you have. The only way I could protest was by refusing to follow the rules.

"Send me the watch commander," I said.

The watch commander came, shouting at me to give back the trash. I tried to talk to him about my neighbor.

"441!" he screamed. "Are you refusing to hand over your trash?"

I knew what would happen next. According to Miller's SOPs, not returning garbage was a violation requiring a cell search. If I refused the cell search, SOPs required an IRF team to remove me from my cell so they could search it. It all meant more work for the guards.

The watch commander and I stared at each other a minute.

"I refuse," I said. He radioed the DOC (Detention Operations Center) and requested an IRF team. Minutes later, a six-man IRF team marched onto the block. These guys were big and looked like they spent a lot of time working out. Each one weighed at least 180 pounds. That's 1,080 pounds of testosterone-fueled force waiting at my door with armor, shields, pepper spray, and a dog. IRF teams had to follow strict SOPs for everything—how they carried their shields, how they walked, how they stood outside the cage, how they stormed the cage. It was scary at first, but now getting IRF'd was like a day job for me. I knew what to expect and just had to get through it.

"441, will you come out of your cell for a cell search?" the guard screamed at me.

"Will you bring my neighbor back from interrogation?" I yelled back.

"On my three!" the IRF team leader yelled.

They pepper-sprayed me first, and that hurt like hell, but once the pain settled, the adrenaline hit. I was ready for them.

As soon as the door opened, all that weight crashed in like a moving mountain. I felt my body fly at the speed of light and for a brief second I was suspended in midair not feeling anything, until I hit the wall and—*boom*—the air got knocked out of me and I couldn't breathe. All I saw were stars.

The SOPs could be interpreted by the IRF team depending on the situation. IRF teams hit our heads against the ground, choked us, kicked us, twisted our fingers, put our faces in the toilet, knelt on our necks, sat on us—whatever they thought necessary to restrain us. They were very creative.

Every brother had a different approach to getting IRF'd. I always resisted. I had to. I'd learned that they would beat me no matter what, so at least when I fought, they had to focus more on securing me than beating me.

SOPs said that each of the six guards was assigned to restrain one part of a detainee's body. One guard was assigned the head, one to each arm, one to each leg, and another to the torso. SOPs were created with the average detainee in mind and didn't account for brothers who weren't completely average. I'd seen IRF teams spend more than an hour trying to follow SOPs to remove a brother who had only one leg or who was too short to have a guard on every limb.

They restrained me with plastic wrist ties and dragged me out of my cell. They took my ISO mat, towel, blanket—all my stuff—and then they put me back in. When the IRF team threw me back, they dropped a pair of handcuffs. No one saw it happen, so I picked them up quickly and hid them in my cage.

At the shift change, the guards realized they were missing a pair of cuffs and couldn't leave until they found them. They went crazy. I sat quietly in my cage hoping they wouldn't do another cage search. If they did, I would have to refuse and then I'd get pepper-sprayed again. I was still burning from the earlier pepper spray, but the AC was so cold in my isolation cell, the burn kept me warm.

I called the new shift block sergeant and asked him to bring the watch commander. The watch commander came and I was happy it was a woman. They were usually nicer to us. She arrived with an Arabic interpreter.

"If I open your bean hole, will you promise not to make any problems?"

"I give you my word," I said.

She opened the bean hole and I told her what happened with the last shift.

"As a show of respect for you," I said, "I want to show you something." I held up the handcuffs. "I'll give them to you if you promise to call the camp officer please."

This shocked her. The earlier shift was in big trouble over the cuffs.

"Do you trust me?" she said.

"I don't know," I said.

"Do you respect me?" she said.

"You've always been nice to us," I said. "Yes, I respect you."

"If you give me these cuffs," she said, "I'll prove to you that you can trust me, too."

I handed her the cuffs. She was very happy that she got them from me without any problem. This would go on her résumé. Five minutes later, the camp officer was standing in front of my cell.

He thanked me for giving back the handcuffs.

"You should thank the watch commander," I said. "She's one of the good ones." Then I told him about how my neighbor had disappeared to interrogation for days. "I'm worried about him," I said.

"You know we have no control over the interrogators," the camp officer said, "but I'll see what I can do."

More brothers on the block started making noise about my missing neighbor. We were in solitary confinement, but we still stuck together when we could.

The camp officer came back a little later with an interrogator, a young guy in a polo shirt. They all looked the same to me. He wanted to figure out how I knew my neighbor and if there was a connection between us.

"Where's the new detainee?" I said. "Have you killed him yet?"

"We're keeping him cool in a nice room with AC," he said.

That really made me mad.

"For two days!" I cried.

"He's refusing to talk to us," the interrogator said. "I gave him a Pepsi and he picked his nose and put it on my pants. We're trying to help him."

"By torturing him!" I yelled so that brothers on the block could hear me. "If you don't bring him back, we're going to turn this block upside down." The block started getting crazy when I said that.

About an hour later, escorts brought my neighbor back.

I watched through my bean hole and was surprised to see him. He was really funny-looking with big eyes and wild, curly hair. Some brothers looked mean with their Guantánamo beards and long hair, just the way interrogators wanted. But there was something about my neighbor that was different. He looked so young and innocent, like this was the last place he belonged. I barely knew him, but he felt like a brother to me.

He went straight to sleep and I didn't bother him.

It felt really good to help someone. It made all the pain of the pepper spray and the harsh cold of solitary confinement go away, if only for a little while. I thought my father and brothers and all the men in our tribe would have been proud at how I stood up for him.

Just before the shift change, the female watch commander came to my cell with new clothes for me. She opened the bean hole and took my old ones, drenched in pepper spray.

"Shukraan lika," I said. Thank you.

"You are a good guy for helping your brother." She looked at me with kind, warm eyes that gave me hope some Americans could still see us for who we were.

The next day, interrogators moved my neighbor from the block again. Before he left, he whispered through the wall to me, "My name is Zakaria. Thank you for helping me."

"I'm Mansoor," I whispered back.

He saw the kind of person I was. So did the female watch commander, and that meant a lot. I felt lost in this terrible place—we all did. But sometimes I found myself, just little pieces, and I tried to hold on to them for as long as I could.

YOU SEE THAT you're in a big mess that's getting messier and there's nothing you can do to stop it. You understand now it's the interrogators' job to make sense of it all and they can't. They don't think you're this Adel anymore, but now they think you're someone else. Still, the questions remain the same: *Where is bin Laden? Where is Mullah Omar? When is the next attack?* You've tried everything with them. You've told them the truth. You've joked with them. But their ignorance scares you more than their sense of humor, and now you realize you're in serious trouble. So you tell them that, yes, you are whomever they say you are and then they want details you can't give them because you can only tell them what they've told you. You feel sorry for them that they are so afraid of you for something you didn't do, but that fades after five minutes short-shackled to the ground, your hands chained to your ankles.

General Miller thinks you've been trained in counter-interrogation techniques. So now the interrogations get worse to counter the counter-interrogation techniques they think you know. Guards bang on your cell door every five minutes and you can't remember the last time you slept peacefully. Solitary confinement. Bright lights. Loud music. Slaps. Extreme cold. Extreme heat. And you've heard that there's worse.

Some around you stop talking to interrogators. You stop talking to them, too. What's the point? You have nothing left to say, and they don't know what they're looking for.

And then two guards come for you and they're really nice.

"Ready for your reservation?" they ask.

"Where?" you say.

But they don't say. They take you to the Gold Building where you met the generals after the revolution and this doesn't make any sense. They don't take you to the nice big room with the blue couch and the fresh flowers. They take you to a smaller room with a long table holding a bottle of water and a bowl of pistachios. The guards chain you to the floor and leave.

You wait a long time and finally an old man with gray hair combed back comes in carrying his backpack. He talks to you in Arabic.

"I'm here today just for you," he says. His Arabic is ugly but he's not worth correcting. "I hear you're a troublemaker. I hear you're a leader. I hear you're a clever young man." He stares at you, making sure you make eye contact. "Making trouble won't help you here, but I can help you."

He takes a copy of the Holy Qur'an out of his backpack.

"I'm learning the Ko-ran." He shows you his own handwriting on the first page and maybe he hasn't studied it enough to know he's disrespected the book by writing in it. He reads to himself for a moment as if he's getting guidance.

Then he looks at you again for a long time. You look hard into his eyes.

"I'm the head of interrogation," he says. "I will meet you just this once. Today, you and I are going to make a very important decision." He closes the Holy Qur'an and puts it back in his backpack.

"I know who you are," he says. He is very serious and there is the tone of truth to his voice that you haven't heard before in all your interrogations. He opens your file, thick with pages and notes and photographs. He flips through, reading to himself. "I know you are not this Adel," he says. "This Egyptian recruiter is too old for you. I know you're not Alex, the al Qaeda general. I know you're just a nobody from Yemen, but today is your chance to change that."

Your heart races. *They know*, you think. *Someone knows who I am. In sha' Allah!*

He studies you, trying to read your thoughts, and you try to betray nothing.

"We have a lot of men here that we know nothing about," he says. "I see you're liked on the blocks. They've made you a block leader. They trust you. You're a natural leader."

He continues with other compliments and lets them sink in.

"That's why I've chosen you," he says. "I need you to help us. I need *you* to work for *me*."

You have never felt such ache in your heart of false hope. Is this what he's offering? Is this your test? You hold up your hand. You are very respectful. *Be mindful of Allah,* you think, *and Allah will protect you. Be mindful of Allah and you will find Him in front of you. If you ask, then ask Allah alone; and if you seek help, then seek help from Allah alone.*

"Work for me," he continues. "I will make your life good here."

When everything has been taken away from you—your life, your family, your freedom, who you are—he now asks you to give away the one thing you have left: your integrity. *Know that victory comes with patience, relief with affliction, and hardship with ease.*

You were raised to respect your elders, to address them with respect, and that's what you do. You use your best Arabic, your formal Arabic, like the men in your country do when they talk to someone who is older and much respected.

"You know from my file that I am not who they say I am," you say. "You know I have done nothing wrong. You know that the men here are not terrorists. So why do you torture us? Why don't you release us?"

He interrupts you.

"What would I tell the White House?" he says. "What would I tell Congress and the Pentagon? Should I tell them we have here only farmers, teachers, students, charity workers, and drug addicts? Do you know what they'll ask? Where are those men who trained at al Farouq? Where are the fighters? Where are the men screaming 'Allahu Akbar'?"

"If you're studying the Holy Qur'an," you say, "then you know He is my witness and I cannot cast my eye toward the sins of Muslims."

He looks at you with a cold eye. "If you work for me, your brothers would never know. I would make you a wealthy man, rich enough to take care of your family for generations. You could live in the US. You would be taken care of . . ."

You hold up your hand again, and this time you don't care if you are being rude.

"No," you say. "If you know me . . . if you really are studying the Qur'an as you say, then you know you are insulting me by asking me to work for you."

With the coldest tone you've ever heard, he says, "There are always victims in wars. If you say no to me now, consider yourself a victim."

You have a choice and it's very simple. Will you betray the brothers around you, the men who were dragged to this hole with you, who have shared their meals with you, who have been beaten with you, who have been tortured like you, who have taken care of you, who pray with you every day—wrongfully accused brothers who had nothing to do with the attacks of 9/11? Will you betray them and lie about them for empty promises and some comfort items? He's just served you the nastiest, hairiest piece of shit on a plate and invited you to eat it. What do you say?

No.

He looks at you, disappointed. "That's not what I expected," he says.

You watch him stand up with his little backpack, holding the Qur'an he desecrated with his own writing in English. You watch him walk to the door. You watch him turn to you one last time.

"Fuck yourself," he says in a funny Arabic way using air quotes. Then he walks out, leaving you chained to the floor.

Consider yourself a victim. You replay those words over and over again. You replay the conversation to see if there was any other way, any other choice to be made. No. You made your choice, the only choice you had, and you cry knowing that there is no easy way out of here now. They'll never admit their mistakes. They'll cover them up. They'll deny them. They'll try to turn their mistakes into opportunities to make snitches, and that means you'll never get out.

AFTER MY MEETING, they moved me to the open cages in Sierra Block, where I told my neighbor I'd been offered a deal to work for the Americans. He told me he had been taken to the same room and offered a similar deal.

"Did he offer you the wine?" my neighbor asked.

"No!" I cried. "Who do they think we are?"

Islam is a practical religion that's woven into the fabric of our daily life. General Miller, this head of interrogations, the interrogators and psychologists all failed to understand the depth and strength of our faith. Yes, we were physically weak, we were beaten, and they would beat us more, but our strength was in our hearts, and our hearts were driven by our faith and trust in Allah. We couldn't be bought with promises of riches. According to our faith, we're all created for a single reason, which is to worship Allah. One way to worship is how you handle hardship and dilemmas in your life. Life on this earth is a test for us, and we should expect anything, even the worst hardships, in our test. At the same time, nothing happens without Allah's permission; nothing moves without Allah's will. If we were at Guantánamo, He had willed it and we would leave when He willed it. But we had free will to choose our path while here.

I went to my cage door and started calling out to my brothers, making a speech. It was messy, just me talking from my heart about what was right and good. I talked the way my father had talked to our tribe. I told them about my meeting and what the interrogator had offered me. I told them we had a choice in how we would survive here.

"We must stand together!" I yelled. "We must not spy on each other. We must not work with the Americans. If they torture one of us, they torture all of us."

The brothers listened and they called out my words from block to block as I spoke. Many of the brothers liked what I said and called out, "Allahu Akbar!" and that's when guards stormed the block and told me to "shut the fuck up!" But I didn't. I continued calling out. I knew I would get punished. I knew I would get sent back to solitary confinement, that I would get harassed and beaten by guards. I knew interrogators would now turn my life into hell. I didn't care anymore. I didn't want privileges or comfort items, things they could take away from me or use to manipulate me. I didn't want to work up the system to level 1+.

I kept calling out to my brothers and soon I heard blocks all around me calling out my words, and that's when the IRF team marched onto the block.

"We must all become level 4s!" I cried. "If we have nothing, they'll have nothing to take away from us!"

The IRF team pepper-sprayed me and stormed my cage. They beat me. They always beat me. I was taken away to solitary confinement and isolation where I couldn't talk to another brother for months.

- NINE -

Zakaria had a bad tooth, and this was the kind of problem interrogators loved. Soldiers beat him all the way here, and somewhere along the way, they broke his tooth. Maybe it was a rifle butt. Maybe it was a boot. He didn't know and it didn't matter. He couldn't sleep or eat with the pain—he couldn't do anything.

As block leader, I asked the guards to send medical staff, but they told us Zakaria had to talk to his interrogators. We were "classified" and that meant every part of our bodies and health, even our teeth, was top secret. We weren't allowed to know what medicine they gave us or what vitamins or shots. If we had a health problem—any pain or sickness—we had to pay our interrogators for treatment. If you didn't have information, you were in big trouble.

Interrogators controlled everything: food, air, clothing, water, light, sun, talking, sleep, rest, knowing the time, news from the outside, where we lived, and our health care. They had a theory that dependence or helplessness or both would make us talk.

Miller had opened Camp 4, where brothers wore white instead of orange, lived in open communal blocks, and had lots of privileges. This was to show us how we could live if we just followed their rules and talked to interrogators. I would never get there, and I was fine with that. I wasn't the only one: many brothers had stopped talking to interrogators. After an interrogator put a Holy Qur'an under his foot, one of the brothers even issued a fatwa that said talking to interrogators was forbidden and cooperating a major sin.

Interrogators loved it when we had problems—one more thing they could control. Zakaria was called for a reservation with his interrogators, who offered to give him pain pills for his tooth. They offered to bring him to a dentist. All he had to do was talk.

Zakaria refused. I was back in Sierra Block, where most of us were being punished for not cooperating or talking to interrogators. Guards said it was a block full of troublemakers, but really we were mostly just guys who couldn't tolerate bullies and rules that made no sense. General Miller was a bully and his SOPs were Shit on Paper.

When Zakaria's pain was so great it kept him from eating, Waddah and I passed him milk from our meals. We poured it through the holes in the fence, from cup to cup, until it got to Zakaria. He lived on milk for a couple days, but the pain kept getting worse.

In protest, several of us refused to eat our food until they treated his tooth. We asked the guards to call the camp commander so we could ask him to help Zakaria. The camp commander didn't give a shit about Zakaria. All he wanted was for him to talk to interrogators.

"Call your interrogators and ask them," he said each time.

Some brothers like Hamzah refused to go to the shower and rec. Hamzah was from North Africa but had lived in Italy and worked for the Mafia. He'd been sold to the CIA by someone who wanted to get rid of him. Hamzah had a gravelly voice full of impatience and the build and confidence to set any bully straight. Refusing to go to shower or rec meant they had to call an IRF team to make him leave, and guards didn't like fighting Hamzah.

Others like Sayd refused to leave their cages for anything. Sayd was a white Russian and former Soviet special ops who was all shoulders. He enjoyed a good fight with the guards.

This went on for days and then we said, "Enough! We can't watch our brother suffer like this." In this block of troublemakers, we knew how to make trouble. In a few days, most of us would be sent back to solitary confinement for another couple of months anyway.

I was finding other tribal men like me who were driven by a moral code that ran in our blood for generations and centuries. This isn't something I can explain or teach. A tribal man is guided by honesty and respect. He's a man who keeps his word. He stands up for what's right and fights for those who have been wronged. At his core, he knows—and feels in every cell of his body—what is right and wrong and knows there is nothing between the two. It's a part of you like your heart or your eyes. This group, we were all from different tribes, but we felt bound as if we were all one tribe. The interrogators had started to call us troublemakers and "the worst of the worst" detainees because we refused to follow their rules and that meant guards had to fight us. But brothers started calling us *aleuyun alhumur*, an Arabic Yemeni saying that means "men of great integrity." The English translation is "red eyes."

"Let us all refuse to come back from rec and shower," Waddah said. He was always suggesting ways to fight the guards. We got rec and shower twice a week, with sixteen brothers going each day, half in the morning, half in the afternoon. This would mean IRF teams all day long and would cause a lot of problems for the guards.

"Let's tear up our meal trash," Yassir said. He was only sixteen when he was brought here, and even now he couldn't grow a full beard. He was here because they wanted information about his father, who was in the Saudi army. They wanted to link him to al Qaeda.

"Let's keep our meal trash!" Adnan said. We all laughed at this. He was really creative at driving guards crazy. They had to account for every piece of trash before the end of their shift. They would have to do cage searches for all of us and that would mean more IRFs. This would kill the guards with work. Adnan was also from Yemen and had a wife and children. He had an amazing mastery of Arabic. He spun beautiful words and phrases that captured exactly what we were feeling. He'd been in a car accident while he was in the Yemeni army and they'd sent him to Pakistan for brain surgery. The Pakistani police picked him up in Islamabad and sold him to the CIA.

We decided to do all of it, and the next day after breakfast, Othman, a Saudi navy man who spoke English, called the watch commander. Othman was really built and liked to fight, especially with the marines. When the watch commander finally came to his cage, Othman said he had a message for the interrogators.

"Oh yeah . . ." The commander didn't have time to finish his sentence. Othman splashed him with a full cup of milk, enough to fill the watch commander's mouth.

"That's for not treating our brother!"

I called the guards and when they came, I splashed them with milk, too.

More brothers splashed guards with milk and water, so the camp officer came to the block to see the situation for himself. He took one step on the block and every brother started spitting at him.

"Treat our brother!" we chanted.

When the guards came to collect the meal trash, Adnan, Hamzah, Waddah, Sayd, and I refused to give it back. This meant they had to send IRF teams to collect the trash. The IRF teams came with one of their dogs, but we splashed the dog with water. They kicked our asses and collected our trash, but it was hard work for them and that's what we wanted.

They didn't serve lunch as punishment for splashing. We still had rec and shower, and the brothers who went refused to come back until they treated Zakaria's teeth.

The IRF team came again with the dog. They beat the brothers at the rec yard and brought them back to their cells. Then the guards called for cage searches. They wanted to take away whatever comfort items we had. Since we were mostly level 4s, all we had was a blanket and an ISO mat.

When they opened the bean hole to restrain me, I snatched the chains from the guard's hands and ran to the back of my cage. The guard turned crazy.

"Treat our brother!" I slammed the cuffs against the cell wall to break them.

They pepper-sprayed me, but I covered myself with my blanket.

The block turned upside down. Everyone was splashing guards now, and the guards ran out. With my blanket and the broken chains, I made a lock for my cage door.

The camp officer came again with the IRF team and the dog.

"Take the shackles off the door and give them back," he said through an interpreter. He was really mad now.

"Treat our brother first," I said.

He went to get a chain cutter, and while the IRF team waited in front of my cell, brothers splashed them with water. All up and down the block, brothers kicked their cage doors and shouted at the guards. The noise in the block was heavy.

The camp colonel showed up next with a bunch of high-ranking officers, but they wouldn't come into the block because there was so much chaos.

The camp officer finally came back with the chain cutters, but when he cut the chain, I pulled it back into my cage. Oh Allah, we were having fun with them. We all laughed. It felt good to be in control.

Before the IRF team rushed my cage and kicked my ass, I hung the other chains on the fence where Othman could pull them through the mesh. While I was busy getting beaten, Othman took one chain and passed the other to Abdullah, two cages down.

"Fuck this!" The camp officer threw his radio to the ground. Now they needed IRF teams for Othman and Abdullah. The block was crazy with brothers yelling and guards fighting. They threw me restrained into the shower and locked me there until the evening shift came. The fighting went on all day.

The evening shift officer came to me and asked if I would return to my cage. I felt sorry for him. He was one of the nice officers who treated us well. It was the interrogators' game to keep a couple officers to play good cop. There were good guards, good doctors, good nurses, and even good interrogators, I won't deny that. They might have been good people at heart, but they were still used as part of the bigger game to manipulate us.

I told the evening shift officer what I had been telling every guard and every commander for days: "Please, treat our brother."

"Okay," he said. "Give me some time and I'll see what I can do."

When he came back, he told me that Zakaria would be taken to the detainees' hospital in the morning.

"The reason it's taking so long is that we don't have a dentist for detainees right now," he said. "But I'm working on it."

To show that I trusted him, I walked back to my cage peacefully, without an IRF team.

GUARDS CAME FOR Zakaria early in the morning. Every brother who'd splashed guards was put on food punishment—no milk and no cups for a long time. We didn't mind. Zakaria was getting treated.

We all sang to him in celebration when he came back. He smiled big, but his mouth was full of gauze. He couldn't talk yet because of the anesthesia and just went straight to sleep. I think it was the first time he slept in a week. I watched him sleep and studied his mouth. Why would his mouth be so full of gauze to fix one broken tooth? He had a lot of blood still coming out of his mouth.

The corpsman came to give Zakaria a painkiller.

"Now?" I cried. "Why wouldn't you bring him painkillers before, when he really needed them?"

"You know I have my orders," the corpsman said. He wasn't bad like some of the guards. We understood that. He had his orders. The corpsman took the bloody gauze from Zakaria's mouth and filled it again with new gauze.

After the third prayer, Zakaria was awake. The anesthesia had worn off and he could talk.

"I don't know where they took me," he said. "They hooded me and covered my ears." He said he waited there for a long time before a doctor came with a bad Arabic interpreter. The doctor looked at his tooth and said he had a cavity and bad teeth. But the doctor wasn't a dentist, and the camp didn't have one, so he couldn't do a filling. The only thing he could do was extract the tooth. He told Zakaria to ask his interrogator to be taken to the base hospital, but since Zakaria had stopped talking to interrogators, they wouldn't help him.

"The doctor spent a long time working on my mouth," Zakaria said. "And he kept giving me shots."

"Show me your mouth," I said.

Zakaria opened his mouth and I almost threw up. There were bloody holes everywhere.

"Are you crazy!" I cried.

He closed his mouth.

"Keep it open!" I was really angry. "Do you know how many teeth they extracted?"

"Just the one?"

"Your mouth looks like the doctor threw a hand grenade in there!" I said.

"Stop joking!" Zakaria was really scared now. "This isn't funny."

"This is real, brother. I'm serious."

Zakaria turned to Ghamdan, his neighbor on the other side of his cage, and opened his mouth again.

"This is madness!" Ghamdan cried. "How could you let that happen?"

"What are you talking about?" Zakaria cried.

"Criminals!" Ghamdan was really mad, too.

"Where are your teeth?" I cried. "Didn't the doctor show you?"

"My mouth is classified," Zakaria said. "The doctor told me that if I wanted to see, I had to ask my interrogator."

I couldn't hold back my tears. I was afraid that they could do this to any one of us. I called the camp officer and an interpreter.

Guess how many teeth that asshole criminal extracted from Zakaria's mouth? Two, you might guess. No. Three. No. Please, go on. Five . . . six? No. Are you crazy, Mansoor? They took eight teeth at one time.

A Black army officer came with a female interpreter. The Black officers were always nicer. I don't know why.

"Show them your mouth," I said to Zakaria.

The major's face went hard. His eyes got wide. He turned away like he couldn't look anymore. The interpreter covered her face.

"Are you sure that happened at the detainees' hospital?" the major asked.

"Are you serious?" I yelled. "You see the blood! You see the holes!"

He looked really worried. He called for a cameraman to take photos.

"Unbelievable!" he said over and over again until even I knew what he was saying in English.

"The doctor shouldn't have done this," the interpreter said. "All we can do is write a report."

"We can't let this happen," I said. "We have to do something."

"Please," the major said. "Let me talk to someone about this first." He walked away. "Unbelievable!"

"They took our brother to a butcher, not a doctor," Hamzah called from down the block.

Zakaria was not a well-educated man. He was just a common man, like most of us, and he believed that America was a great country that had the best doctors and hospitals. America was supposed to be the best in the world for everything, so a tooth should have been easy. Like all of us, he also thought that all doctors were the same, that they were good people who cared about all people.

I had thought that way, too, once. I had piercing kidney stones and the interrogators had used them against me. They had sent me to the hospital and pretended they were going to cut off my genitals to cure me. The interrogators had a good laugh about it. In Camp X-Ray, at the very beginning, I saw a brother taken to the medical tent to be treated for frostbite on the tip of two fingers. He came back with no fingers at all. Maybe Zakaria wasn't the most aware brother in the camp—we were all learning here—but he paid dearly for what he learned.

I saw fear in all my brothers' faces. Who was this America holding us?

Some brothers decided that day not to ask for health care anymore, no matter what happened. Others decided to stop taking the medicine the camp gave us.

By the end of that day, the camp moved most of us in Sierra Block back to solitary confinement in Oscar Block. What had we accomplished? Zakaria couldn't eat because of the pain in one tooth; now he couldn't eat because he was missing eight teeth. No matter what we did, we would always lose and lose more.

Weeks later when I came out of solitary confinement, I got news that the Black major and the female interpreter were redeployed elsewhere. They had filed their report and then disappeared. We all learned something else from Zakaria's teeth: even officers and interpreters couldn't question the interrogators here.

- TEN -

Guantánamo was an upside-down world where nothing made sense, and that's the way the interrogators liked it. It was a place where salt was more valuable than gold, daylight existed only in our dreams, iguanas had more rights than we did, and the rules changed every day. We weren't allowed to know the time, but time is all we had—day after day in a never-ending cycle of interrogations where the interrogators tried to outsmart our supposed advanced counter-interrogation techniques and every second they couldn't meant the United States was under imminent threat of another catastrophic attack. It was a place where they'd rather believe lies than truth so long as it supported what they already believed. If our lives weren't at stake, it would have been funny.

But the interrogators and camp admin took whatever we did or said very seriously, no matter how ridiculous it was. At Guantánamo, even the most absurd jokes had real consequences. That didn't keep us from joking around though. Our jokes could be an innocent distraction or a dangerous game, depending on who was in on the joke. Either way, it was something to do, and sometimes the only thing to do, when we weren't waiting around for the guards to harass us or the interrogators to kick our asses. Our jokes were the only things we could control, that the interrogators couldn't take away from us, that reminded us we were human.

The Americans were scared of us and we could use that against them, often with unexpectedly delightful results. On one of those

115

stormy nights during Guantánamo's rainy season, a Yemeni brother had a cold and was performing incantations known as Ruqyahs over his water bottle as a way to heal himself. Some brothers did this instead of asking their interrogators for a doctor. They recited short Surahs from the Holy Qur'an or Allah's beautiful names over their water bottles or cups, then blew into the water. Then they drank the water or passed it on to other brothers who were feeling sick.

New guards were always really confused by this no matter how many times we tried to explain it. They were told all kinds of things by the camp admin when they first arrived, like we were all crazy killers and religious extremists. But they never told them about this.

One of the new guards noticed this brother had covered himself with a sheet and was holding a water bottle to his lips and whispering. Like all of us, this brother had really long hair and a beard—we couldn't cut them—and maybe looked a little scary.

This guard watched him for a long time, nervous.

Lightning flashed, and this brother recited his verses louder and then the thunder clapped.

"What's he doing?" the new guard asked. "What language is he speaking?"

"He's performing an Islamic healing," Othman said. He was always trying to help the guards with his English, even when it wasn't helpful.

Hamzah called the new guard to his cage. He had a wicked smile and I knew he was going to cause some trouble.

"Our brother here is a sorcerer," Hamzah whispered. "He's calling his jinns for help."

"What are jinns?" the new guard asked. She was really scared now.

"Jinns are demons," Hamzah said.

They both looked down the block at our brother reciting the Qur'an to his water bottle.

"Demons?" the guard said.

"You know," Hamzah whispered. "Shape-shifting spirits made of fire and air. Like Aladdin. He's just summoning the Two-Thunder jinni who controls thunder and lightning."

All the blood drained from the guard's face.

"Hey, brother," Hamzah called in Arabic. "I told her you're a sorcerer. I told her you're calling your thunder jinni to help you."

With the next lightning flash, the sorcerer recited the verses even more loudly and now rocked back and forth like he was summoning his jinni.

The new guard watched him closely. When the thunder clapped again, she jumped and muffled a terrified cry.

Crazy lightning flashed and the sorcerer spoke louder. Thunder hit one, two, three times in a row, each time closer and closer, louder and louder.

"Oh my God!" she cried. "Oh my God, oh my God, oh my God!" The new guard ran to the block sergeant and told him what was going on.

Soon the sorcerer had a big audience of guards watching his performance, all freaking out as he spoke louder and louder.

Lightning flashed. Thunder rumbled. It seemed to be on top of us and all around us.

"Tell him to stop," the sergeant said to Hamzah.

But the sorcerer kept talking. He kept rocking. Thunder kept clapping.

"This guy is crazy!" the guard cried. "He's going to kill us all."

He was such a good performer, even some brothers were worried now. Did he really have a thunder jinni?

The sergeant called the watch commander, and when he saw what was going on, he shouted at the sorcerer to stop or he'd call an IRF team to make him stop.

Our brother stopped. He had finished his incantations anyway. He took the sheet off his head and calmly handed the watch commander his water bottle. He was a good actor, this brother.

The thunder didn't stop though. It lasted all night long. So did our laughter. The new guard got a nickname: "Thunder Girl." The sorcerer got over his cold, but of course, he was punished—he wasn't allowed to have a water bottle for three months.

NOT EVERY JOKE was so harmless. During one of my stays in Quebec Block, where we weren't allowed to have anything except our clothes and an ISO mat during the day, I was in cage 25 and opposite me, in cage 24, was a Saudi brother. We were at the back of the block, where if we stood on our beds, we could see some makeshift housing for the Filipino workers who built and maintained the camps. These workers were like machines, always moving, always building.

"Let's have some fun," the Saudi brother said. He spoke English and called for the guards. "I saw a guy out there with a camera," he reported. He pointed up to the hill and the Filipino tents. The guard strained to get a good look. He seemed really concerned and radioed the camp commander.

This immediately put the entire camp in a state of emergency.

Humvees with armed soldiers and dogs swarmed the hill where the Filipinos lived. Even from where we were, we heard soldiers shouting at the workers. Soldiers lined up those poor workers against the fence and made them get down on their knees, their hands on their heads, just like they made us do every day. Then the soldiers searched each worker in the worst way. They searched tents, turning that place upside down. This went on for hours. What was so funny and tragic to us wasn't what happened to those poor workers. It was that the interrogators wouldn't believe that we were sold to the Americans for bounty money, but they'd believe us when we told them there was an al Qaeda spy in the workers' camp taking photos. To do what—break us out?

The Saudi brother laughed as he watched. I didn't like it. I didn't like that those workers, who hadn't done anything wrong, were treated like criminals. I imagined they were scared and confused and wished they had never come to this place.

The Saudi brother bragged about what he did, and other brothers gave him a hard time. Our lives were hard and we didn't need to make life hard for others who were innocent.

"What's the point?" Mana'a said.

"The guards drive us crazy," the Saudi said. "I wanted to give them some work."

"Yes, but you just hurt a lot of innocent guys," Mana'a said. "If you want to make them work, make a problem here with your own body. Fight with an IRF team. This is how you can make them really work."

GENERAL MILLER TRIED to take everything away from us, but we still had our humor and we used jokes to dull the pain of uncertainty and cruel conditions. Sometimes our jokes were dark. We had to laugh, otherwise we would've been paralyzed by fear.

Even though Miller made it against the rules to talk to each other, there was no way to enforce it. The cages were open. You could hear a brother breathe, we were so close. So we still talked and talked all the time, calling out to each other down the block or even to neighboring blocks and yelling at the guards. Any time of day, you could hear brothers in all languages calling, crying, shouting, passing gossip and rumors, and even planning protests. Brothers at the front of the block by the gates would call to the rest of the block when guards changed shifts, when meals arrived, or when there was news or trouble.

When the vacuums arrived, Ali, one of the most cautious and soft-spoken Saudi brothers, was at the front of the block and called, "Allahu Akbar!"

"What's this good news?" brothers called back to Ali. The only news we were used to was bad news, and Ali seemed excited.

"They brought us vacuum cleaners to help us clean our dirty cages!" Ali called.

"What's a vacuum?" Farhad called back. He was an Afghani brother who'd been sold as a Taliban fighter for $1,000 by a rival farmer. He hadn't seen much of the world outside of his village and farm. I tried to explain it to him, but he didn't understand why anyone would need such a machine. Why not use a broom?

"They're tall and shaped like a woman," Ali called out. "They look like very elegant ladies."

"Who requested these vacuums?" Omar asked. "The Americans wouldn't just bring us something to be helpful."

"Trust me, brothers," Dan called. "Later today they will give us the carpets to cover our cage floors." Dan was a young Yemeni like me who'd been rounded up in Afghanistan and sold as a fighter. He was from a rich family in Sana'a and never learned how to clean. He was one of the laziest brothers. "These ladies will clean the carpets. I'm very optimistic that in no time we'll get TVs and video games in our cells, too."

We all laughed at Dan. He lived in his daydreams, but sometimes a dream was the best place to be. We knew there were no rugs coming. Of course there weren't. And worse, we knew the camp was up to something, we just didn't know what. So we played along with them, knowing the joke was on us and hoping it wasn't.

If you saw our cages, you'd wish we had rugs, too. We hadn't even been in Camp Delta for a year and the cells were corroded and rusting. We had asked for prayer rugs. A vacuum would be very handy to clean prayer rugs. And the guards could use them to clean the walkways when we tore up our garbage and threw it at them. They hated cleaning up after us. In this upside-down world, those vacuums made a lot of sense.

In no time, speculation about carpets and vacuums circulated all throughout Camp 2 and came back to us with a confirmation that, yes indeed, each brother in Lima Block got a carpet and a new vacuum to help clean his cage. The wonders of DNN always delivered.

The brothers who spoke English asked the guards about the vacuums.

"We're not allowed to tell you," they said. "But you'll find out soon enough." They were too happy. These guards had a division patch with a 9/4 on it, so we called them the 9/4. They were the worst of the worst guards. They were like spoiled kids in the camp and had a green light to do whatever they wanted. The night before, they had thrown our dinners in the garbage right in front of us and then kept us up all night, banging on our cages.

We tried to ignore the 9/4 and passed the day talking about the carpets we would get. We were mostly level 4s, so all we had in our cages were ISO mats that we used for everything. We prayed on them, covered ourselves with them when we used the toilet, slept on them, ate our meals on them, walked on them . . . everything. They smelled terrible and were stained brown with rust.

A carpet—now that would fix so many problems. If they came today, we could have them in time for our Saturday night program.

For a few hours every Saturday night after our evening meal, we escaped our miserable situation by singing songs together, reciting poetry out loud, and telling each other stories. This was one of our last connections to the lives we lived outside Guantánamo and it helped ease the fear and hardship of life in prison. We heard so many beautiful voices those nights singing in different languages— English, Pashto, Urdu, Persian, Arabic, Turkish—it was like traveling to each brother's home. Anyone could sing, and sometimes we would all sing together, all forty-eight brothers in a single block. Sometimes another block joined in and sang one verse while we sang another. Sometimes the guards joined in, too. This really made us laugh.

The Saturday that the vacuums arrived, brothers went to rec and to shower as scheduled and still the carpets didn't arrive. We prayed. No carpets. Dinner was served and still the carpets didn't arrive. The vacuums remained by the front gate. It would have been nice to have our new carpets in time for our singing program, but we couldn't wait. An Afghani brother started the Saturday night program with a lovely poem about the first time he saw the sea.

The guards from the 9/4 walked up and down the block laughing at us, imitating the brother reciting the poem. They were always trying to provoke us. We just ignored them.

After the Afghani brother finished his poem, Bahr began singing a song that we all knew. We let him sing out the first verse, then we all joined him. It was such a beautiful and joyous sound, all of us singing together, happy to have each other and our songs, even though we were in cages.

As we sang, the camp officer and guards entered the block and began to move the vacuums throughout the block. We stopped singing and moved to the front of our cages and watched.

"What are they up to?" Dan called out.

The camp officer ordered the guards to place eight vacuums equally spaced down the block so that we each had one close to our cage.

"Where are the carpets?" Ali called out, and we all laughed. But it was a nervous laughter.

"Welcome," Dan sang to a vacuum as it passed his cage. He addressed it like it was a lady. "She won't talk to me! I think these elegant ladies are a little stuck up."

"Or they were given very strict orders not to talk to us," Adnan called out.

Omar looked worried.

"I can't wait to get my hands on this lovely lady," Dan said.

We sang the news to other blocks that the vacuums were being set up.

"This is the first real big change," Waddah said. "Finally they are listening to us."

"I would let her stay in my cage if she wants," Dan said.

"I'll bet that Dan would pull her into his bed with him and hug her all night," Bahr said.

"At least I'll have something to hug," Dan said. "Anything would be better than looking at your hairy face when I go to sleep every night."

Dan called the camp officer to his cage.

"Please, can I have one just for me?" Dan asked. He was kidding but maybe serious, too.

"Of course," the camp officer said. He laughed really hard, then called the guards. "Hey! Bring another one over here just for cell 24."

Dan was clearly proud that he would have his very own vacuum. The guards placed one right in front of his door. He admired it up and down.

"This is a very fine-looking lady!"

"Those are really big vacuums," Omar said. He was worried that we had so many.

While the guard ran electricity to all the vacuums, we went back to our Saturday night program.

Dan asked Bahr to sing a song of celebration to welcome his lovely lady. Bahr started off on a beautiful song. But he didn't even finish the first verse before guards turned on Dan's vacuum. It was loud and high-pitched. Another vacuum turned on, then another. Together they created a chorus of angry screaming that drowned out our own singing.

We all stopped singing.

"No, no, no, no!" Dan cried. The vacuum in front of his cage screamed right at him. I was in the cage next to him and couldn't hear anything he said over the noise. I watched him plead with his vacuum. He motioned for her to stop. He shushed her. He got on his knees and begged. I laughed for a moment, but I realized how bad this could be.

I couldn't hear myself think, let alone talk or sing. Dan covered his ears with his hands and retreated to the corner of his cage.

One of the guards walked up and down the block handing the other guards earplugs. We begged them to turn off the vacuums.

"We have our orders," they said. "They'll be on until you go to sleep." They laughed.

We didn't want to fight with them. All we wanted was for them to turn off the vacuums so we could have our one night of songs. It was the only night we had to look forward to every week.

Yassir, my other neighbor, called to me. With the vacuums on, we could only talk to our neighbors, and even then we had to get really close to the mesh walls and yell. Yassir told me that Adnan had come up with a way to get the vacuums to stop, but many of us needed to act together at the same time.

I passed Yassir's instructions to Dan, and Dan passed them on to Omar, and so on down the block.

We filled our sinks with water, and then with our cups we showered the vacuums. We flooded the corridor and soon vacuums began turning off.

"You're a nasty lady!" Dan called to his vacuum.

The officer came out and ordered the guards to cover the vacuums with plastic bags and raise the cords off the ground. It wasn't long before the vacuums were screaming at us again. They screamed like that for hours, and just before the last prayer, guards turned them off. My ears rang and I had a headache. The day was over, and it was too late to continue with our Saturday night program. The interrogators had finally found a way to take away the last thing in our lives that brought us joy.

In the morning, I was moved to solitary confinement in November Block with the other brothers who had splashed the vacuums. Waiting for us there in front of each cage was a new vacuum.

Before the escorts pushed me into my cage, I kicked the vacuum as hard as I could and it crashed to the floor. The guards hit me hard against the wall, then pushed me into my cage. As soon as the door closed, they turned on the vacuum and it screamed at me.

The vacuum never stopped. It screamed at me every hour of every day for I don't know how many weeks. I had no comfort items in my cell. No books. No Qur'an. I had no way of passing time either. Nothing except my ISO mat and my shorts. The light was on all day and night and cold air blew from the vent, freezing me in my cell. All I had was that screaming vacuum, stabbing my brain. The headaches never ended. I had chest pain, ear pain, eye pain that got so bad my vision blurred. I was nervous and angry all the time. Sometimes I threw up. Sometimes I blacked out and when I came to, I found myself shouting and screaming at nothing. Sometimes the guards leaned the vacuum against my wall, which made everything vibrate and hum so that my whole body went numb. I heard strange voices in my head I knew weren't there. This went on for months.

I filled my ears with toilet paper. I tore pieces from my ISO mat and shoved them in my ears. I shoved them so far in, I had to go to the nurse, who pulled everything out.

"If you keep doing that," the nurse said, "we're just going to leave it all in there."

"I can't sleep," I said. "I can't think. Every single second those vacuums scream at me."

"I can't help you with that," she said. "All I can do is tell you to stop putting this stuff in your ears!"

The only way to get even a little peace was to cup my hands over my ears. But that did very little.

The vacuums were so loud, the guards on the block wore special earmuffs.

One nice sergeant worked on the block sometimes. He trusted us enough to move us to shower and rec without handcuffs and shackles.

"I know you guys won't do anything," he'd say. We all respected him.

On his shifts, he turned off some of the vacuums to give us a little peace. He couldn't turn them all off—that would have gotten him in trouble. But it was much better without all of them screaming at once. Sometimes he took me for an hour or so to the rec yard, where there weren't vacuums, though I could still hear them. Their screaming carried everywhere.

Sometimes other guards broke down and gave us earmuffs to wear, especially when they saw brothers who were young, younger even than me. I could see on those guards' faces that they didn't like the situation but they couldn't do anything about it. If they got caught helping us, they'd get punished.

How could this go on?

I saw Adnan in the November Block rec yard one day on my way to the shower. A long time had passed since I'd seen him.

"What brought you here, brother?" I asked.

"I did something bad to the vacuums in the open cages." He was really happy with himself. "It was so bad, the camp officer had to remove them from the block." If there was one brother who could silence the vacuums, it was Adnan.

"Tell me, brother. Quick!" I said.

He laughed really hard.

"In the middle of the night," he said, "I pulled a vacuum to my cage and cut off the cord using the cage. The guards went crazy. They searched every cage. They asked every brother if he knew what happened to the cord. I told them it was me. I told them I chewed it off and I refused to give it back. So they sent an IRF team to beat me and search my cage."

"Where did you put it?" I asked.

"I cut it up into tiny pieces on the mesh cage, then I flushed it all down the toilet."

"What'd you tell them you did with it?" I said.

Adnan smiled. He was very proud of himself. "I told them that I ate it! That's why they brought me here."

We all called Adnan "the Legend" after that, a nickname he would live up to until the end.

THE VACUUMS WERE so abusive, the camp admin had doctors check on us from time to time to make sure we were still healthy enough to be interrogated. These beasts were everywhere now, even in the interrogation rooms. A doctor asked, "Have you noticed any new health issues?"

This really surprised me. I mean, I was in really bad shape. I couldn't think straight. I had lost a lot of weight. I had no meat on my arms or legs. I couldn't remember the last time I slept. The skin around my eyes must have been dark blue and black.

"I don't know," I said. I told him about blacking out and hearing voices. "You tell me if something is wrong. Maybe everything?"

He asked me all the questions he was required to ask: Do you feel like hurting yourself? Do you feel like hurting others? Do you feel like killing yourself? I couldn't focus enough to say anything but no.

He thought I was healthy enough to go back to solitary confinement, and the vacuums went off for a little while. *Oh Allah!* What
peaceful quiet I had. I even heard myself breathing again.

Then I heard screaming and crying from down the block. I had
heard a lot of screaming and crying since meeting the Americans,
but this was really loud—the loudest ever—and it scared me. I recognized that voice as Farhad's, the Afghan who had never seen a vacuum. It sounded like he had really lost his mind. I heard guards and
then the psychologist. I heard him taken away. The way he broke
down made me afraid for myself. I wondered if it was just a matter of
time before the same thing would happen to me. Then the vacuums
started screaming again.

I saw Farhad passing to the rec yard weeks later.

"Brother," I called, "what happened?"

"I don't know," he said. "I just lost control. I felt my soul fighting
to get out of my body. I tore at everything. I tore off my clothes. I tried
to cut my veins with my teeth to let my soul out. The psychologist
tied me down and gave me a shot that put me to sleep. She wanted to
extract my four canines." We all knew about my Afghani neighbor in
Echo Block. The psychologist actually had his canines pulled.

When I was called to interrogation that week, I found a new interrogator. We were always getting new interrogators. They were
mostly young like me and didn't know anything. We started from
the beginning again. We always started from the beginning. But now
they were adding to my file as brothers broke down and said whatever the interrogators wanted them to say.

"Do you want to tell me what you were doing in Tora Bora?" he
asked.

"I wasn't at Tora Bora," I replied.

"That's interesting," he said. "We have a brother who identified
you at Tora Bora. Said he saw you giving orders."

"Giving orders to who?" I said.

"You tell me," he said, and I knew where he was going. I stopped talking and started praying to myself. That made him mad, so he left me short-shackled and freezing in the room for a couple of hours with the AC on high.

"Start talking to me," he said when he came back, "and I'll take you out of that noisy block." A light went off for me. They'd believe anything.

"No!" I cried. "I don't want to go anywhere! And if you silence my elegant lady . . ."

"Elegant lady?" He looked confused.

"My beautiful lady with the beautiful voice," I said.

"The vacuum?"

"Don't you dare disrespect her!" I cried. "If you take me away from her, I'll spit on you. I'll spit on every guard. I'll never talk to you if you take me out of that block!"

The new interrogator looked confused and maybe a little worried. The psychologist came in next and I talked about my lovely elegant lady to him, too. Then they moved me to India Block, where there were no vacuums. As soon as I reached the block, I threw myself to the ground and refused to walk to my cage. For this to work, I had to really commit.

"Take me back to November Block!" I cried. "I want my elegant lady." The guards dragged me to my cage.

It was paradise in that block without the vacuums. I slept for the first time in a long time.

Oh, how I enjoyed the quiet away from those nasty, noisy, tailed ladies. Every day, I asked the guards to bring me my lady.

"Please," I begged. "Bring me to my beautiful, elegant lady." They thought I was crazy. That's the thing about the Americans. They believed anything but the truth.

They were experimenting on us, and I was experimenting on them, pretending to lose my mind.

I spent a month on vacation in India Block, but I still couldn't think straight. No matter how much I ate, I kept losing weight. I slept, but I always felt like I needed more. I thought that maybe the noise from the vacuums had permanently rewired my brain. I talked to my neighbors sometimes, but it was hard to think straight or even understand what brothers were saying to me. I had a hard time concentrating. I forgot things. I'd be talking to my neighbor and forget what I was talking about in the middle of my sentence. This was common with all of us who had spent time in November Block with the vacuums. It's like the sound had burrowed into our minds and had broken pieces out. Most brothers in India Block had never heard the vacuums scream, but they noticed how I had changed.

"You're distracted all the time," one brother said to me.

He gave me a simple riddle to solve and I couldn't concentrate long enough to solve it. I got mad at him. I was angry with everyone. But he was right. It was hard for me to know what I was thinking about all the time. My mind jumped from one thought to another. I couldn't hold on to one no matter how hard I tried. My eyes hurt when I tried to focus, but I could still hear that screaming inside my head.

When I got my mind back just a little, my interrogators moved me to Romeo Block, where I found the vacuums again, still screaming like crazy. Of course they were. Adnan was there. So were Waddah, Dan, Bahr, and Omar. All the brothers who were with me on that last Saturday night. As I approached my cage, I kicked the vacuum as hard as I could. It fell over and stopped screaming. Before I could stomp it, the guards threw me to the floor, then dragged me into my cage.

Romeo Block had changed. The cords on the vacuums were hidden. And now there were clear plastic barriers in front of the cages, so we couldn't splash the vacuums or the guards.

We lived years with those vacuums. Only a few blocks had them, but they were almost always in whatever block I was in. They followed me, screaming all the time. It killed my concentration. Even to this day, I can't concentrate when there's even the faintest sound of a fan in the room.

Whenever Farhad, the Afghan, saw one of the vacuums, he spit at it. Why would anyone invent such a terrible thing? he asked. He's still not convinced they actually clean. He thinks all they do is torture. I don't blame him. The vacuums pushed me toward the edge of insanity and almost broke me. The cold calculation of the torture and cruelty of the vacuums really enraged me. The camp didn't want us to talk to each other because they wanted us to talk to them. If that's what they wanted, I decided to play a joke of my own.

YOU KNOW EXACTLY what the Americans want. They can't find Osama bin Laden or Mullah Omar or the dirty bomb they think al Qaeda has hidden somewhere ready to go off, otherwise they would have stopped asking you the same questions over and over again. *Where is Osama? Where is Mullah Omar? Where is the dirty bomb?* You've only finished high school but you're smart enough to know that it's really hard to get a dirty bomb, and why are they asking you?

You were sold as Adel in Afghanistan, an identity they made you wear until they found another. Then you became Alexander, a battle-hardened general, again much older than you, but one of the other brothers identified you in a pile of photographs after he had been kept awake for days, shackled in a room with flashing lights and screaming music. You don't blame him. He had to name someone, and if it wasn't you, it would have been another brother.

"Why am I really here?" you ask.

"You tell me why you're here," they say.

"Because you think I know about a dirty bomb?" you say.

"So you know about the dirty bomb?" they say.

"That's not what I said."

You tell them what you know. You tell them what you think they want to know. You tell them nothing. You stop talking—you and so many of the brothers.

You know you have done nothing wrong, have harmed no one, and this gives you strength. Now when they call you for your reservation, you sit or stand or squat, whatever they make you do, and you recite a hadith to yourself. You pray. You recite verses from the Qur'an to yourself in your head. You used to say them out loud, but they stuffed a sock in your mouth and duct-taped it shut, they beat you. It's okay. Allah will understand. You pray and this transports you out of this room that smells of sweat and urine and despair; it transports you to mountains in Raymah or up to the moon or out into the vastness of the universe, all created by Allah, and you don't hear them anymore. You don't hear their questions or their insults. You don't feel their slaps. You don't feel your body shake as your muscles rebel against the squatting position they forced you into, and this makes the interrogators furious and weaker, even if they don't know it.

Some around you can't handle the beatings, the pain, the sleeplessness, the uncertainty. They can't handle the isolation and the constant screaming of the vacuums and the starvation and the sleep deprivation. They can't handle the darkness of the tunnel that has no light and they break down. They work for the interrogators even though they don't want to. They say yes when interrogators ask if a brother is al Qaeda. They identify brothers they don't know in photos. They make up names and connections. They confirm or verify identities and information that can't possibly be true. They lie and lie about hundreds of men, and when they lie, they get rewards. They get better food and better cages. They get moved to level 1+ and then to Camp 4, where the life is easy and there's talk of getting free.

It's hard to watch your brothers suffer while these snitches tell lies about men they never knew, including you. But you understand. You don't blame them. You blame the interrogators asking them to lie and then believing them. You blame General Miller, who created this machine and feeds it. And one day when you're in November Block in isolation with the vacuums screaming, you think of a way to teach them a lesson.

"Let's play with them," you say to Waddah that night when the vacuums go off. "We have nothing to lose. I'm here and they're here." And that's when the fun begins.

You call for a reservation with your interrogators and that makes them very happy.

"Why'd you call?" they ask.

"I'm ready to cooperate," you say. "I have some important information."

They're all smiles, your interrogators, an old guy and a woman, all pasty and pale.

Over the next three days, you make up all kinds of stories with your brothers at night about the dirty bomb they're looking for, and in the morning you feed them to your interrogators. Your interrogators are so happy, they eat it all up, greedy for more. On the third day, at the end of your session, you tell them you have one more really important detail.

This feels good. They don't know what pain lies ahead. They don't know that you are in control. You want to savor this moment a little longer. They wait. You take one last sip of cold water.

"Everything I've told you over the last three days . . ." You pause for a moment. You take in their eager faces. "Everything I told you was absolute bullshit." You watch the words hit like bullets in the chest.

Happiness turns to panic turns to anger and then they're just crazy. They're so mad they can't talk to you. They storm out.

They call you the next day for your reservation and you go but don't talk. You sit there and recite verses from the Qur'an out loud. You do this every day for a week and then someone older comes to talk to you. *This person is in charge*, you think. He must be in charge to be so calm and thoughtful.

"Why'd you do that?" he asks.

"Why are you holding me without telling me why?" you ask. "Why do you torture my brothers? Why do you believe obvious lies and then torture us to say they're true? Why do you make snitches who will say anything to make you happy?"

"How do you know they're lying?" he says.

"Your problem isn't my lies," you say. "It's that you want to hear my lies and make them true. You know that your snitches and spies have been lying to you. And you've been torturing men because of those lies. I told you lies to teach you a lesson, to show you how easy it is to lie to you."

This makes him very angry.

"Fuck you!" he says. "I'm going to break you next."

"We will see." You smile your biggest smile. "I will cut my tongue before talking to you again."

The old woman interrogator comes in cursing you.

"I'm gonna take your shitty ass back to the US and make you my servant. I'm going to shave that disgusting beard and I'm going to make you into my slave. You'll be cleaning my home, scrubbing my kitchen, cooking for me, holding my bag . . . Your ass is mine."

You look away as she yells at you. You don't say anything. And this makes her even more furious.

"Why'd you do it?" the other interrogator asks. He's tired. "Is it because you hate America?"

"I wanted to learn how to be like you," you say. "I wanted to learn how to be an interrogator."

He slaps you. You didn't think he had it in him. He slaps you so hard and so fast it's shocking, and not much can shock you anymore. He kicks your chair from underneath you and throws you to the floor.

"Shackle him," he tells the guards.

They chain you in the worst position. Your whole body shakes. He turns the AC up high and takes a pitcher of ice water and pours it over you.

"I'll teach you how to be a good interrogator."

"Okay!" you say. "Thank you!"

He slaps your face until you bleed.

"They trained you well," he says. "But I'm going to make you cry like a bitch!"

You laugh at him. Then spit in his face. It's a good one, mixed with blood.

The guards strip you naked. He pours more water on you and leaves you chained to the floor, squatting with your hands in front of you.

The interpreter says, "He's been doing this for fifteen years and you're the first one to make him look like such a fool."

How did this become about him? you think.

Guards come in every hour to pour cold water on you and make sure you're awake. You pray. You recite hadiths. Days pass like this. You're miserable but you really enjoyed seeing those assholes so angry.

They try hard to get you to say you weren't lying. They're desperate for you not to lie. Sorry things didn't work out the way they liked, you tell them.

"You're going on the blacklist," the old woman says.

You don't know what this blacklist is. You're already in this prison; what could be worse? You're young, you don't give a shit about anything. *If you challenge me,* you think, *be prepared to bang your head against a wall with your blacklist.*

"You're going to spend the rest of your life here!" the tired old guy yells at you.

The angrier he gets, the happier you are because you know you've beaten them.

"By Allah," you say, "I will leave Guantánamo. And you will be the one holding my hand and leading me to the airplane. One day you criminals will be found out." You're serious when you say this. You don't doubt it for a second. You believe these criminals will be caught, that they'll be stopped, and that you'll all be set free.

This old tired guy looks at you, surprised.

"Who the hell are you working for?" he says.

"Allah," you say.

"Someone will break you," he spits. "Someone will break you soon, Osama's guy."

You recite to yourself a hadith: *And if they were to gather together to harm you with anything, they would not harm you except with what Allah had already prescribed against you. The pens have been lifted and the pages have dried.*

You are here because Allah has willed it, and with His blessing, one day you will leave. In a land of sick jokes, that is the only truth.

- ELEVEN -

Now that I was on the interrogation blacklist, I was in deep shit—not the usual face slaps, short-shackles, and humiliating genital searches—deep, deep shit where interrogators and guards got creative with all kinds of nasty techniques. We were all suffering and sitting on a bomb waiting to go off.

One of the worst tortures was sleep deprivation, which went on for months or even years. But guards had a special treat for brothers on the blacklist. They called it the "Frequent Flyer Program." To keep me awake, guards stormed my cell, beat me, restrained me, then ran me to a new cell in another block, where they'd leave me just long enough to fall asleep, then they'd storm into my cell again, beat me, restrain me, and run me to another cell. This could go on all night or for days and weeks. Sometimes they even made bets on how fast they could run a detainee through a certain number of cells in one night.

I wasn't the only one in such deep shit. Brothers all over the camp were refusing to talk to interrogators and suffering for it. The nastier the interrogations got, the more brothers refused to talk.

One Afghani brother, Nadeem, was in the sleep deprivation program for nine months. He lost a lot of weight, around sixty pounds, and had only about one hundred pounds left. He was a little older than me, maybe twenty-one years old.

Word about his condition spread through DNN and we started to protest. The brothers in Camps 1 and 4 didn't respond. They had it good and didn't want to risk their privileges. Camps 2 and 3, though, that's where things started to fall apart.

As usual, we started to protest peacefully by putting in formal complaints with the camp officers to stop the abuse and religious harassment, especially the desecration of the Qur'an. They didn't respond, so we started refusing our food and medicine. Then we refused to go to rec and shower. The camp admin still didn't care, so we had to move to the next level, which was to refuse to come out of our cages for anything, especially interrogation. We had nothing but IRF teams, and so the guards had nothing but work.

A majority of detainees were Afghani brothers like Nadeem. The Afghans were quiet most of the time, keeping to themselves and not getting involved in our protests. And that's what they did despite Nadeem's condition—they kept quiet. I don't know why. The camp was messy, but without the Afghans, it wasn't messy enough.

The interrogators wanted Nadeem to admit that he was an al Qaeda leader, and they really pushed him, but things didn't completely erupt until one of the interrogators put the Holy Qur'an under his foot. It's important to understand that the Afghans took the treatment of the Qur'an very seriously. When a guard threw a Holy Qur'an to the ground and stepped on it, he woke a sleeping beast.

The Afghans put their hearts and souls into their work. They started fighting early in the morning, right after the first prayer, and didn't stop until after the last prayer. They banged their cages and windows all day long. They yelled. They spit. They splashed. They turned the camp upside down. Our Arab resistance was nothing compared to what the Afghans did. This went on for over a month before the camp admin decided to crush us with IRF teams. They beat us badly. They showered us with pepper spray. They made our meals smaller. They kept us awake all night with searches.

The Afghani brothers in Quebec Block thought the camp took it too far, so they did, too. When things only ever get worse, you can lose all hope and lose control of yourself. The camp admin doesn't respond to peaceful protest or hunger strikes or fighting, so you ask yourself, what can I possibly do to make my captors care about my shitty situation? The Afghani brothers in Quebec Block thought they had the answer. They organized a mass suicide where they would all hang themselves and throw the camp into complete chaos.

They did it in waves throughout the day so that the IRF teams and guards would have time to cut down each wave of brothers and take them to the medical unit. It was shocking, even for us. All day long "Code Snowball" echoed throughout the blocks as more than sixty brothers hung themselves by their sheets. When one brother was cut down, another hung himself. The guards made the situation even worse by pepper-spraying the Afghani brothers before cutting them down.

Word spread quickly to other blocks about what the Afghans had done, and more brothers started hanging themselves. There were Code Snowballs all over the camp until finally a state of emergency was called.

The camp admin loved us so much, they didn't want us to die. Each brother had to be brought to the hospital for a special review to make sure he was okay and wouldn't try to kill himself again. One of the brothers wasn't cut down soon enough and went into a coma. We didn't think the camp admin could hide something this big from the outside world.

Colonel McQueen, a broad-shouldered, no-nonsense Black man who was the camp's warden, tried to calm the Afghani brothers. He promised that guards and interrogators wouldn't desecrate the Holy Qur'an again. None of the brothers believed him. They demanded to hear it directly from General Miller. But General Miller was a chicken, and that night he spoke to the camp through the loudspeakers. He said that the interrogator who desecrated the Holy Qur'an had been kicked out of Guantánamo, and that guards wouldn't mishandle or even touch the Holy Qur'an again. We had heard many stories like this at Guantánamo, and while it calmed things down for a time, we didn't believe him. We all knew those Afghani brothers didn't really want to kill themselves. They just wanted to send General Miller a strong and dangerous message that we were at a breaking point and if conditions didn't improve, things were going to get really messy.

The Afghani brothers got their message to Miller; the rest of us had to wait a little longer. We got our chance when he made a surprise visit to Lima Block. He was known to walk the blocks, but when he walked blocks full of Redeyes and Afghans—and we had both— they usually placed plexiglass barriers in front of our cages first so we couldn't splash him. But on this day they didn't.

"The Big Nasty is here!" the brother at the front of the block called down.

Miller was short and bald, and walked with an unmistakable arrogance. We knew he was the one who tortured us every day. We had all talked about what we would do if he ever walked our block. Everyone got ready.

"You have shit?"

"Please give me shit."

"I need just a little!"

Unfortunately, this is not something you can just make on command. And it's hard to hide. Because of the smell, guards knew when you saved it. Luckily I had a cup of urine left over from the previous night of fighting with the 9/4. It smelled very nasty. I'm sorry to tell you that this was our weapon of mass destruction. I'm not proud of it. But it's all we had.

Miller strutted onto our block, all chest and shoulders in an arrogant march like he owned the place. He didn't even look at us, but we looked at him and smiled.

"Hello," we said. We played good detainees, like we were soft.

When he got to the middle of the block, a brother called, "Allahu Akbar," and all the brothers threw what they had at him. Urine. Dirty water. One brother had a cup of shit. General Miller was close to me and I splashed him with my nasty urine right in his face. The guards went to cover him, but they were too late to shield him from most of it. His uniform was wet, his face covered with spit, dirty water, pieces of shit and toilet paper, urine, soap. It looked very lovely on his bald head.

"White trash! Stupid redneck! Idiot Rambo! Donkey ass! Room service!" we yelled.

We danced and celebrated. We kicked the cage doors, the sinks, anything that would make noise, and our celebration spread to the next block and the block after that and soon all the blocks joined our party and you could have heard "Allahu Akbar" as far away as Sana'a.

"Today," I said to my brothers, "I am honored that the great idiot Miller sipped some of my very fine urine."

Omar didn't like what we did.

"You didn't just throw feces on General Miller," he scolded. "You threw feces on the entire American army. On America. They won't let you do that."

He was right and he was wrong. We threw shit on the American army that tortured us. We threw shit on the general who made the army think that way. But that was not America and we knew it. We knew not to see America through the filter of Guantánamo, even though most of the guards still saw us through the filter of 9/11.

It was one of the best days at Guantánamo. We were cut off from our families and the world and tortured until we would admit that we were terrorists. And yet the great General Miller had tasted our feces and our urine. We were inside of him. We knew we would be punished badly for what we did. But they couldn't take that away and that's what mattered.

That night they gave us double meal portions for dinner and we were so happy to fill our stomachs. Usually the food was very little, and we were always hungry. We should splash the general every day, we joked. But we also felt something was not right. We all got tired very quickly and the block started to quiet down. I started to get ready to fight. I filled my sink with water and soaped my floor, but my body was getting heavy and all I wanted to do was lie down and sleep. Then the guards turned off our water and closed our windows. I called out to my brothers. The block was quiet. Almost everyone was asleep. The guards had drugged our meal. I tried not to fall asleep, but I did.

While I slept, I had a vivid dream that I was dragged from my cage by barking dogs from hell, that my body burned with pepper spray, and that guards danced on my body, kicking and punching as they laughed and sang. I dreamed they dragged me to solitary confinement in India Block by my feet.

That's where I woke, the heat of pepper spray still burning my skin. I had a bad headache and bruises all over. I was sore, and my body was so heavy and tired I couldn't move. My nightmare was real.

Still, splashing Miller was worth it. When guards brought us our meals, we'd ask, "Where is Miller? Maybe he wants to share our meal with us again."

We scratched WHERE'S MILLER into the Styrofoam clamshells they brought our meals in. We called it out to guards when they passed by our cages. We wouldn't have to wait too long to find out.

- TWELVE -

As Miller escalated the conflict across the camp, we were always looking out for what he would do next. Construction wasn't anything new: Guantánamo was a living, breathing monster that was always growing, expanding, adapting, changing. Construction workers were constantly working on the blocks. The salty air corroded the metal, and they were either repainting the blocks in the same bland green or replacing parts of the cells to make them stronger. But they'd been working on Romeo Block for a long time, at least a month nonstop. It was their experimental block, always staffed with the worst guards, and no one wanted to go there.

So what were they doing in there now?

One day, after the third prayer, we heard IRF teams shouting and dogs barking in Romeo Block. We called out to the brothers there to find out what was going on. Right away, one of the guards started shouting at us.

"Shut the fuck up!"

"Hey, idiot," Hamzah yelled at the guard. "Watch your mouth or I'll break it." Hamzah had the deep, gravelly voice of someone used to getting his way all the time. He had no patience for asshole guards. All the other brothers on Tango Block started calling out to our brothers in Romeo Block.

Our brother Azani called back from Romeo. Azani was from Yemen and one of the camp's calmest and quietest brothers. He always

143

followed the rules and never protested, even when guards did the most humiliating things, but he had stopped talking to interrogators, too.

"Please, brothers!" Azani called. "Help me! Guards stripped me naked and took my clothes. They say it's the new rules in Romeo."

General Miller and the interrogators thought they were clever. They were moving the weakest and most compliant brothers to Romeo, one of the worst blocks, to break them and make them talk. The interrogators had done this before. They had moved compliant brothers to Tango or Sierra, blocks full of Redeyes, knowing they couldn't stand the craziness and would do anything to get moved to a quieter block. It was hard being on our block. There were IRFs and cell searches all the time and these brothers couldn't handle it. They weren't snitches. They were just brothers who avoided conflict. We called them brothers of absolute patience.

More brothers cried out from Romeo Block.

"They're using IRF teams to strip us," a brother called out.

This had been a big problem since the beginning of Guantánamo— guards and interrogators taking our clothes. It was humiliating. Brothers couldn't offer their prayers if they were naked.

From Romeo, we heard IRF teams barking orders and shouting. Our young brothers cried out for their clothes.

Tango block went dead silent.

"They're baiting us," Omar said. "They're cracking down on co-ordinated protests, and then they put all of us in a block together?" Omar knew how Miller thought. "But we can't let them do that to our brothers."

There were around seventy Redeyes in the camp, guys from all different parts of the world, different ages and religious mindsets, different personalities. We weren't an organized group; we were more like a tribe, and we had a wild reputation across the camp. Everyone knew who we were—other prisoners, guards, interrogators, even the commanders.

I called a war summit. There were twenty-three of us on the block and we all agreed that we had to help our brothers. Our plan was simple: we'd pull the guards to our block and fight them here to make them stop what they were doing in Romeo Block.

We all filled our sinks with water—the first thing guards did during a riot was turn off the block's water. We hid our Qur'ans and toothbrushes to keep them safe from pepper spray. I rubbed my floor and bed and walls with soap to get ready. We prayed.

General Miller had his SOPs and we had our DSOPs, detainee standard operating procedures. First, we asked the watch commander to call the camp officer so we could register a formal complaint and talk, but the camp officer refused to come to our block. Next, we called the guards names and splashed them with water.

"Chicken!" we yelled. "Donkey!"

In response, they turned off the water, then shuttered all the outside windows to keep us from calling to our brothers in Romeo Block. But it was too late. Brothers in Sierra and November Blocks relayed news of what was happening to other blocks. DNN was quick.

Omar called one of the nicer guards to his cell and asked Othman to translate for him.

"Your General Miller is trying to make us fight you," Omar said. This guard had a palm-tree patch on his arm and wasn't from the 9/4. "Look around you in the camps. You have boys and old men. Farmers. Look at me with my one leg. Does it look like we want to fight? No. Your General Miller wants chaos. He wants us to fight. So what does he do? He makes you enforce rules that make no sense. He puts the most compliant brothers who never cause any problems in Romeo Block and takes away their clothes. Listen!"

"They're just following the new SOPs," the guard said.

"Yes!" Omar cried. "He makes you punish us because of illogical SOPs."

This guard thought really hard about what Omar said.

Another guard, one of the nastier ones, pulled the nice guard away and pushed him off the block. When the nasty guard came back, he danced up and down the block mocking us.

"General Miller is making us fight!" he sang like a little girl. "Shut the fuck up, haji motherfuckers!"

Waddah splashed him with toilet water.

The nasty guard returned fire, showering all of us with pepper spray. This is how things would escalate. After the initial burn of pepper spray, you have a rush of adrenaline. There's no coming down once that starts, and I wondered if they knew that. Abdul splashed the nasty guard with number two and that shut him up, but then everything broke down. More guards stormed onto the block with pepper spray and we splashed them with anything we had. We hit and kicked our cages, we shouted. The block turned into a sloppy, shitty, peppery hot zone.

"Please!" Omar yelled at the guards. "Don't get involved."

Othman yelled out, "If you walk through our block, we'll splash you with number two!"

The guards left the block wet and messy. We all chanted, "Send us the general!"

A guard came back in and told us the general refused to talk to us.

"Okay," we said. We tied our blankets in knots at one end, then soaked them in water. This was something we had learned from the Afghani brothers when they rioted. With just a little water, the blanket became a hammer. When they all hit the floors and doors, it made a fierce thundering boom.

I used my hammer to break off the bean hole doors from my cage. I held them up for brothers to see and soon others were hammering their bean holes, too. The guards went wild when they saw how many of us had broken them off, and they called Code Yellow, one of the highest-level emergencies.

All their energy shifted away from Romeo to our block, just as we planned. But now Camp 3 filled with hundreds of soldiers, medical teams, dogs, officers, interrogators, civilians, all kinds of crazy people. Many IRF teams armored up. At last the idiot General Miller himself came. They had mobilized an army to fight us.

One of the bigger idiot officers, a guy who was really well built, tried to enter the block. He didn't get far. There was too much splashing and spitting. They sent an Arabic interpreter in next.

"They want to talk to you," he said. "But first, 441 and all the others who broke the bean hole doors have to hand them over."

"Fuck him," Hamzah said. "If he wants to talk, we'll talk about Romeo Block first, then we'll discuss our metal doors." Hamzah had no patience for the general. "They want to see our brothers naked in Romeo Block? Send them here and they can look at my cock."

The interpreter took out a small notebook from his pocket and wrote down everything we said.

"Tell the general that if he wants my door," I said, "he can come and get it himself."

Guards in raincoats brought in plexiglass barriers and placed them in front of our cages. We let them cover every cage and think they were in control. Maybe they forgot that we had broken the bean hole doors.

The camp's army major came in and asked us to give back the metal doors. Hamzah, who spoke English, explained to him how stripping our brothers in Romeo was not only a religious problem, it was just inhumane.

"You tell the chicken general that if he wants to walk around naked, fine!" Hamzah said. "Maybe he wants to show off his cock. Tell him those brothers can't pray like that."

"I'm not here to listen to your dictations," the army major said. "SOPs are SOPs. No clothes in Romeo. Now give me the goddamn metal."

We wanted to solve the problem, but we were dealing with crazy people, and those killers only understood one language: the language of force and strength. So we refused.

General Miller and the colonel stormed onto the block full of arrogance, like they could do whatever they wanted. They had IRF teams with dogs and shields to protect them.

The general stopped at Omar's cage with an interpreter.

"Are you the one trying to turn my guards against me?" General Miller yelled. "Do you want my guards to revolt against me?"

"I was just telling your guards why they shouldn't fight with us," Omar said.

Miller listened to the interpreter and he looked like he was going to erupt. He surveyed the block as if he were assessing a battlefield. He turned away from Omar and charged down the walkway, safe behind the plexiglass. At the middle of the block, he stopped.

"Now you listen!" he yelled.

We reached through our bean holes and pushed the barriers over.

"Allahu Akbar!" we shouted.

We splashed the idiot General Miller and the colonel and the interpreter and all the rest with shit and dirty water. The IRF teams scattered everywhere like wet chickens. Oh Allah! It was lovely seeing them flee like that, bumping into each other, stumbling to the ground. Some of them got stuck in the back of the block. Their pretty beige uniforms were stained yellow and brown, and the only way out was to pass by us again.

We all laughed hard at how easy it was to scatter them. Arrogance makes you forget how weak you are. We had no doubt that they would kick our asses soon. But for just a few minutes, we had chipped away at their confidence. Maybe they would listen to reason now.

They didn't. Guards set up big fans at the gate then emptied canister after canister of pepper spray into the wind until we couldn't breathe. We could handle the pain of pepper spray on our skin, but when we couldn't breathe . . . there was nothing we could do. One of our brothers, an older Palestinian, had asthma and he collapsed, unable to breathe. We thought he might die. We had no choice. We had to stop the fight to save our brother.

IRF teams went to each cage and showered us with pepper spray, then beat us until we couldn't move.

They came for me with six guards and a dog. I'm not tall or big. I'm just five foot four and I'd lost a lot of weight because of months of sleep deprivation.

"I'm not afraid of your dog!" I yelled.

"Good for you!" the team leader yelled back.

I had actually trained with guard dogs in Yemen. When they charged in, I snatched the dog and gave him a nice big hug that made him whimper instead of bark, and then he went still in my arms.

"Save the dog!" the guards screamed. "Save the dog!"

The entire team jumped on top of me, but my floor was so slippery from the soap and pepper spray that they all fell. When they had me restrained, they didn't beat me, and I was glad for it. Instead, they dragged me to the rec yard, where they threw me to the ground shackled. More guards came and they all piled on top, holding me so I couldn't move. The officer knelt on my neck, pulled my head up by my hair, opened my eyes, and showered each eye with pepper spray. The world went black in a blanket of pain. I thought I was blinded forever. Now they beat me, kicking, punching, throwing me around like a plastic toy. I didn't feel the pain after the first couple of kicks. My spirit left my body and watched from above, listening to the solid thud of boots on ribs, skin splitting, ribs cracking. When they were done, I felt the sole of a boot on my face.

"That was for the dog," the officer said.

The IRF team dragged me by my legs to a cage in Sierra Block. It was hard to breathe and I knew several of my ribs were broken. I couldn't see and didn't know if it was because of the pepper spray, because my eyes were swollen shut, or because there was so much blood on my face. The blood in my mouth tasted of death.

By morning, they had moved all of us to Sierra Block. Then they came back for me. My face was so badly beaten and swollen, I couldn't open my eyes or mouth. The IRF team came again and shackled my hands and legs. They dragged me back out to the rec yard and beat me again. It didn't matter. The old pain numbed the new pain. When they dragged me back to my cage and threw me in, I stood up tall to show them that they hadn't gotten the best of me. I stood to show my brothers that we didn't have to fear them. I spit at the guards and they charged back in, all six of them, and slammed me against the wall. They pounded my head against whatever surface they could connect with and then put my head in the toilet and flushed. The pepper spray got worse with water, and now my face and eyes burned like fire. When they left me, I couldn't stand. They had broken my ankle.

It wasn't my intention to hurt the dog; I could have killed it if I had wanted. That dog had bitten so many of us so many times. It was strange to see how much love and respect they had for the dog, the dog they had trained to terrorize us.

They left us in Sierra Block, naked with no blankets in the middle of winter, with only the pepper spray to keep us warm. After the IRF teams finished with us, they went back to Romeo Block and finished stripping the rest of the compliant brothers. Sierra Block was next to Romeo and we listened to our brothers stripped naked, one by one, while getting their asses kicked.

Believe me, we didn't want to continue. We were all in bad shape, but we had no choice. We had to show them that we couldn't be beaten. The guards turned off the water so we couldn't wash before prayer. We agreed that we would all refuse to leave our cages for everything: searches, shower, recreation, reservations. They served us a nasty breakfast with no spoons, but most of us couldn't open our mouths or chew. We tore up our Styrofoam plates into small pieces and threw them all over the block floor.

"Room service!" we called. "Come clean for us!"

They just laughed at us. They didn't even bother to clean the walkway. Instead, they went from cage to cage asking us to return our spoons.

"You didn't give me a spoon," I said.

"Detainee 441 is refusing to return his spoon!" the guard yelled. This was a violation, and according to SOPs, it required a cage search.

I refused to leave my cage, which meant they had to send an IRF team to remove me before they could search my cell. We all refused, and they were ready for us with IRF teams. I don't think the camp admin even slept that night. They were busy planning. I saw General Miller himself in the yard helping the IRF teams gear up.

"This is not good," Omar said. "No, it's going to be very bad."

The IRF teams marched into the block wearing raincoats and face shields. General Miller trailed behind them. They stomped their boots on the steel floor, their footsteps in unison like a beating drum.

"Welcome," Waddah called out. "Unfortunately, we don't have shit for you today, but we have this." He threw the rest of his breakfast. They didn't care much.

"Chicken! Chicken!" we all called together in English. "Shake your ass. Shake it. Shake it off!" I'm sure we sounded very funny in our bad English.

They came for me first. The commanding officer said to the guard filming us, "ISN 441, are you coming out for cell search?" They had to document everything to prove that they had followed SOPs and that we deserved what we got.

"Where is your dog?" I yelled in English. Then in Arabic I said, "I'm protesting the new SOPs in Romeo Block. Give clothes to our brothers!"

The commanding officer spoke to the camera. "ISN 441 refused to be compliant with the camp rules." Before he was done, a guard hit me with pepper spray. They opened the cage door then pushed in all at once, slamming me into the wall with their shields. I felt like I had been hit by a car.

The IRF team kicked my ass, shackled me, and dragged me to the rec yard.

They stripped me naked, then shaved my body, my beard, my head. We hadn't been allowed to cut our hair or beards for years. When the barber cut my hair, it was no regular haircut. He shaved a cross on my head. On other brothers, he shaved devil horns, Stars of David, stripes. He shaved one brother to look like a horse, a stripe of hair running from the middle of his head down his back. They shaved just one half of another brother's head and beard, leaving long hair on one side. They gave another brother a mustache like Hitler. When we saw each other, we all laughed. We were hungry and miserable, but we laughed at each other and that lessened the pain just a little. We were all Redeyes laughing at each other as much as at General Miller for thinking that silly haircuts and good beatings would break us and make us talk to interrogators. That really pissed him off.

General Miller stopped in front of me.

"Why the fuck is he smiling?" General Miller yelled at the interpreter. "Fucking smiley troublemaker."

That made me smile even harder.

WHEN THEY CAME to move us to solitary confinement in Oscar Block, we refused to walk.

"Give pants to our brothers in Romeo Block," we said again. And again, the IRF teams came. Again the pepper spray, again they stormed our cages, shackled our arms and legs. Instead of carrying us, they pushed us onto our backs, then dragged us by our leg shackles.

When they took Othman, he sat up so that when he passed by our cages he looked like a kid driving a car. "Beep beep!" he called.

"Beep beep!" we called back. We drove our pretend cars all the way to Oscar Block. As we left Camp 3, we heard our brothers in other blocks joining the protest, refusing to leave their cells. At Oscar Block, the guards took our clothes, just like they did in Romeo. Some brothers were left with only pants, some with just a shirt, depending on how much they hated us. The psychologist, who was always asking us if we wanted to kill ourselves, told the guards to strip me completely naked and to leave me with nothing but my plastic ISO mat.

That night, the guards turned off the blinding lights and it was black in our cages. To do head counts, guards had to open the viewing window on our door and shine a bright light into each cage.

After the shift change, I heard a terrifying scream at the top of the block.

"Devils!" a woman cried. "There are devils in the cells!" One of the new guards had started doing the head count. No one had told her about our haircuts. When she shined a light into our cages, all she saw were naked men, beaten and bruised, their hair shaved with calculated cruelty.

"Devils!" she cried.

THEY LEFT US in our new "devil look" for days, weeks maybe. They brought camp staff, civilians, and many visitors to Oscar Block to see us. The guards opened the viewing windows on our doors so delegations could walk past and look at us like we were in a zoo. They laughed at us, but I also saw fear. What kind of men were they holding?

The interrogators tried everything to get us to talk. "Cooperate with us," they kept saying, "and we'll give you pants. We'll move you to another block."

None of us talked. It wasn't a holy war between East and West. We thought this was clear by now. It was a battle for our humanity, to prove that we weren't just animals.

Even the Red Cross laughed at us when they came.

"They aren't beating you or torturing you like in Arab countries," the Red Cross guy said. "They are using normal circumstances to try to make you talk. You should just talk. It would be better for everyone."

"Why don't you come and live with us?" I said. "Come live naked with us, get beaten, suffer from no sleep and from hunger. Then you can tell me it's just normal circumstances and not torture."

You couldn't tell by looking at us, but we'd won a small battle. I thought General Miller was trying to accomplish two things: force the compliant brothers in Romeo Block to start talking again to interrogators, and stop more organized protests from happening. And he failed at both. It was simple: we had nothing left to lose by not talking to interrogators, so we didn't. The harder General Miller tried to force us to talk, the more we resisted. Even worse for the camp admin, most brothers who were talking to interrogators before Romeo stopped talking after our protest.

We had been fighting battles against the camp admin for years. Now Miller was bringing us to war.

- THIRTEEN -

We didn't start the fight the night we destroyed Oscar Block, and we hadn't planned on escaping either. After the riot for Romeo Block, the interrogators moved half of the Redeyes to other blocks, leaving only twelve brothers in a block that held thirty-six. We were the youngest of the Redeyes and the ones interrogators had labeled the worst of the worst. We had all been moved around a lot since Camp Delta opened and this was the first time we were all together—only us—on a block. It was Waddah, Abdullah Alajmi, Khalid, Sayd, Hamzah, Adnan, Yassir, Mana'a, Ali, Othman, Yousif, and me, 441.

A tribal code had brought us together. Respect for respect. Shit for shit. We never started a fight, only joined when someone disrespected us or harmed our brothers. We didn't have a leader and none of us gave the others orders. We all knew what to do and just naturally worked well as a team.

We knew something was wrong at the shift change that night. Instead of a regular shift from the navy or army, we got one made up of the worst guards from all over the camp, guards mean and nasty enough to have earned nicknames like Fat Ass and Lazy Rabbit. They started in on us right away.

"242," Lazy Rabbit barked at Khalid. "Do you want to eat?"

"Yes," Khalid said.

"242 refused," Lazy Rabbit barked.

They put all our meals on the ground outside our cages and then twenty minutes later threw them all away in front of us. We couldn't fight every single time guards harassed us. If we did, we would have been fighting every minute of every day. But we had our red line, and the guards knew this. We decided to be quiet until after we finished our prayers, then we would deal with this shitty shift. We prayed the last two prayers of the day at one time while guards banged on our cell doors and mocked us. When we were done, we filled our sinks and soaped our floors.

Waddah asked for the watch commander so we could register a formal complaint about the meals. Lazy Rabbit refused to get him. We banged our cell doors. They turned off the water. Fast Turtle danced up and down the block mocking us. We cursed them. They turned off the AC and ventilation. We baked in our cages and banged on the doors some more. They shot pepper spray into our cells and called for cell searches. We refused. They called the IRF teams. It was business as usual. But the IRF teams didn't come. That meant they would wait until later and come when they thought we were sleeping.

Yassir was on hunger strike, and when the nurse came for his nightly checkup, we told him to leave with her. The guards had made it clear the night would be messy. When Yassir left his cell, the guards searched him in front of the nurse and pulled his genitals really hard. He hit the guard and they all kicked his ass bad. Now we were just eleven.

When he left, we yelled to each other through our doors to make a plan. All we had in our cells were our orange uniforms, thin plastic ISO mats, flip-flops, and some of us had one towel. Our plan was simple—destroy our cages from the inside. We'd never tried this before—everything was made of steel welded together. But Abdullah had figured out how to make a better hammer than the ones we used during the Romeo riot. He told us to roll our flip-flops into a ball, then wrap them tightly with our shirt. Then we wrapped the ball in a towel, each layer making the ball bigger. Next he told us to tear our pants in half, put the ball inside one leg, and roll it tightly into a bigger ball. Then we put that ball inside the other pant leg and tied it off; it was long enough to hold and swing like a hammer. We dipped the ball in water and that made it even heavier. Now we were just in our shorts, but we had a hammer strong enough to break anything.

The guards turned on the ventilation system again and put huge fans in the middle of the block to keep us from talking. It didn't matter. We had our hammers and our plan.

Fast Turtle flickered the bright lights and laughed like a little boy. I had to close my eyes or I'd get sick. Finally, he got tired and turned them off completely, and that's when we got to work.

We divided into two teams. The first distracted the guards by kicking the doors, while the second team hammered our sinks. Those poor babies didn't stand a chance. Abdullah's hammer was a beast. The guards were used to the sound of us kicking our doors, and that gave us cover for our real work. We kicked, we pounded, we jumped off our beds to land our hammers even harder. We beat the hell out of those sinks and finally they broke. Because the guards turned off the water, nothing happened when we pulled them from the wall. I pulled out pipes and pumps and scrap and threw them all over my cage. I sliced my hand badly, but I didn't care. I didn't even feel it.

"Mission accomplished!" we sang.

I went to work pounding through the ceiling fence to get at the lights.

"Hi, sweetie," I said to the light fixture. "It's time to put you to sleep."

All night long, we worked on our cages with Lazy Rabbit and Fat Ass walking up and down the block, mocking us for being so loud in the dark.

"Are you angry?" Lazy Rabbit cried. "Poor babies are hungry?"

"Go to sleep, kiddies," Fat Ass spit with a mouth full of tobacco. "Go to sleep so we can play tomorrow."

"I've almost broken the toilet out of the ground," Abdullah called out. "Wrap your towels around the sink and make a hammer out of it. Then jump off your bed and hammer the toilet."

Then Abdullah discovered something that changed everything. Breaking the toilet from the floor would open up a hole big enough for him to go through.

"We can escape!" he called out.

"Allahu Akbar!" we cried.

Sweating from all that work and no AC, I took a break and listened to the *boom*s and *bang*s. It sounded like heavy-duty construction. But it was our song, a new rhythm for our block, and some of us even sang along.

When Abdullah had almost finished with his toilet, we talked about what we would do when we got out. One brother suggested we hide on the rec yard roof and cover ourselves with the green tarp.

"They would never think to look there," he called out.

Waddah suggested we fight the guards with all the metal we had pulled out. Mana'a suggested we sneak out, and when the guards came to fight us, go back to our cages.

We knew there was no way we could actually escape from the camp. The most we could do was escape from our cages and maybe the block. We didn't want anyone to get hurt. And we didn't want to hurt anyone. We just wanted to show Miller that he couldn't cage us, even with the strongest American steel.

Our plan was to break all our toilets by the time the guards usually settled down to sleep for a couple hours. We could finish breaking the toilets, rest for a little, pretend we were asleep, and then escape.

"I'm done, brothers!" Abdullah called. "Let's go!"

The rest of us needed more time. Finishing the job wasn't easy. The cut on my hand was deep and bleeding a lot now. My cage was covered in blood. I ripped up my towel and wrapped my hand, but it quickly bled through. I kept working, holding my hammer in the other hand and jumping off my bed onto the toilet with just one leg, keeping weight off my broken ankle. Nothing could stop me.

"We have to go out together," Waddah called.

"Are we sure about this?" Ali called. "One of us could get killed." He was always the cautious brother, thinking and planning ahead.

"Let us at least try," I called out. "It would be a shame in the history of this hell if nobody tried to escape."

Abdullah was quiet. We thought he was just resting. We continued working on our toilets. Then all of a sudden, we heard guards shouting.

"Code Black, Oscar Block!" guards yelled. "Code Black! Detainees escaping. Repeat. Detainees escaping."

We celebrated and congratulated each other. We danced and laughed.

"I'm sorry, brothers!" Abdullah yelled. "I went out through the floor to find a good way for us. I was only halfway out when Fast Turtle opened a window and saw me."

"You were supposed to wait," Waddah called.

"I just wanted a quick look!" Abdullah cried. He really was sorry.

"Still," Othman said, "may Allah reward you."

Oscar Block filled with guards, civilians, dogs, camera crews, day shift guards, soldiers with guns—it was like the entire world had been called to us.

As guards piled into the block, we threw all the stuff we had pulled from the walls and floor out into the open for the guards to see.

They tried to turn the block lights back on, but most of us had broken our light fixtures.

Two IRF teams stormed Abdullah's cage and kicked his ass. But he put up a good fight. He hurt one of the guards with a piece of his toilet.

I went back to work on my toilet. I really wanted to finish. Miller had arrived in the yard, and I was running out of time.

"Hey, General," Hamzah called. "Do you want to buy some stuff? You seem like a rich asshole. I have a Guantánamo sink, specially made in America. Original. A little beaten-up but very valuable. I'll even guarantee it. How about a light? Good for sleeping, and also from America. I'll give you a deal. Just one cup of shit on your face."

We all laughed.

"Turn on the light!" Lazy Rabbit yelled at my door. He was shining his big flashlight on me through the window.

"New rules!" I said. "Straight from the general. The light must stay off." I showed him the broken light fixture. "Are you afraid of the dark! Go to sleep, Lazy Rabbit!"

This made the brothers laugh. They started throwing things in the cages, making all kinds of noise. The soldier with the video camera came to my door and recorded me through the viewing window. I took this chance to send a message to whoever would watch.

"Yes, we did this," I said in Arabic. "Not because we're bad people. We did this because the camp admin forced us to do it." I described all our treatment under Miller. I was still bleeding a lot, so I wrote 441 in blood on my wall for the camera. Then I started working on my toilet again.

"Send us the general!" brothers all up and down the block chanted.

"They don't negotiate with terrorists," one of the interpreters said.

We discussed our options while the interpreters listened. We wanted them to hear.

"Please, brothers!" Waddah called out. "Let us fight them first, then we can talk. The worst thing they can do is to kill us. We've been protesting and fighting for years trying to get them to stop their hideous policies. Tonight, the highest-rank chickens are here. They're the ones responsible for torturing us."

"I'm with you," Hamzah said. "We should fight!"

Othman cautioned patience, so did Mana'a. In the end, we agreed, all of us, to fight.

All the civilian staff left the block and three guards were placed in front of each cell and three on the outside, just in case we went through the toilet hole. For eleven half-naked, beaten, starved, sleep-deprived brothers, there were at least seventy-two guards just by our cages. They all had either bats or shotguns or rifles.

I went back to work on my toilet. I wanted so badly to finish before the fight. The guards outside my door took out their pepper spray.

"Spray me," I yelled, "and I'll throw shit and metal at you!"

With a final blow, I broke my toilet. It was beautiful seeing that hole in the floor. It didn't matter what happened now, I'd won my battle.

I picked up the toilet plate and threw it toward the door. That's when the guards outside shot me with rubber pellets through the sink hole. They were serious now.

"Assalamu alaikum," someone said in a funny Arabic accent. I knew that voice. It was one of the nice navy officers. I guessed they wanted him to play a good cop.

"Wa alaikum Assalam," each one of us called back.

We asked Waddah to talk to him for us.

"I'm here to help you," he said. "The general and the colonel are very mad. They're talking about doing things that won't be good for you. You understand they could do anything."

"If you are going to talk like this," Waddah said, "then tell the general and the colonel to fuck themselves. Tell them to bring their chicken guards to move us. We're not afraid."

We knew the general and colonel were listening.

"We are here if they want to talk to us about our issues," Waddah said. "But if you want to just threaten us—go!"

The navy officer left and came back after a few minutes.

"Please," he said. "I'm talking to you man-to-men." He asked if he could open the viewing windows so we could talk and hear each other better. He asked us not to do anything to him if he opened them.

"What about the guards?" Waddah asked.

He ordered the guards to step away from our cells, then opened the windows and knelt down on his knees so that he could talk to Waddah better through the window.

"Please," Waddah said. "Don't kneel like this before me. I don't like it. We kneel only for Allah. Please, have them bring you a chair."

This really moved me.

When the navy officer was seated, Waddah began talking to him.

"Check the AC," Waddah said. "It's been off all day and has made the block like an oven. Check the water. They turned it off so that we couldn't wash before praying. Take a deep breath and tell me what you smell. Pepper spray. They spray us all the time. It's all over our walls and the floor. It's on our clothes."

"I can smell the pepper spray," the navy officer said.

We took turns explaining what happened throughout the night and how it began as soon as the guards threw away our meals.

"I'm sorry that happened," the navy officer said.

Waddah told him to bring the general and the colonel to talk to us so that they could hear what the guards had done.

"They won't come," the navy officer said. "They think you want to control them and force them to do things."

We sat silent for a few minutes.

For once they were right. We wanted to force them to see us as human.

"How can we finish this mess?" the navy officer finally said.

"It's simple," Waddah said. "The interrogators need to stop the torture and mistreatment."

"I mean this mess here, tonight," the navy officer said.

"They sent you to take all this metal from us, right?" Waddah said.

"Yes. But I really want to help," he said. "I don't want you to get hurt."

"You kill us every single second of every day," Waddah said. "Every day you try to make us into the bad guys you think we are. Every day you send these guards to fight with us."

"You will all be moved to another block," the navy officer said. "You won't see these guards anymore."

"What we want is simple," Waddah said. "We want to be treated like humans."

The discussion went on for a long time. Some brothers still wanted to fight. Some believed that what we had done that night would make the camp admin reconsider how it treated us. I was tired; the adrenaline had stopped flowing. I looked around at my cell and what I had done, what they had made me do. The blood scared me. I wanted it to end. I didn't want to fight anymore.

"Let us finish this in a peaceful way," Ali said. "They will hurt us more than we can hurt them. And we will still be here."

"We'll come out peacefully," Waddah said. The navy officer knelt down on both knees and thanked us. This would be a huge achievement in his file. Let him have it.

We took apart our hammers so no one would know how we destroyed our sinks and toilets. I was really tired. I had bled a lot. The camp admin sent the nicest guards to move us. They knew we wouldn't attack them. I told the navy officer I wanted to be last.

"Don't fight, brother!" Othman called to me. I didn't want to fight. I just wanted to walk through the block, look into every cell, and see what we had done. I left my cell wearing just orange shorts. It looked like bombs had exploded.

I heard my brothers laughing and singing as they went through the block gate. I thought they were making fun of the guards.

"I'm sorry you came so late to the party!" Waddah called.

"Come dance with us the way the guards did all night," Mana'a yelled.

"If you need a demolition team," Hamzah said, "you know who to call."

When I got to the gate, I understood whom they were talking to. Spilling out of the Oscar Block yard were hundreds of people—guards, soldiers, interrogators, interpreters, nurses, psychologists, and even people in civilian clothes. They had so many IRF teams in armor I couldn't even count. Every branch of the military was there: army, navy, air force, and marines. In my three years of detention, I had never seen anything like it. Beyond the gate were armored Humvees with high-caliber machine guns and troop carriers with soldiers in full gear. There were camera teams everywhere. And in the middle of it all was the colonel, still in his pajamas, and the general in his shorts.

We were eleven skinny guys with barely any meat on our bones, no clothes but our orange shorts, and heavy chains on our wrists and ankles. I must have looked like a tiny bald bird, just a few feathers covering my ass. My escorts towered over me with their helmets and armor and big cans of pepper spray pointing at my face.

I looked all around me and just smiled. I wanted to jump up and scream. No, I wanted to fly. The guards had been cracking down on us so hard for so long because they were following orders. And here were the people who gave the orders, in their pajamas because we had made them get out of bed. I wanted to dance around them and yell, "Welcome to the terrible life you think we should live."

"Wow, wow, wow!" I said. "Hello, hello." I greeted them in my bad English, then switched to Arabic. "We are so honored you could join us here tonight."

The guards walked me into the middle of the crowd. The colonel was barking orders into a radio.

"Colonel!" I called. "I like your pajamas. Very nice. Can I borrow them, please? Just the pants. I'm a little cold in just my shorts."

The interpreter translated and I heard someone laugh. At least someone else was enjoying the show.

"Who told you to break the block?" the interrogator asked. "Who helped you plan the escape?"

"You did," I said. "We work for you."

"Who's your leader?"

"The general, here, is our leader," I said.

They didn't think that was funny.

"Escape?" I said. "Us? From here? Noooooo. Why would we ever try to do such a thing when we are in such safe and caring hands?"

I turned to General Miller, who was across the yard.

"You search our asses every day!" I yelled. "You desecrate our Qur'ans! You torture us. You shower us with pepper spray like it's water." This got his attention. This got everyone's attention. "You hold us without telling us why. What do you want us to do, General? Tell me! What should we do?"

Everyone was looking at me now.

"We didn't try to escape," I yelled. "We dug holes in the floor so we could get some water to drink and air to breathe."

"Who's your leader?" the colonel asked again.

"I'm our leader," I said. "No one is our leader." I pointed at my brothers. "They are my leaders. We are all leaders. None of us are leaders. Now it's my turn to ask you a question: What do you want from us?"

Nobody answered me.

I was tired. I had lost a lot of blood. I hadn't eaten in more than thirty-six hours. I didn't know what I was saying anymore.

"General!" I called. "Colonel! Please, can I have a Humvee? Just one. You guys have so many. I think I need something to drink. Yes.

Something to drink. Where is your hospitality, General? Don't you have a tribe? I'm sure you shame them."

"Get him to the clinic," the colonel ordered.

"Hey, General!" I screamed. "Where are your pants? Are you being punished in Romeo Block?"

I was young and full of raw emotions and I didn't have much experience in life. I had been shattered inside and out, abused, mistreated, so far from everything and everyone I loved. But that night, I felt less hurt. I don't know how to explain it. All that hurt had come out for the camp to see. We made them see us. We made them gather the full strength of the world's strongest army for eleven skinny guys with homemade hammers.

THE COLONEL ORDERED that I walk the half mile to the clinic and not be carried. I limped with my broken ankle and shins bleeding from the tight metal shackles.

As we left Camp 3 and walked through Camp 2, I called out loudly to my sleeping brothers and told them what happened.

"We destroyed Oscar Block," I shouted. "We almost escaped."

"Allahu Akbar," a brother called back.

More brothers started asking questions. But the generators came on and drowned out our voices.

Once we got outside of the camps, everything was so quiet you could hear the guards' boots crunching the gravel. The march was bloody, the shackles digging deeper and deeper into my legs. The light of the Humvee shone bright on our backs. As we walked, I stole a glance at the night sky, where I saw stars for the first time in years. I felt a light chill from the wind on my bare skin. I smelled the sea and breathed in the salty air. For these brief seconds, I wasn't at Guantánamo. I wasn't detainee 441. I was Mansoor, looking up at a beautiful sky. I couldn't hold back my tears, tears for the life I'd lost and the one that had replaced it.

The nurse was waiting for me at the clinic and I was happy to see her. The guards took me to a small room, laid me on my back on a stiff hospital bed, and cuffed my hands and feet to the bed. I shivered uncontrollably from the AC. I was so cold I couldn't even talk. "Shit!" the nurse cried when she saw me. "Call the doctor!" She turned off the AC, then brought me a thin foil blanket. The nurse asked a guard to uncuff one side of my body so that she could cover me, but he refused.

"We have orders," he said.

The nurse argued with them and then argued with the officer standing in the hallway.

"I need the doctor in here," she cried and then hurried out.

"You have a good nurse," the interpreter said. She was a very nice Arabic woman.

"Just move me back to the block!" I yelled. "Bring your riot team because I'm not walking."

The nasty officer ordered the guards to uncuff me from the bed. The riot team waiting in the hall stormed in and piled on top of me, bending my legs to be cuffed with my hands behind my back. They lifted me up and started to carry me out of the clinic. "Put him down!" the doctor ordered. The nurse and nice navy officer were at his side.

The nice navy officer ordered the IRF team to put me on the bed with only one hand and one leg cuffed, then he ordered the nasty officer to leave the room.

I was shaking like hell now.

They wrapped me with two foil blankets so that only my head was sticking out. I looked like a piece of meat in tinfoil, ready to be cooked.

The nurse had the doctor look at my legs. She left and came back with a bottle of vanilla Ensure. She poured a cup full and handed it to me.

I thanked her for her kindness and then asked for one more.

She laughed and brought it. I felt warmer after two Ensures and that foil blanket. "How are you now?" the nurse asked.

"Ready to break another block," I said. The clinic was crowded with guards and staff and camera guys and interpreters. Everyone laughed, even the guards. It was nice to joke around with so many people out in the open like that.

"They called it off!" one of the nurse's assistants called out. The entire room seemed to exhale all at once. The guards started taking off their armor.

"They just called off the base-wide state of emergency," the interpreter said.

"A full state of emergency! For us?" I said. "Are you serious?"

"Do you know what you and your brothers did?" she said. "Everyone across the entire base was woken up and put on alert. They announced that all detainees had broken out of their cells. Sirens sounded all over the navy base. People were panicked."

"We just broke a few sinks and toilets," I said.

"The president will hear about this," the interpreter said.

"How did you cut your hand?" the nurse asked. "I need to write a report."

"Do you want to know everything," I said, "or just the part where I cut my hand?"

"We all want to hear the whole story," the interpreter said. "But we can't ask you to tell us that."

Did they really care? Or did they just want answers for their reports? It didn't matter. I told them everything anyway so that they would know we were not animals. They all listened closely, even the guards in the room. Sometimes they laughed. Sometimes they were upset.

Of course, I left out the one detail they all wanted to know.

"How did you guys break the block?" they asked again and again.

"That's classified," I said. I turned to the nurse who had been so nice. "I'll call you next time so you can join us."

You can't imagine how good it felt to be talking and laughing and not worrying about guards telling me to shut up.

"Did you really ask the colonel for his pants?" one of the older civilians asked.

They finished treating me and the nurse brought another Ensure with some pills for the pain. We were stalling now, trying to steal every last minute before going back to the camp. I wanted to stay in the clinic forever and sleep.

I smiled at the nurse. "Thank you," I said. "You're a good woman."

"I'm going to walk you back to the block," the nurse said.

"It's not necessary," I said.

"She has to," the interpreter said. "She'll have to write in her report that you were escorted to your cell safely and with injuries addressed."

I'll never understand you Americans, I thought. *You torture us and then walk us home to make sure we get there safely.*

It was early morning when we stepped onto the dirt road leading back to Camp 1. The bright sun burned my eyes and warmed my skin.

I was happy that long night was coming to an end. All I wanted to do was eat breakfast and go to sleep. But the guards stopped at the Camp 1 gate. They turned me to the left toward the Brown Building for interrogation.

THE COLD METAL chair froze my ass as soon as I sat down. The guards chained me. The AC said it was sixty-two degrees, and soon I was shivering uncontrollably. I didn't want to shiver, not now. I didn't want my ugly interrogator to think I was afraid or weak. I conjured memories of swimming in the mountain hot springs in Yemen with my friends. I felt its warmth and held on as long as I could, but the roar of the AC brought me back. I didn't know how long I would have to stay like that. Minutes. Hours. The cold made my wounds ache and throb. I imagined diving into a volcano and swimming in molten lava.

The door slammed open violently. They did the same shit every time. At least this time it only took the interrogator thirty minutes to come in.

The interrogator was an old guy I called Tired Jack. He always looked run-down in the same dirty clothes and sunglasses, like he needed a shower. He wasn't the worst of them. Next in was the asshole Iraqi interpreter. Then two women in military uniforms and sunglasses; one was blond, the other dark-haired, and I thought she might be Arab. The last one in was a pissed-off mule of a marine.

I had to pee. If I had known I was going to interrogation, I never would have drank all that Ensure at the clinic. I asked the Iraqi interpreter to call the guards so I could use the toilet. He didn't even look at me. He just translated what I said in a really nasty way.

"MP!" I shouted. "MP! Toilet!" I kept shouting this until Tired Jack tried to stop me.

"Start talking and then they'll let you go to the toilet," the interpreter said.

I couldn't hold it anymore and knew they wouldn't let me leave. So I just let it go. I moved my leg so I wouldn't pee on my new bandages.

"Why are you smiling?" the asshole interpreter asked.

I was so happy and so warm. One problem solved. I'm not proud of peeing myself. This was just a part of life with interrogations. What would you do?

I gave everyone a solid look, straight in the eyes, so they knew how much I despised them.

"You have a rough night?" Tired Jack started. "What happened to your hand and legs? Get a little hurt?"

He let that sit for a while, knowing I had nothing to say to him. I didn't talk to interrogators. They knew this.

"You try to kill some guards last night?" Tired Jack was always trying to get an angle. He said a lot of bullshit like this when we fought the guards. "You trying to play the hero?"

I didn't answer him. I didn't even look at him.

"We're just here to talk to you," the Mule said. "We want to know what happened last night. How you injured yourself."

"What are you smiling at?" Tired Jack said. "Just look at yourself sitting there in your own piss, naked, wrapped in bandages."

My pee was turning cold. The warmth never lasted long.

"Talk to me, Mr. Commander," Tired Jack said. They were still trying to get me to confess that I was some kind of al Qaeda general. "Tell us how you organized it all."

I laughed at them.

"You have an impressive file here," the blonde said. "Block riots, hunger strike . . . Seeing you here, pissing yourself, you don't seem to fit your profile at all."

"I thought I was going to meet a big guy," the marine mule said. He rolled up his sleeves showing his arms, all muscle. "Start talking to us and we'll let you go. Your friends told us everything. Sounds like you're really important. We just need to hear it from you."

When I didn't answer, he started talking bad about my family. There is one thing you don't do to a Yemeni tribesman (or to any Arab): you don't talk about their family. I'm very serious about this. Not even as a joke.

"Close your mouth, America's slave," I snapped. "You're just their nasty bitch."

He cursed me, so I spat in his face.

When I did that, everyone in the room panicked. Guards came in and put a mask over my mouth and gave the interrogators face shields.

I yawned, I was so tired.

"Rough night?" the Mule said again, like it would be funny the second time. "Just tell us what happened."

"You should just ask General Miller," I said. "He was there." That was the last thing I said.

They went around in circles for hours. They tried everything with me. They really wanted to know how we destroyed everything.

Finally, the Mule stood up and got right in my face. "I'm not afraid of you," he said. "None of us are. We've all met guys like you. And they all end up screaming like girls." He grabbed my head in his hands. I felt his strength—he could have snapped my neck with a single twist. I just laughed. I couldn't help myself. I was in so much pain. I was cold, hungry, tired . . . I couldn't stop laughing.

Tired Jack tried one last trick. He brought in a set of orange clothes and a hot breakfast.

"Your choice," he said. "Talk now and you can have some breakfast and your beautiful orange clothes." He started eating my breakfast and using the orange uniform as a napkin to wipe his mouth. There was no way I was going to talk now. Our breakfasts were shit—powdered egg, oatmeal, poorly prepared with no salt. I really enjoyed watching him try to eat it.

They took my chair and made me sit on the floor and then left. Hours passed like this. The Mule came in at one point.

"Osama bin Laden trained you well," he said. "Did he tell you to escape, too?"

"Yes!" I said. "And he's waiting for us out there."

That really pissed him off. They could tell bad jokes and I couldn't? Tired Jack had the guards shackle me in a painful stress position. And then the psychologist came in, a skinny white woman with dead eyes.

"How did you hurt yourself?" she asked. "Did you cut your wrist on purpose? Were you trying to kill yourself?" I just lay there, silent. And then she asked the only question they actually cared about: "How did you destroy your cell?"

The Mule came back one more time with the blonde and the Arab. My eyes were closed and I was reciting the Qur'an.

"I see how it is," he said. "You know what? I'm going to go to the beach now with these beautiful women. We're going to swim, have a few drinks, then we'll have sex all night long. And you? You'll be lying here in your own shit."

I stayed in that room all day. Hour after hour. I peed several times and went from warm to cold each time. I offered my prayers like that. It was one of the longest days in my life. When guards came for me, my skin was blue. I couldn't get up or walk. I felt like I was one step from death.

They forced me to walk and I was okay with that. I went slowly, focusing on one step at a time. Outside, in the blistering heat, my body thawed and I let the warmth of life wash over me. The sun warmed my soul and brought me back to life. I looked forward to rest, finally, in India Block. That's where they always sent us for punishment.

In Camp 1, the guards escorted me past India Block and I stopped immediately.

"No!" I shouted. I knew where they were taking me and I refused. I threw myself to the ground and refused to get up. The IRF team came and six guards kicked my ass to secure me, then they carried me to Delta Block, the BHU, where psychologists made our worst nightmares come true with shots that paralyzed us, medicated us, beat us, and so much worse. I screamed and cursed. I tried to resist but I had nothing left.

I spent two months in Delta Block before I was moved to India Block. They said the cut on my hand was a self-inflicted wound and that I had tried to kill myself.

NEWS OF THE Oscar Block epic spread like fire throughout the camp. Brothers in other blocks and other camps told us that they saw real fear on guards' faces. They never expected something like that to happen in solitary confinement, where the cages were solid steel and there was no way to coordinate an attack.

Not all our brothers were pleased with what we did. The camp admin came down hard on all of us. They intensified the search procedures and the patrols around the camps with Humvees and armed soldiers. The SOPs became tougher, too, and guards carried pepper spray all the time now. Some brothers got hurt because of what we did, and we were sorry about that. Some brothers said that we proved to them that we were animals.

They brought many civilians to the camp and paraded them through Oscar Block. "Look how determined they are to hurt us," they said. "Even when imprisoned, they're extremists. They're terrorists and they won't have mercy on you here or on the battlefield. Imagine what they would do if they got out." Then General Miller or the colonel would spin a story for the visitors about how America's heroes stopped us from escaping and saved the day.

In return, brothers teased the guards and camp staff about how strong we were, even though we were tortured and starved. All we had to do was say, "Oscar Block," then laugh like crazy. One brother named himself Oscar.

It wasn't long until other detainees started breaking their sinks and toilets. The camp admin started rebuilding blocks to make them stronger.

When they were done rebuilding Oscar Block, General Miller collected all twelve brothers who were there that night. He brought us to Oscar Block and put us in the same cages. They had triple-reinforced the floor, replaced those shiny sinks with a small enclosed faucet operated by a very small button. The cage doors were twice as thick and so was the fencing covering the light. Now you needed a real bomb to destroy the cage.

The next day, guards brought each one of us, one at a time, out into the block yard, where we found the colonel, interrogators, and camp officers. Just like the last time we were all together, my brothers and I joked and teased the colonel and his staff.

"Hey, Colonel," I called out. "Do you want me to sign your pajama pants?"

He just stared at me through large sunglasses.

"You have your pants on this time!" Waddah called. "I miss seeing your dirty pajamas."

They took a photograph of each of us. The nice navy officer later told Waddah that the colonel hung framed photographs of all twelve of us, the worst of the worst Redeyes, in his office. I guess he wanted to be reminded of the men who brought the most powerful country in the world, maybe that ever existed, to its knees for just one night.

I thought they were afraid of us after that night, but Omar told me differently.

"What would the world say if you guys managed to escape?" Omar asked me. "Did you think about that? They would say the Americans couldn't control a handful of ragged detainees on an island. They would say the Americans couldn't even secure their own military base. Escaping would have been like shitting on the Americans and on George W. Bush. General Miller and Colonel McQueen weren't afraid of the Redeyes. They came running that night because they would have been fired."

Whatever the case, twelve skinny brothers sent a strong message to the camp that they could beat us, crush our bones, starve us, detain us in the darkest, deepest hole, but they would never break us. They would never tame us.

CAMP V

CAMP VI

CAMP ECHO

BUILDINGS AND STRUCTURES

- (A) Alpha
- (B) Bravo
- (C) Charlie
- (D) Delta
- (E) Echo
- (1) Control

USES

- Experimentation
- Operations
- Punishment
- Solitary Confinement

PART 3

HUNGER

- FOURTEEN -

In the summer of 2004, everything seemed to be turning against us, even the weather. We had all kinds of problems—heat that baked us in our cages, thunderstorms and wild rain that came from nowhere, and winds that felt like they would pull the roof from over our heads and blow us away.

It was around this time, when the mesh cages were like ovens, that a brother in Tango Block called out that officers were walking the blocks telling brothers they were going to be moved soon and wouldn't need to take any of their things with them. This was big news! I mean, this was really big news. The only time they moved someone like that was when they were going to be released. DNN lit up with calls from every block and soon we heard that around seventy brothers from all over the camp were on this list. There had been several groups of detainees released recently, including a big group of Pakistanis and Afghans, but nothing like this. The guys on the new list were from different countries and backgrounds and ages. Redeyes, compliant brothers, Afghans, a boy who was only fourteen when he was brought to Guantánamo. The list made no sense, but nothing at Guantánamo ever did. And nothing ever happened that wasn't meant to make our lives harder. We knew this. But still, we always had hope and so we started to gossip.

"I saw a huge airplane in the sky," a Saudi brother called out. "I saw it while I was in the rec yard. Maybe that plane was for these brothers."

"I think they're going to release those brothers," Dan said. "Why else would there be a plane like that? Where else could those brothers go?" Dan would believe anything that made him feel better.

A rumor spread like wildfire that an officer had informed some brothers that being on the list meant they were going home. By the end of the day, officers had come to Romeo, where they were keeping me and other Redeyes in nothing but shorts. The officers went to my neighbor, Hamid, and told him he was on the list. Hamid tried to keep calm, but he couldn't stop smiling.

"At last, I'm leaving this hell," he cried. I congratulated him. I didn't trust the admin, but still it hurt knowing I wasn't on the list. His joy became mine, and I was happy for him.

None of us slept that night.

"I hope they won't shackle me or beat me," Hamid said. "I don't want to arrive at home with bruises." He thought about that for a minute and then smiled wildly. "Even if they do, I don't care. I'm going home!"

He paced his cage nervously, talking out loud to himself.

"I wonder if my family will be waiting for me at the airport? I wonder if there will be reporters or cameras? I wonder if the guards will let me take a shower before the flight. I wish I could cut my hair. Do you think they'll give me a white uniform? Isn't that what they give brothers who leave? I hope they get me the right size. Do you think I should tell the guards my size?"

We told him he shouldn't ask the guards any questions.

"You don't want to give them any reason not to take you," Waddah called out.

"You're right," Hamid said. Then he was off daydreaming again. "I'm going to hug my mother first. Then my wife, my kids, and finally my sisters. They'll have sleep medicine on the plane, right? I'll need to sleep. I can't sleep. I can feel my blood running in my veins."

"Now I understand why those idiot interrogators have been torturing us so badly these past months," Shah said. "They wanted to
squeeze every last drop of information from us before setting us
free."

My feelings were mixed. I was so happy to see another group of
brothers leaving this hell and so sad that I wouldn't see them again.
We had been through a lot together and survival made our bonds
strong.

When the guards came for Hamid, he practically ran to them.
He had the most beautiful, happy smile I'd ever seen. Guards shackled him, then covered his eyes and ears and led him out, the same
SOPs for brothers who had been released before. Rumors spread
that escorts were using the white van, the one used to take brothers
to the airport.

DNN was active all day with brothers across the camp calling out
news of who had been taken away and when. Late in the morning,
a brother came back from the rec yard and said he had seen a huge
plane fly overhead.

"That must have been our brothers!" he called out to the block.

I imagined Hamid and all seventy brothers in white clothes getting off the plane in their home countries and the new lives that
awaited them. "When are we going to leave?" we asked each other
in the days that followed. I imagined myself walking into my village
with everyone calling out to me. I imagined my mother wrapping me
in her arms and kissing my cheeks, telling me how old I look with my
beard. My father would make a special feast of fresh fish from the Red
Sea. As much as I wanted these dreams to come true, I didn't allow
myself to believe they actually would.

We tried to get some news from the guards about our brothers,
but all they said was that they had left the camp, just like the other
groups that had left.

In the days after Hamid left, those of us who remained talked about what we would do when we were free. I would get married and go to university. I would start a computer business. I would pick up my life right where I left it just a few years ago when I left for Afghanistan. Dan said he would go on a long motorcycle ride through the mountains and then write a movie about this place. Others said they would write books so that the world would know what happened to us here. This seemed like a good idea to me, and I thought about all the moments we had experienced in this place that no one knew about. But I didn't want the world to just know about all the bad things that had happened to us. I wanted them to see who we were and how we had survived through friendship and brotherhood.

One thing was certain: we would appreciate every tiny part of our lives we had taken for granted before. Fresh air, sunlight, clean water. Guantánamo would forever remind us of these simple pleasures.

Time slowed as the weeks passed and we heard nothing about our brothers or our release. The days got hotter and longer. Storms came out of nowhere, pounded the roof and flooded the yards, and then disappeared just as quickly as they came. But nothing stopped the machinery of the camp. Guards still treated us terribly. Escorts still dragged us to interrogations. More and more brothers stopped talking to interrogators and the punishments got worse with more brothers being put on sleep deprivation.

"This must be the last squeeze," Shah said one day when he came back from interrogation. He hadn't slept in weeks and had lost a lot of weight. "They're just getting us ready to leave."

I wasn't so optimistic anymore.

And then officers appeared again in the blocks. They were army officers in nice uniforms with high ranks, and we thought they were coming to tell us that they had another list of brothers to be released.

An officer came to my cage with an Arabic interpreter. I was wearing only orange shorts—they still wouldn't give me more clothes.

"ISN 441," the officer said. "You are to appear before the Combatant Status Review Tribunal, the military review tribunal to determine your combatant status."

"What is he talking about?" I said to the interpreter. I was only twenty-one years old. I didn't understand what these words had to do with me. "Combatant Status Review Tribunal?"

"They will determine your status as a fighter."

I wasn't in the military. I wasn't a fighter, and now I had to appear in a court to determine what kind I was?

"If it's a court," I said, "will I have a lawyer?" I was young but I wasn't completely ignorant, and other brothers had talked about how they wanted the Americans to accuse them of a crime so they could prove their innocence. But this didn't sound like that at all. I wouldn't have a lawyer, so it sounded like just a new interrogation technique.

"Criminals!" Hamzah called out. "They're working for the interrogators."

A few days later, escorts came for me. My tribunal was just like an interrogation, but without the beating and the stress positions. Officers asked me the same questions interrogators had asked me thousands of times, year after year.

"Are you an al Qaeda commander?"

"No," I said.

Days later, the officers came back to my cage and told me the tribunal had determined I was an "enemy combatant." They showed me a piece of paper to make it official.

"What does that mean?" I asked.

"It means that you are Osama bin Laden's commander," the officer said. "And that we consider you an enemy of the United States government."

"Okay," I said. "I am very honored, but you should ask al Qaeda if they will accept me first."

In the days that followed, all the brothers were taken to their tribunals. Just like the interrogations, it didn't matter what we said. Almost everyone was determined to be an enemy combatant.

"Please, sir, can you give me this piece of paper?" Hamzah said to the officer in his most serious voice. "We aren't allowed to have toilet paper and I need something to clean my ass."

We didn't know it at the time, but officially declaring us as enemy combatants was their way of holding us indefinitely without saying why and not treating us according to the Geneva Conventions. Instead of getting ready to release us, they were justifying holding us forever, according to American laws.

Soon lawyers were representing some brothers from the UK, Germany, and other European countries to help them file writs of habeas corpus. I didn't know how these things worked, and I didn't understand how that could help me, and it didn't matter anyway because lawyers didn't come for me. Some brothers were told that their cases were so weak, they were better off just confessing that they were al Qaeda or Taliban. This made no sense since so few of us were. I tried to get a lawyer through a neighbor who had one, but his lawyer said he wouldn't represent me because I was an al Qaeda leader. This cut me deeply. Even the lawyers had already decided who I was without meeting me.

It made me sad and confused, and like everything else in those days, it really upset me.

IT UPSET THE sea, too. It stirred up a summer wind that blew so hard, the camp admin had to take down the green tarps that covered all the fences and kept us from seeing the sea and the outside world. The officers came onto the blocks again, and this time they told us a hurricane was heading toward the camp and the guards would be evacuated along with the staff. We would be left locked away in our cages.

For the first time, our blocks quieted down. No guards, no chains, no banging and clanking. The song of our daily lives changed that day so that the wind could sing to us. Without the green tarps, we looked out our windows and saw the sea, the vast and beautiful sea, dark and angry, and the sea saw us, too, and raged at what it saw: hundreds of men in metal cages.

"Allahu Akbar!" an Afghani brother called out when he saw the sea for the first time. "Allahu Akbar!" brothers called out, thanking Allah for the wonder of this beautiful sea.

When the calls quieted down and we were alone in the camp, we faced our friend the sea in silence. We watched him flex his muscles and bend the world with his strength. We listened to him howl and whistle and punch the rocks below with powerful waves. When the cells and cages began to fill with water from the storm surge, some of us were afraid that the sea wanted to carry us away with him. It was scary how mad the sea was and how loud the wind screamed and pulled at our roof. And just when we thought our friend would take us, he calmed down and soon we caught a glimpse of Allah's tranquil beauty.

Those hours without the tarps were like a vacation. When the storm passed, the sea looked refreshed and calm, the blue so deep it burned my eyes. Out on the horizon, a huge ship sailed silently by. It was such a strange and beautiful sight, that lone ship on the open sea. We all waited for something magic to happen, maybe that ship would come and free us. But the ship passed, too, and we were alone again.

After three days, workers returned and put the green tarps back up, blocking our view of the sea.

Then the guards came back, and the noise started again. We had loved the sea, and now we loved him even more. The sea had scared away the Americans and left us unharmed. Knowing he was there, we were a little less alone.

IT WASN'T LONG after the hurricane that I saw Hamid. I thought I was dreaming when the guards brought him back to my block. He was so skinny I didn't recognize him at first. Hamid was gone, so how could it be him? He was just skin and bones with no life in his eyes.

When the guards left, we let loose a storm of questions.

"We drove for a long time," Hamid said. "And I just wished the driver would hurry up and get to the airport. I didn't want to miss the plane!" He told us how when the van stopped, it didn't sound like they were at an airstrip—it was too quiet. He was led blindfolded through a maze of hallways and gates and the guards kept calling someone named Control to open the doors. When the guards stopped Hamid and removed his leg shackles and blindfold, he was standing inside a white concrete cell—a real prison cell, not like these rusting cages—with bright lights above, a cement floor, a real metal toilet, and a sink with a mirror.

Hamid got very serious and he looked like he was going to cry. I had never seen a man this broken. Then he told us how the guard called Control one last time and asked him to secure cell Charlie 105. And that's when his door slid shut.

Hamid sat quiet for a long time, staring off like his mind was still living in this cement box.

"Brothers," he said, "I was in that cell until just recently. I had only a sheet and thin plastic mat. There was no call to prayer, no way to know what time it was. It was freezing in that cell. I waited and didn't sleep. When guards brought breakfast, I asked them when I would be leaving, and they just ignored me."

He told us how the food was so little that he had counted 471 grains of rice in one meal, not enough to fill half a Styrofoam cup.

And they made him take the food with his back to the door and his arms behind his back.

"Two meals passed," Hamid said. "Then four, then six, and still no escorts to the plane. Eight meals turned into sixteen, and that's when I realized we weren't going home. This was just their way of moving us to another prison. I stopped counting meals and lost track of time. The freezing killed me. I was always hungry."

Even after what we'd seen, it sounded like a nightmare. The only way to talk to brothers in other cells, he told us, was to lie down on his stomach and call out under the door, but the echo was so bad they couldn't understand each other anyway. He said that he didn't see anyone for weeks except guards. There was no rec, no shower . . .

"There is no hope in that place," Hamid cried. "I started to go crazy!" He told us how he started to experience all kinds of things he'd never felt before. And that's when the interrogations started. He couldn't sleep. He felt aroused for no reason. His thoughts raced all night. When he called to other brothers, they said they felt the same things. One of the brothers was a doctor and said the camp was putting drugs in their food. So they all stopped eating prepared foods. "I just ate fruit and bread," Hamid said, "and the symptoms disappeared!"

He never left his cell, except to go to interrogations. He was beaten and sexually assaulted, and he said other brothers called out the same experiences. They started to hunger-strike and to fight with the guards, so the guards put big fans outside their doors.

"It sounded like a helicopter hovering inside my head," Hamid said, "and it never stopped. I lost a lot of weight. I started having hallucinations. I found myself crying and shouting and banging on the door. I wished I was crazy so I wouldn't know what was going on anymore. I wanted to disappear from my body."

He told us how one day, when he was finally left in the rec yard alone, he took off his pants and hung himself.

"I'm sorry, brothers," he cried. "I know this is a sin but I couldn't live like that anymore!" Guards pepper-sprayed him and cut him down. Then they took him back to his cell, stripped him naked, and left him with nothing, not even a sheet to keep him warm.

"Of course, the interrogators came to talk to me after that," he said. "They knew I had finally broken. I was crazy. I told them, 'You know what? I am Osama bin Laden. I'm the one who planned 9/11.' Whatever they asked me, I said yes, I did it. I told them, 'I am al Qaeda. I am Taliban.' I have never been to Afghanistan in my life and they knew that but I didn't care."

He told them he was planning to kill himself no matter what they did if they kept him there.

"I'm happy to be back in these cages," Hamid said. "At least I can see you and talk to you."

When he finished speaking, we were all silent.

We had passed months celebrating our brothers' release, thinking we were next. All that time, they were being tortured in a way none of us could have ever imagined.

We were in Romeo Block, the worst block in all the camps, and now we'd learned that there was a worse place for us.

Soon, more brothers returned to other blocks and brought with them similar stories. We heard they took Abu Fatima to the medical clinic where they took his vitals, gave him white clothes like detainees wear in Camp 4, loaded him onto the plane, flew him around like he was going home, then brought him back. Abu Fatima broke. When he returned to our camp, he cried all the time. He wasn't the same ever again. Some brothers were put on boats. Some were driven around. They told all of them they were going home. It seemed like every block got their own report from that new, scary place. This is what the camp admin wanted. They thought they would finally break us.

WHEN THE OFFICERS came to Romeo Block again with a new list, I knew my name was on it. They wanted me to hear how bad it was first before taking me. The guards came for me with shackles, goggles, a blindfold, hood, and earmuffs.

"There's a white van!" a brother at the front of the block called out. My heart pounded in my temples. How would I survive this?

"I don't give a shit," I called out. "Let's go. Let's try something new!"

My brothers laughed and cheered, and that gave me strength.

"Lion!" they cried.

But inside, I was dying. Really. I was so scared.

"Let's go," I said to the guards. "Hurry up. I want to get there. I heard there's nice cold AC and a good toilet."

I learned to pretend to love what I hated to confuse my interrogators.

Through the hood and earmuffs, I heard the muted roar of brothers singing to me as I was escorted off the block. I prayed silently to Allah.

Allah, oh Allah, you know I'm tired. Allah, oh Allah, you know I'm weak and scared. Allah, oh Allah, please help me and don't let them win. Allah, oh Allah, please preserve me of all evil.

Camp V was named as if it was just another camp, but it wasn't. It was just like Hamid had described it. Cold. Cruel and lifeless. Camp V had an administration wing and four blocks like toes on a chicken's foot: Alpha, Bravo, Charlie, and Delta. Each block had two floors, and each floor had two rows of six cells facing each other. Everything was operated by Control, the tower in the middle of the camp. From there, they controlled all the gates, the cell doors, the block doors, the lights, the AC, the speakers.

Alone in my cell, I looked at myself in the mirror for the first time in years. *So, that is how old you look now,* I thought. I didn't recognize myself with the beard and the hair pointing in every direction, both peppered now with a few gray hairs. I stared at my face for a long time. I opened my mouth and looked at my teeth and tongue. I touched my nose and lips. I felt my ears. I ran my hands through my hair and played with the points. I tried to make myself look nicer, but I couldn't do anything with that wild hair. I was bored and made faces at myself. I made funny faces, angry faces, happy faces, all kinds of faces—I even tried the faces I made at interrogators to see what it looked like from the other side. I talked to this crazy guy in the mirror and I liked him. He was me. And I didn't see anyone else for a long time.

Right away after the first meal, I started feeling strange things happening to me. I couldn't sleep. My mind raced in circles all night long. I felt aroused like I'd never felt before. Where did these strange feelings come from? That feeling of sexual energy was new, but I didn't masturbate because it's a sin. Every part of my mind and my body was confused, and that's when they came to take me to interrogation.

The interrogation room was cold and lifeless, too, but there was a couch and a female interrogator sitting there.

"Come sit with me on the couch," she said. She was being nice, and I didn't trust her.

I sat on the floor and refused to talk. Instead, I recited the Qur'an to myself and ignored them.

At the next interrogation, she was there on the couch again, and again I sat on the floor.

"Do you think about me?" she said. "Come over here and talk to me. I want to be here for you."

I couldn't even look at her, not one glimpse. I prayed and my prayers took me out of the moment, out of the room. She got tired of my praying and started talking dirty to me. I can't even repeat what she said.

"Why are you sitting on the floor like a dog?" she said. She tried everything to get me to sit with her.

Then two more interrogators came in, one of whom was an FBI agent. They were both new and didn't know their asses from their faces. They tried their good interrogator/bad interrogator routine, with one offering me water and something to eat, the other forcing me into a stress position. But not a single sound came from my mouth.

This went on for days, weeks, I don't know how long. After so many years of interrogations, I had learned that praying and reciting the Qur'an completely shut off all my senses so that I didn't hear, I didn't see, I didn't feel anymore. I just existed in the moment but outside the moment. Interrogators could talk for hours. They could do all kinds of humiliating things to me and they did. But it didn't matter anymore.

They got angry and ordered all the stuff removed from my cell. Then they had guards bang on my cell door every couple of minutes nonstop so that I couldn't sleep for more than a couple of minutes at a time. This went on forever.

In another interrogation, one of the interrogators said, "Our hammer came down hard on the first group we moved to Camp V. We're bringing it down even harder on you. How do you like our hammer?"

Sometimes they turned off the fans in the hallway, and I lay down by the door and called to the others. That's how I found out Waddah was on my block, and Yousif, too. Together with a Saudi brother, Kamal, and a Tunisian brother, Hashim, we made a pact to bring the interrogators and the camp to their knees. The interrogations and the torture were hell. But holding us in these concrete tombs without us knowing when or if we would ever get out—it was like being buried alive and having our souls ripped from our bodies.

They had built a new prison, a solid prison that was all solitary confinement cells meant for isolation and sensory deprivation. They'd sent us there to keep us apart from each other. To punish us. To keep us from organizing. If we didn't figure out a way to fight back, what would they do next? We'd thought the permanence of Camp Delta was terrifying after Camp X-Ray. Camp V was a nightmare come true.

We needed to fight back, but how? We had tried fighting with guards by ourselves. We had tried organizing block riots but we knew they would never let us do that again, and our bodies were broken. We had tried hunger strikes, sometimes with others, but they had been easy to isolate if the camp moved quickly. Now we had an idea for something bigger. We thought they were terrified of brothers committing suicide or having anyone dying here. So we would organize a camp-wide hunger strike, one that would harness the Americans' fear of hundreds of brothers all refusing their meals and bringing themselves close to death until the camp admin changed the camp or let us go. In Camp V, the five of us made a pact that if one of us went on hunger strike, we all would join, and together we would spread the hunger strike across the entire camp.

- FIFTEEN -

It wasn't easy organizing a hunger strike across more than thirty blocks in so many camps with men who spoke so many different languages. It was just a matter of time before they moved me out of Camp V. They brought me to Papa Block in Camp 3. I heard right away that Yousif had refused his meals, then I heard that Waddah had, too, then Kamal and Hashim. Brothers on my block asked me to wait and join their hunger strike led by an older Egyptian whose Qur'an had been desecrated by interrogators. I understood what they wanted but told them I couldn't wait—I'd given my word to my brothers. They understood. We all understood that something bigger than ourselves was taking shape and that soon we would all be striking together.

I refused my next meal. With the five of us on hunger strike, word spread quickly and soon the air was electric with the news of a camp-wide hunger strike.

Going on hunger strike is like entering a dark tunnel, where the light at the end is death. You don't know how many days or weeks or months or even years you will be in that dark tunnel, but you know you will claw your way toward that light, always getting closer. There is no peace in this darkness, only restlessness. You travel with death every inch and every second.

In the beginning, there is the pain we all feel in our stomachs when we are hungry. Your stomach growls and yells, begging for food. But soon, that gnawing is replaced by the pain of your dreams. I had vivid dreams of the meals my father made when we broke our fasts after Ramadan—lamb mandi with perfumed saffron rice, the meat so soft it melted in my mouth. I regretted every grain of rice I'd left uneaten on my plate. You let yourself go in those dreams, enjoying every imaginary bite, even if it tortures you more. Then your stomach shuts down as your body begins to consume itself, starting with fat. If, like us, you were already given little food, you'd have almost no fat for your body to eat. That would be okay; your situation would be worse if you were in good shape. In that case, you'd feel the pain in every muscle and every cell your body consumes. Days pass and now you don't sleep well. You're agitated and restless and you have to stand up and walk or do something to keep your mind busy. You begin to have vision problems. You lose your ability to concentrate or focus. You feel confused. More days pass and it becomes hard to breathe and your heart beats fast with the slightest movement. Your muscles shrink. Your cheeks hollow. Your mouth dries out and smells nasty and tastes worse. You can't get rid of it. Weeks pass and now you can't walk or stand. You have no energy. *Allah, oh Allah*, that was the worst. You have no muscles. Your head aches all the time. You feel your ears closing and have a hard time hearing. Talking is a problem, too. Your voice has changed and when you talk, you sound like you will cry. You won't. You crawl further down the tunnel toward the light and now you have a hard time holding your head up. After four weeks, the hallucinations begin. You hear strange voices. You travel back in time as if your current life and your past life are one; the events mix and transport you away from your dark tunnel. You are just skin covering bones. You run your hands over your face and feel deep sockets around your eyes where muscle used to be. Your hair falls out. Your joints ache and feel loose in their sockets. Your hands shake and still you crawl toward the light. What's strange is that your stomach doesn't hurt anymore; there is no hunger. When you try to talk, you struggle to find the right word, or even a word at all. Your temper shortens, you move between peace and distress in the snap of a finger, feeling that each cell in your body is dying slowly, day after day.

Please understand, none of us wanted to die. But we understood that by going on hunger strike, we were choosing to set off on a slow and painful journey to death. At some point, we looked at our options and knew we had no other choice. We could do nothing and die forgotten in this terrible place or we could die trying to bring attention to our indefinite detention.

I wouldn't wish this journey on anyone. Please, don't go down that tunnel. You won't be the same person when you come out.

When I began my hunger strike, interrogators moved me to solitary confinement in India Block so that I couldn't get other brothers to join. It was too late. Brothers across the camp had already started refusing their meals and boycotting routines like showers and going to rec. The camp got dirty fast with IRF teams.

The summer sun was hot, and around twenty-five days into the hunger strike, I started fainting. I weighed less than one hundred pounds and there was nothing left for my body to consume. I was in bad shape. The new colonel ordered me moved to the detainees' hospital, which they only did when they thought we might die. The medical staff didn't want to give me an IV infusion because it would allow me to continue my hunger strike, so they waited until the last possible moment, just as I was starting to lose consciousness and couldn't move at all. The good American doctors had become experts in dealing with hunger strikes.

But this time, there were too many of us in bad shape needing IVs. Through DNN, we learned that brothers in every camp, even the compliant brothers in communal living in Camp 4, were on hunger strike. Mr. Hunger Strike was very happy with his work. Every day we heard Code Yellows called for brothers who had fainted or were too weak to stay in the cages. Within a couple of weeks, the camp admin shut everything down—no rec or showers or medical appointments.

Even interrogations had to stop. They didn't have the staff to handle so many brothers who needed care.

What had started off as a smoldering ember fanned by a few brothers caught fire and spread across all five camps. We were hundreds of brothers starving ourselves in unity to protest being held secretly for three years without cause, for being tortured with impunity and harassed by the world's strongest country with no realistic end in sight. Brothers joined the strike because what else were they to do?

The clarity of these days comes and goes. I had stopped drinking water and was moved to the detainees' hospital where I found Yousif, Waddah, and Hashim. We were the tip of the spear and now we were all close to death. The senior medical officer (SMO) came to us with a warning.

"I'm telling you," the SMO said. He had fear in his voice. "In the next forty-eight hours, if you don't do something to stop this hunger strike, you'll have a dead body here."

General Miller was gone now, and the new commander, Colonel Bumgarner, walked the blocks asking brothers what we wanted to end the hunger strike. This was his way of talking to us unofficially and getting a sense of what brothers wanted. He came to us at the hospital with a new interpreter and cultural adviser he called Zak to discuss why we were striking. The new colonel was a tall fat man with a bald head and funny accent. He wasn't arrogant like General Miller or Colonel McQueen, but he seemed like the kind of man who liked to hear himself talk and thought he could solve any problem with straight talk. Zak had worked for General Miller in Iraq and had been an adviser to interrogators and military personnel there. General Miller liked Zak. We learned right away that Zak was more than just a cultural adviser. He advised interrogators on how to use our faith against us.

Brothers across the camp had different reasons for striking, but there was a core list of demands that hadn't changed since the very beginning. It was simple, and we told him what we wanted:

1. Respect for our religion and to be able to practice according to our faith. This also included an end to interrogators and guards desecrating our Qur'ans.
2. Fair trials with real legal representation rather than more of these military hearings where they tried to get us to confess to the accusations they'd made against us.
3. Proper food fit for humans and clean water. (The water was always dirty and tasted contaminated. The food was never enough, often old and inedible, or clearly not halal.)
4. Access to sunlight and to not be forced to go months in cells with no natural light.
5. To know why brothers sent to Camp V were treated so much worse than others, and why they were sent there for so long, in some cases for more than a year.
6. Basic human rights, including an end to regular and humiliating genital searches and access to real medical treatment.
7. Contact with our families—to be able to write to them, receive letters, and have calls.
8. An end to General Miller's system of levels that determined a detainee's privilege, and that detainees be treated equally.
9. Oversight by a neutral body that could observe our treatment and situation and report publicly about the conditions at Guantánamo.

We told Colonel Bumgarner and Zak that they should negotiate with Omar, who was on hunger strike in Camp V. Omar was selfless and humble but strong and knew how to mediate between all the different groups of men in the camp.

When Colonel Bumgarner and Zak came to Omar, they listened to the demands he made, then told him they wouldn't negotiate with him until he could promise that brothers in all camps would agree to stop splashing guards. We were hundreds of men starving ourselves to call attention to our humanity, and they wanted to talk about a few brothers splashing guards? Really? Omar said no.

Omar was a reasonable man and a good negotiator who knew he couldn't start with such a base demand on their part. And I think that's why Colonel Bumgarner stopped negotiating with him. I don't know how it happened, but Colonel Bumgarner then went to Kamal, a Saudi brother who spoke English and wanted to be the leader of all the detainees. Kamal liked to hear himself talk, too. He had an attorney who represented dozens of other men, all on hunger strike, brothers from European countries who spoke English and were able to tell their stories about the hideous things the Americans had done to us. This gave Kamal some leverage. There's no doubt that he wanted to help and thought he could, but he just didn't know how to do it properly.

Waddah, Yousif, and I were surprised when Kamal came to us to talk. He had already visited brothers in Camp V. This was a big deal, Colonel Bumgarner letting Kamal walk the camps with escorts to talk to brothers about the hunger strike and splashing. He wasn't even wearing ankle shackles! He said that the White House had personally given Colonel Bumgarner permission to make changes to the camp that Kamal had negotiated. He said they would make sure we were all treated according to the Geneva Conventions.

"Brothers!" Kamal said. "The colonel assured me he will live up to his word if we call off the hunger strike. This is a victory for us! They're even going to create a council of brothers to negotiate better conditions." Kamal was proud of what he had done, but we were confused.

"What happened to Omar?" Waddah asked.

Kamal was offended that we had asked Omar to negotiate for us.

"My attorney is talking to the world for us," Kamal said.

"But he's not our lawyer," I said. "I don't know him. We're negotiating for our lives."

"Trust me, brothers," Kamal assured. "The tables have turned. Some of our British brothers have been released and the world is watching. If Bumgarner doesn't make changes within two weeks, we will go on strike again. The *New York Times* is writing about us. So is *The Guardian*. They say hundreds of us are on hunger strike until death if necessary."

This all sounded good, but maybe too good to be true. I was hesitant about Kamal. I couldn't deny it. Many brothers were. He was with us for the pants rebellion of Romeo Block but had disappeared when things got messy. I didn't know and trust him the way I did Omar. Sometimes Kamal seemed more interested in being a leader than solving problems. But he had gotten our story out. The camp was negotiating with him, and they had never done that before. The strike seemed to be working and we held our breath.

I was suffering badly and Waddah asked me to stop the hunger strike to prove to the colonel that we would all stop if he kept his word. I didn't want to stop and risk ending my strike too soon, but I did. I knew I was close to death. A part of me was relieved to stop, and to see an opening in the tunnel that didn't lead to death. But I didn't trust the colonel to keep his word and that worried me. I didn't want to lose our leverage.

After recovering for a few days on an IV and Ensure, I was taken back to Alpha Block in Camp Delta, where I told Ali, Mana'a, Yassir, and others the good news that Kamal had negotiated a temporary end to the hunger strike. We were all uncertain but hopeful.

We felt a change in the camp that was hard to read. Some of the lower-level camp staff and guards had had a difficult time treating us so badly. I could see that they wanted conditions in the camp to improve. But most of the senior staff and higher ranks weren't happy with the negotiations. They even refused to admit that there were negotiations at all, because that would put us on an equal level with them. A female army general told one brother, "It hurts the way you twist our arm and force us to improve living conditions in the camps."

The camp settled into an uncertain calm for a few weeks as we got better food and fresh water. The admin promised to stop desecrating the Qur'an and to respect our religion. Guards stopped mocking us when we prayed. Almost all brothers stopped hunger-striking and six men formed the council—they were Saudis, Egyptians, Algerians, mostly scholars and intellectuals, men like Abdul Assalam, who was the Taliban ambassador to Pakistan.

We suspected that the camp admin wouldn't follow through on their promises to improve conditions, and why would they? But we had to try. We wanted this to work. What other options did we have?

It really seemed that maybe our lives would be better. And then it all came to an end.

The next council meeting was broken up by guards, and then Hamzah was beaten badly during an interrogation. His interrogator battered him with a metal chair and threw a small refrigerator at him. Then a guard threw his Qur'an to the ground. Hamzah had the same attorney as Kamal, so it was strange that they would even take him to interrogation now, just as we were negotiating the end of the hunger strike. I thought it was an act of sabotage. I thought the interrogators didn't want to give up control over the camp. If Colonel Bumgarner made conditions better, what leverage would interrogators have? There were forces at work that were beyond any of our control.

Even though Hamzah was being held in Camp V, word spread quickly about what had happened. It hadn't even been two weeks since the end of the strike.

The negotiations failed. I went back on hunger strike right away. Many of us did; we had lost something. The power of our unity maybe, and the morale it brought us. We'd lost our hope that the Americans could see us differently. Our demands weren't extraordinary. We had asked only for basic human rights, and the Americans thought even that was too much. If we couldn't change the conditions of the camp with hundreds of men on hunger strike and the world watching, how could we ever change things? I had come close to death and for what? Still, I had to continue the hunger strike to the very end. I had no choice.

Around the same time, the US Congress passed a law that allowed the camp admin to force-feed us in order to keep us alive. Colonel Bumgarner didn't care if we were healthy or being treated humanely so long as none of us died. I was put on force-feeding along with other brothers who were in bad shape. At first, it was done without re-straints and detainees didn't resist them. Twice a day, nurses numbed our throats and threaded lubricated tubes through our noses and into our stomachs. Then they fed us two cans of Ensure. It was enough protein to sustain us and keep us from dying, but nothing more. Most of us didn't boycott the force-feedings at first. And some brothers chose to drink their Ensures. We were all learning as we went. We didn't want to die. We wanted change. And with the force-feeding, we were still maintaining the hunger strike.

Weeks passed like this in an unstable cease-fire between hunger strikers and Colonel Bumgarner. But when he realized he wasn't go-ing to break the hunger strike like this, he came up with new and creative ways to harass and humiliate us that couldn't be tracked by the Red Cross. He gave us oversized pants that fell to our ankles if we didn't hold them up. He moved hunger strikers from block to block and in and out of solitary confinement so that it was difficult to know who was on hunger strike and where they were. When the Red Cross representatives came, he moved us around even more to hide us. I was so weak from not eating and now guards woke me up every fifteen minutes. Everyone cracked down on us, especially the interrogators.

My body was so broken down, escorts had to move me on a cart to interrogations. One time, I was shackled to a chair at a table and the interrogator came in with his lunch.

"Do you mind if I sit?" he said, very polite. "I didn't have a chance to eat."

He sat down and took out his lunch, a McDonald's grilled chicken sandwich, and started eating. The food smelled so good it drove me crazy.

"Mmmmmm," he continued. "This is so good! I love this. Oh, God! You'd love this. Here, want to try?" He put the food right in front of my nose. Wa Allahi, it smelled so good! It took every ounce of strength to ignore him. "Oh, right. You're not eating. This is really good though. Mmmm. It's just sooooooo delicious."

Allah, oh Allah. I closed my eyes and put my head down and recited verses from the Qur'an. I thought about the vastness of the sea and how my mother and father and my little sister were on the other side of the ocean. I pondered the magnificence of the universe and Allah's world and how perfect everything was. The complexity of how birds fly. How we see the stars flicker in the night sky. The rotations of the planets around the sun and the moons around the planets. The rising and setting of the sun every day. I imagined flying up into outer space and traveling the universe, lost in the magnificence and beauty of Allah's creation. It was mystical. It was spiritual.

And then I felt something hitting me and I looked up to see the interrogator spitting sunflower shells on me. They were creative, these interrogators. But we were stubborn, and we had more at stake. It might sound difficult to ignore the food and suffer all that pain, but our lives depended on it. Our faith and innocence gave us strength, and they could never strip that away from us.

Hours passed like this and finally, when the interrogators had tried everything to get me to talk and were angry and frustrated with how little they had accomplished, they threw their food on me and stormed out. These were the small victories we captured and carried with us back to our cages.

Our bodies had become the battleground for control, and toward the end of 2005, I started boycotting the force-feedings along with other brothers. The camp admin could send the IRF team to beat me and restrain me, but they couldn't legally restrain me for a force-feeding. I lived only on water for thirty, forty, fifty days or maybe more. There were maybe a hundred brothers still on hunger strike and they went as long as possible without giving us IVs or infusions. We were all drawing new battle lines.

I was moved a lot. I was confused and weak. But I remember certain moments. I remember being in my cage in Golf or Alpha or Romeo Block with no visits from the medical staff for weeks, only guards and interrogators. I remember crawling close to the light at the end of that tunnel, and when I was reaching for it, the guards took me to the medical clinic. I remember nurses trying to give me an IV infusion, but my veins collapsed with every try. Finally, after more than two hours of trying, jabbing needles everywhere in my body, they got a small vein in my foot. I remember the feeling of the cold IV fluids shooting into my body and shaking uncontrollably from the cold. I remember asking for a blanket and the response they gave: "If you feel cold, then start to eat."

Three guards came to move me. I thought they were going to move me to the hospital but instead they took me to an empty block holding only four other brothers.

When guards came back for me the next day, I couldn't walk and they had to carry me. "He's dying," they said. It was like hearing them talking about someone else, not me.

They took me to a medical space where I thought there would be medical staff to feed me the way they had in the past.

Instead, an old doctor was there in a uniform who told me he was another colonel.

"Who's this?" he asked the guards.

"Detainee 441, sir."

I had met many assholes in this place and could detect them right away by the way they held themselves. This guy was a really big asshole. He grabbed my file and came close to me.

"Sir, are you detainee 441?" Every word dripped with arrogance. All business. He had a job to get through and that's all he cared about. "Do you know why I'm here?"

"No," I said.

"Sir, I am here at the request of the White House," he said. "I am here to make sure that you eat. Do you understand me, sir?" He didn't wait for an answer. "Sir, I don't care about your hunger strike. I don't care why you were brought to this place. I don't care if you think you are innocent. I don't give a shit that you say you have been mistreated. I care about one thing and one thing only. Do you know what that is, sir?"

It seemed like he was talking just to hear himself talk.

"I'm here, sir, to stop your hunger strike," he said. "That's it. Sir, do you understand what I'm telling you?"

Again, I didn't answer.

"Now, sir," he went on, "I'm asking you to stop this hunger strike and begin eating. I want to help you, sir. I'm asking you to help yourself, because tomorrow there will be no more asking. Tomorrow you will eat. No question about it."

I tried to tell him why we were on hunger strike. I told him about the torture and the abuse and desecration of our Qur'ans. I told him about the genital searches.

"Suit yourself," he said, and he walked out.

He was serious and cold. His firm insistence that I would eat tomorrow scared me. He reminded me of the men in the black site. I was taken back to the block, and I told my brothers what the doctor had said.

"Don't worry," Yassir said. "He's just trying to scare you." He started making fun of the colonel for calling me sir. We didn't think anything more about what would happen to us tomorrow if we didn't break our hunger strike.

I hoped Yassir was right—that this doctor was only trying to scare us. The world knew that we were on hunger strike to protest our treatment and to be seen as humans. Why would the Americans refuse this?

Two days later, guards came to me, acting strangely nice.

"Hi, 441." They laughed. I didn't feel good about that. I figured, okay, here we go. They are going to take me to the hospital like before and give me an IV.

No. The guards carried me to November Block, to a solitary confinement cage where a group of nurses and corpsmen was waiting for us. They were all very serious, stern. Beside the nurses was a thinly padded chair with a body harness, armrests with restraints, and a high back with restraints for the head. It was the same chair Americans use in executions. Next to that chair was a six-foot wall of Ensure cases. Guards pushed me into the chair. They tightened the chest harness so that I couldn't move, then strapped my wrists and legs to the chair. Every point of my body was tightly restrained—I couldn't move at all. One of the male nurses stood in front of me holding a long, thick rubber tube with a metal tip. Another nurse grabbed my head and held it tightly while the male nurse forced that huge tube into my nose. No numbing spray. No lubricant. Raw rubber and metal sliced the inside of my nose and throat. Pain shot through my sinuses and I thought my head would explode. I screamed and tried to fight but I couldn't move. My nose bled and bled, but the nurse wouldn't stop.

"Eat!" the nurse yelled. "Eat!"

He kept forcing that tube deeper into my nose. I coughed and gagged. I was so weak I couldn't fight anymore and just gave up. I thought I would choke.

"Eat!" the nurse yelled. "You want me to stop? Eat!"

There was no way I would.

It took him a long time to get that thick tube into my nose. When the entire tube was down my throat and in my stomach, a corpsman brought five cases of Ensure from that wall and put them at my feet.

"This is your breakfast," he said. "Enjoy!"

The corpsman opened the first can of Ensure into a bag connected to the tube. When the first one was done, he poured another, then another . . . He kept opening cans and pouring them in until my stomach and throat were full and Ensure poured uncontrollably out of my mouth and nose. I thought I would drown in Ensure.

"If you throw up," the corpsman said, "then we'll start from the beginning with a new case and fill you up again."

He opened more cans of Ensure and poured them into the bag. The other nurse braided a pen between two of my fingers and squeezed them together, bending and bruising my fingers in the most painful way.

"Eat!" the corpsman said. "Eat!" He kept saying this and the more I struggled, the more everything hurt. I felt pain in every part of my body. This torture lasted until the entire case was gone.

When they were done feeding me, the nurse pulled hard on the tube and ripped it out of my body. It felt like a knife coming through my nose and it bled badly. Blood ran everywhere. I couldn't breathe and my stomach was so full I thought I would explode.

The nurses and medical team left. So did the guards. They left me there, tied to that chair alone. They'd mixed laxatives with the Ensure and I needed to use the toilet really badly, but I wasn't allowed. This was their special kind of humiliation. I hadn't eaten in months. Everything they forced into my stomach was going straight through my intestines. I tried to hold it all in, but I couldn't. When the guards and nurses saw, they all laughed at me.

Hours passed like this, strapped to that chair in my own mess. Finally, they moved me to a very cold cage with only a single piece of plastic on the bed.

The nurse came to the cage door and asked me to take off my soiled shirt and pants. I did. I thought they would bring me clean clothes, but they didn't.

"You're being punished for throwing up during your feeding," the nurse said.

Allah, oh Allah. Help me. They are going to kill me.

They brought me back to that chair four more times that day, and each time they threaded that fat tube into my nose, then poured an entire case of Ensure into my stomach.

"Eat!" they screamed.

"Please," I cried. "You'll kill me!"

This made them laugh and they slapped me harder.

After the fifth feeding, they left me in the chair all night in just a pair of soiled shorts in my own mess. The next day, I was called five times again. *Allah, oh Allah.* I couldn't take it. I thought I would die.

Their intention was clear: they wouldn't stop feeding us like that until we ended the hunger strike.

I didn't want to let my brothers down. I heard brothers crying out, breaking, saying they would end their strike. I tried to resist. I did. I was strong and lasted two days, and then I heard Waddah call out to me from down the block.

"Brother," he called. "Please stop. They will kill you. It's okay. We are stopping the strike."

It was a relief to hear Waddah's words. I stopped my hunger strike that day. All of us stopped except for two brothers who were badly wounded during the force-feeding when the corpsmen pulled the tube from their throats. It was a relief to stop. And I hoped it wasn't for nothing.

The world knew what happened. Attorneys documented it and so did human rights organizations. But it didn't matter. The colonel had broken the hunger strike without a negotiation. I'm sure he got a nice star in his file for that.

- SIXTEEN -

We were in Camp 1's Alpha Block, where Colonel Bumgarner had moved a lot of the Redeyes and troublemakers. He preferred the risk of keeping us together to the risk of us organizing other detainees. Tensions in the camps had been rising ever since the end of the hunger strike. A brother was found unconscious and full of prescription drugs, and the colonel snapped. He shut down all of Camp 4 after searching through a Qur'an for hidden pills set off a block riot. He moved all the most compliant and cooperative brothers to Camp V, the worst place at Guantánamo. Nothing this man did made sense.

So we didn't know what to expect when Colonel Bumgarner called our brother al-Etaby for an appointment. The colonel had Zak with him, the cultural adviser. He was supposed to advise the camp on things like religion and food, but he truly hated us and told the colonel the Redeyes were a terrorist cell planning operations in the camp.

"He's crazy, this colonel," al-Etaby called out to us after they met. "I mean really unstable. Really arrogant. This guy is dangerous." Al-Etaby was one of the more educated brothers at Guantánamo. He spoke English well, even better than Zak.

According to al-Etaby, the colonel wanted to talk about a rumor he'd heard a few months before that a detainee dreamed we would only be released from Guantánamo after three brothers died. We'd all heard about this dream. We'd all thought about it and analyzed it and concluded it meant nothing. We talked a lot about dreams. Dreams were important to us, and I was considered a good dream interpreter, but this dream was just a joke. The fact that the colonel mentioned it made it even less important to us.

I WAS IN a cage close to Yassir, and farther down the block were Mana'a and Ali. Everyone on the block had been part of the hunger strike, and most of us were preparing for a second wave that we planned to start soon. We were only eating the fruit and vegetables in our meals or skipping our morning meals. Corpsmen weighed us every day and checked our health to make sure we weren't losing weight. They were being very careful trying to prevent another hunger strike. If they thought you were on strike, you'd get moved to isolation.

It was the first time in a long time that they had put so many Redeyes together in one block. Yassir, Mana'a, and Ali had all been with me for the pants rebellion of Romeo Block and the destruction of Oscar Block. We were among the last brothers to stop striking.

The night everything changed, I remember the guards gave extra food to anyone who asked for it, and I passed my fruit down to Yassir. We had our evening meal and I remember the block was strangely quiet after that. Yassir sang a little. He had a beautiful voice, one of the most beautiful in the camp. I remember the guards were changed out in the middle of a shift and that was strange. I remember thinking how unusual it was that the block was so quiet and how all the brothers were tired and falling asleep. Most nights you would find some brothers awake all night reading, talking, praying, being taken to the rec yard or to the showers—usually all night long. The camp sometimes put sedatives in our meals when they were expecting trouble, but there was no trouble that night and no reason for it. I remember how strange it was that guards closed the rec yard early.

It was also strange that I fell asleep early and that I slept deeply without being woken up by guards or by brothers being taken to appointments or reservations. There were always brothers coming and going from the block. I slept deeply like that until I was woken by a female guard screaming. I woke up afraid, my heart pounding through my chest. I heard block gates slamming and guards stomping down the corridor. It blurs now as I remember looking down the block and seeing guards carrying Yassir out of his cage. His hands were tied behind his back; his ankles were tied, too, and a cloth was sticking out of his mouth like he'd been in an interrogation. I tried to get a better look and I could tell there was something wrong with his neck.

There were so many guards and so much noise I didn't know what was going on. I wondered if I was in a dream and then I heard brothers crying.

"What's going on?" I called out.

"Yassir is dead!" a brother called back.

I collapsed to the ground on my knees and cried. How could Yassir be dead? This had to be a mistake. How could my brother who had been so kind, who had been by my side through so much, who had never talked about suicide—how could he be dead?

I heard a Code Red called, but not Code Snowball for an attempted suicide. The block filled with more guards, and then I heard more cries. Brothers called out that Mana'a was dead, too, and so was Ali. *Allah, oh Allah.* How could this happen?

The block was in chaos. All the brothers were confused and afraid. The guards were confused, too. Some guards thought it looked like a suicide, others thought it didn't and couldn't understand how those brothers ended up like that. Nothing made sense. None of those brothers had talked about suicide. None of us had. We had just survived the hunger strike together. Conditions in the camp had gotten better, and we were preparing to strike again for even more changes.

Two guards were ordered to stand in front of each cage and we weren't allowed to talk or use the toilets. The guards said they wanted to stop any more of us from killing ourselves. Colonel Bumgarner stomped up and down the block, yelling and cursing like he was crazy.

I cried all night. We all did.

Four escorts came for me.

"Move!" they barked. They pushed me from behind. They were so angry, and why?

"Where?" I asked.

"Shut up!"

Of course they took me to interrogation. The room was already freezing, like it had been prepared for me. Waiting for me were two interrogators, a man and a woman. Their faces were hard and angry, and I wondered what they had to be mad about. I was the one devastated with grief. We had just lost three brothers and the camp was calling it suicide when we all knew that was a lie. Suicide is a sin in Islam, and didn't the interrogators and camp admin understand that yet?

"What happened tonight?" the man thundered. He had the voice of someone who doesn't know what they're talking about so they just say it loudly.

"I don't know," I said. I tried not to cry. I didn't want them to think I was weak.

"Who had those detainees killed?" the woman said. "Were they forced? Was it a pact? Did you ask them to do it?" The question made no sense to me.

"Why don't you ask the colonel?" I said.

I heard a lot of noise out in the hallway. The interrogators left the room and all the noise moved down the hall. They never came back. They left me there for hours in that cold room until an IRF team came to kick my ass and move me to solitary confinement in November Block.

Colonel Bumgarner turned into a crazy cow, furious at everyone. He declared a state of emergency in every camp and deployed IRF teams to every block.

Overnight, the colonel completely reset the camp with strict new rules intended to prevent us from killing ourselves. Whatever the guards said—that was the new rule. If we said no to anything or refused to comply with an order, guards called a Code Yellow and a new Quick Reaction Force stormed the block. These were like IRF teams, but worse. If I looked a guard in the eye and he didn't like the way I looked at him—Code Yellow and QRF team. I was beaten by QRF teams at least four times that day. Every camp fell into total chaos.

In solitary confinement, they did everything they could to raise the level of our misery. Fans howled behind our cages all day and all night so that we couldn't talk to each other. They put bigger and nastier vacuums in front of our cages and never turned them off. The temperature changed from freezing cold to boiling hot hour by hour. Guards banged on our doors whenever they walked by. They didn't let us sleep. The new SOPs in solitary confinement said that guards had to look in on us every sixty seconds. At night, they woke us up every fifteen minutes to make sure we were still alive.

Not all guards were like that. There were always good guards. Every rotation had men and women who couldn't make sense of their mission and the SOPs. But after our three brothers died, even the nice guards turned on us.

"I'm sorry," one guard said. "We all have new orders. Everything has changed."

Something happened with the hunger strike and with our brothers' deaths. Something changed all across the camp. Now it was like we really were at war.

"Time to kick some ass," I heard guards say outside my cell, as if it was some kind of game.

Everything they did seemed like it was meant to kill us. Guards played with my body like a toy. The nasty vacuums screamed and the big fans roared at me all day; the noise buried me, burrowed into me, pressed down on me. There was no relief, no comfort—we couldn't talk or sing to other brothers the way we had in the past. Whatever restraint, what little sense of humanity the guards once had was gone.

One night right after the deaths, I heard a brother screaming a few cells down from me. I knew he'd been beaten badly and the pain I heard in his screaming killed me. I banged on my door and cursed the guards, who rushed to my cell. They smiled and their smile said, *Let's have some fun.*

You know what? I didn't care anymore. No matter what I did, no matter how hard I tried to stay calm, no matter what I said, they were going to kick my ass anyway. That's how it was now. There was no talking. There was no protesting. There was only force and violence. Fine, I said.

"Come here, chicken!" I screamed at the guards. "Call your fat-chicken colonel!" I screamed.

My English was really not so good, but I knew a lot of words, especially curses, which I learned from the best teachers—guards. I think they understood the tone. Code Yellow. QRF. They pinned me to the wall and then threw me to the ground. They piled on top of me, teasing me, mocking me, yelling at me in English the way I yelled at them.

"Chicken!" They laughed. "Donkey!"

They dragged me to the toilet, slammed my face in, then flushed it. They laughed hard, having so much fun. Blood was everywhere. They'd broken my nose.

They dragged me out of my cage, searched it, then pushed me back in. A few minutes later they were back.

"Do you want to go to rec?" They smiled. I knew there was no good answer.

"Yes," I said. If I said no, I knew there'd be another QRF team. They put the shackles on my hands and ankles so tight that they dug into my skin.

"Is that okay?" they asked.

"Yes," I said. Remember, there was no "no."

They pushed me hard all the way to the rec yard, and by the time I got there the shackles had cut deep into both my ankles.

At the rec gate, the nastiest guard searched me in the worst way possible. He grabbed my genitals hard and pulled.

Allah, oh Allah. I knew they would throw me to the ground and beat me if I did anything. I knew they would beat me if I did nothing. I said to myself, I will stay calm and as soon as they are calm, I will get one good knee or headbutt to the nastiest guard. After that, by Allah, they can do whatever they want to me. But as soon as I stepped into the rec cage, the nasty guard stopped me.

"Time's up!" he said.

"What . . ." I said. I didn't even finish before—

"Code Yellow in November Block rec yard," he spoke into his radio. Before he was even done calling it, a QRF team stormed onto the block.

Everyone had big red canisters of pepper spray the size of fire extinguishers. The guards circled the outside of the rec cage so that I was completely surrounded. Guards all around me showered me with pepper spray. It came from every direction and knocked me to the ground right away. It burned like nothing I had ever felt. I couldn't see. I couldn't hear. All I could focus on was the fire burning every inch of my body. The guards kept spraying until I was completely drenched and their canisters empty. I couldn't breathe I was coughing so hard, and I thought I would drown in fire. I tasted death.

Where do we go in these moments of pain, when the world turns black? We always turned to Allah. I prayed to Allah to guide me, to protect me, to help stop this madness and hasten my release.

Guards dragged me back to my cage and threw me in. I heard a compliant brother, Hamam, screaming down the block like he was going crazy, and I started screaming, too, so that guards wouldn't send a QRF team to beat him. I don't know what I was screaming or whom I was screaming at. The camp. The guards. The colonel.

"Shut the fuck up!" The guard banged on my door.

I beat the door and screamed any words that came to my mouth.

The QRF team came again and piled on top of me. Choked me. Pulled my genitals.

This cycle went on for days, weeks maybe, and then the block went silent one day. The vacuums stopped screaming. *Allah, oh Allah.* My whole body relaxed. When I looked out of my viewing window into the hallway, I saw a Red Cross representative walking down the block accompanied by officers. The vacuums had disappeared. I called out to them and motioned them to my cell door. I wanted them to see my condition.

"Please," I said. "I have been beaten badly and covered in pepper spray. My nose is broken." I spoke quickly in Arabic to get out everything that had happened since Yassir, Mana'a, and Ali had died.

"No Arabic," the Red Cross representative said. "I'm sorry."

"Nose broke," I said with my broken English. "Help."

"Someone will come talk to you in Arabic," he said. But we both knew that was just a lie that he had to say. There would be no representative speaking Arabic. The Red Cross cared about us as much as the colonel did.

I stopped eating after that. I wasn't on hunger strike. I wasn't planning one. I still accepted my meals but I couldn't eat. I quickly lost the little weight I had gained back since the hunger strike. How do we slide toward the edge of despair? We inch toward it, little by little, so slowly it looks like we're not even moving. I stopped drinking water, too, and that's when I started hallucinating, struggling to unblur the world around me. I prayed to Allah. *Allah, oh Allah. Please give me clarity. Allah, oh Allah. Please accept my soul if I die in this place. Allah, oh Allah* . . . The world went black and when I opened my eyes, I was in the medical clinic with an IV connected to my arm.

"You almost died," the doctor said. She had kind eyes. A guard stood behind her. "I'm recommending that your interrogators move you out of solitary confinement."

"He's there on Colonel Bumgarner's orders," the guard said.

"And what if he dies?" the doctor asked.

The guard had no answer.

THE COLONEL WASN'T done with me yet. They moved me to Romeo Block, which was newly redesigned to look like an experimental laboratory for rats. Really, it was like a battle arena, where guards and detainees fought every day like it was their job. The front of every cage was covered with thick glass, and then inside the cage was the same mesh as before, but it was covered with another smaller mesh that was almost impossible to see through. Every second cage was empty, holding only a vacuum screaming nonstop. The scariest part was seeing all my brothers in these cages, like crazy skeletons, some just in orange shorts, some in weird green robes. These were suicide robes and they looked like long tank tops that went to your knees. Velcro straps at the shoulders connected the front to the back. There was no way to rip or tear them. No way to hang yourself with them. All the brothers had long beards and hair, everyone was very skinny. You could tell that they weren't fed. Their faces bruised and their hands raw, you could tell they'd all been fighting the guards.

"Welcome back to the worst of the worst," Waddah called to me.

Allah, oh Allah. All of Romeo Block reeked of pepper spray.

Brothers up and down the block called out to me over the roar of the vacuum machines.

When I got to my cage, the guards unshackled me and demanded my clothes. Brothers cried out, excited at the possibility of a fight. I was still in bad shape and not ready to fight, but I couldn't show I was weak. I refused to hand over my clothes. I think we know what happened next. QRF team. Pepper spray. All the brothers on the block stomped the floor and banged the cages, cheering me on. The noise was madness.

"Keep them busy so they don't beat you," Waddah called out.

"Don't worry about Mansoor," Omar called. "He knows how to handle them."

All the guards coughed from the pepper spray, and I knew right away they were inexperienced trainees. I almost felt bad for them, amateurs going up against a professional.

When they charged in, I jumped out of their way and they hit the wall. *Boom!* They fell into a pile on the ground.

Brothers cheered.

From my bed, I jumped onto that sad pile of men and started punching whatever I could. My brothers shouted and laughed. I grabbed a helmet here, pulled a visor there. I didn't know what I was doing. My adrenaline was rushing and I thought I might faint at any moment. I saw the cage door was open and darted for it, but I hit a wall of pepper spray and then guards dropped me to the ground. It was over now. They piled on top of me, knelt on my neck, and restrained my legs and hands together behind me. They carried me like this to the rec yard, the guard in front holding me by my throat so that I couldn't breathe. In the yard they cut my clothes off me, laughed at my skeleton body, and then put me in a suicide smock. They were always finding new ways to humiliate us. When I was restrained again, guards gave me a couple more kicks, then carried me back to my cage.

I wasn't done. I needed to finish strongly to show my brothers I wasn't weak.

The cell pull-out can be tricky for new guards. They have to take the restraints off and back out quickly before you can move. These guards were slow and I was able to grab one of them by his armored vest. It ripped in half and the five guards pulling him fell out of the cage and the block sergeant slammed the door shut, leaving that poor new guard stuck in my cage alone with me.

"Pull me out!" he screamed.

Brothers cheered. Brothers laughed. "Pull out!" they mocked.

I charged him. I threw punches and kicks everywhere while he was stuck with his back against the door. As soon as they opened the door to pull out the guard, I threw the vest and it hit the officer standing outside the cage barking orders. Those vests are heavy and it hit him hard and knocked his cap off and made him drop his radio.

"Allahu Akbar!" brothers shouted. "Push in! Pull out! Pull out! Push in!" It was crazy with all the noise.

Again, pepper spray. Then the guard was pulled out.

"May Allah bless you," Waddah called.

"Are you trying to kill my men?" There was the colonel again, yelling at me in front of my cage.

"Hello, fat chicken," I said in my best English. "No one wants to kill your chickens."

"My men are here trying to help you!" the colonel yelled.

"Like you helped my three brothers?" I said.

"Help us!" Omar called out. He was the block leader on Romeo Block. He pointed to me. "This is your idea of helping us? Look at him! Look at his face. You should be ashamed."

The colonel didn't answer.

"You're the killer," I said. I didn't look at him. I didn't want to give him the respect he craved.

The colonel stormed out. I think he had accomplished what he wanted.

The rest of the day, guards from other blocks came and looked at me, like they were told to make sure they knew who I was.

THAT NIGHT, A young female sergeant came on as watch commander, and the first thing she did was open all the windows on the block to air out the pepper spray. She even opened the brothers' windows that had been ordered closed for days as punishment. We called her Mole because she had a beautiful mark on her cheek. She had always been fair and respectful and never harassed us. She was one of the only guards who didn't change after our brothers died.

When she was done with the inventory, she went to Omar.

"You've heard what happened today?" he asked.

"I've heard." She smiled.

Omar was very polite with her and asked if we could clean our cells and get the men to rec early so we could sleep.

"You know the rules about rec," she said. The new rules were that half the men on the block had to go to rec during the day, the other half at night. Going to rec meant lots of noise: shackles rattling, doors opening and closing, guards talking and barking orders. With a bad shift, it was impossible to sleep. "We have to do rec at nighttime, unless you refuse."

"We don't want to refuse," Omar said. "We just want some peace."

"Okay," she said. "If your brothers cooperate, we can hurry through rec and showers early. I'll tell the guards to be quiet later."

Mole told Omar that she had been warned not to help me. She told him that the colonel spoke to everyone on the night shift and told them that 441, Smiley Troublemaker—that's me—was the most dangerous detainee at Guantánamo. He told them that I had tried to kill an officer earlier that day. He meant the vest I threw. Labeling me like this was a really big deal. It meant extra punishments and more harassment from guards. It meant I was a target. We knew the colonel wanted guards to clamp down on us for what had happened that day. They needed to punish us. But this took it really far.

She was hesitant about helping me at first, but Omar asked her to talk to me and then decide for herself if I was dangerous.

"Oh shit!" she cried when saw me. "What happened to your face?" There was blood all over my face and smock. There was blood on the floor and on the bed. I couldn't see her that well, my face and eyes had swollen so much.

"Poor Mansoor," Hamzah called. "No one can tell if that is your ass or your face!"

Some brothers offered kinder words of sympathy. Most joked and laughed, trying to make the situation better and to cheer me up.

It hurt to laugh. I thought I had a broken rib. But I smiled.

"I'll get you some new clothes," Mole said. "Promise me you won't cause any trouble."

I promised. It was humiliating to have to assure people that I wouldn't hurt them after getting beaten. It hurt being asked not to cause a problem when that's all they ever did. Was it really that hard to understand why we did what we did?

WHEN I WAS told that I was to appear at an Administrative Review Board hearing to determine if I was still an enemy combatant, I imagined going before the colonel and telling him he was a criminal. I didn't know what this hearing was or how it was going to be different from the last one or even why it mattered. No one explained it to us. Other brothers, even ones who had attorneys to help them prepare, said these hearings were still nothing more than dressed-up interrogations where the board asked the same questions interrogators asked. The Americans didn't present any accusations or charge any of us with crimes. They just read out loud the lies interrogators had forced out of us under torture. This was their justice? Only a few brothers had ever been reclassified and released, and they were mostly from European countries or from Saudi Arabia, and they were only released because their governments pressured the Americans.

So what was the point? I decided to give them what they wanted. I would give them their jihadist. I would give them their al Qaeda fighter.

Before my hearing, the camp admin asked if I wanted to prepare a statement to read to the review board.

Of course I did! I hadn't had a pen or paper in years and couldn't wait for the chance to write my statement. I would write it personally to the colonel and General Miller. I was taken to a room and given a pen and paper, and over three days, I wrote a thirteen-page letter to the board in Arabic. I was direct in my accusations of the Americans. They were criminals for what they had done to us and to Muslims and I wanted them to know it. Each night I recited to my neighbor, a brother from the UAE, what I had written.

"Mansoor," he cried. "You're crazy to write such things. They'll kill you."

"They're already killing us here," I said.

"They'll keep you here forever!"

"They've already told me that I'll be in solitary confinement for seven years," I said. "What will they do after that—just let me go? They've made up their minds about who I am. Look at the people who run this place. Colonel Bumgarner, General Miller. These people are crazy! They'll never let me leave."

I was young and devastated from losing my brothers. The Americans had already decided who I was, even though they knew better. I'd spent years trying every way I knew to protest my detention and our treatment. I had learned who my enemy was and that's what I wrote.

"I hope the colonel is there to hear my statement," I said.

My neighbor laughed. But I was serious.

The day of my review, I refused to wear the white clothes they gave me and instead wore the orange jumpsuit. "Let's be honest," I said. "I never get to wear the white of a compliant detainee. Why would I wear it today?" They took me to a room with a bunch of high-ranking officers and an interpreter.

They asked if it was okay to call me Abdul Rahman Ahmed, one of the names interrogators called me now. There had been so many names, I couldn't keep track of them all anymore.

"Call me whatever you want to call me," I said. "It doesn't matter. I've told you who I am and you still call me by this name."

They had all these formalities to make it seem like it was a court, but we all knew it was just a show and meant nothing. I had no lawyer. They had no charges. They asked me if I wanted to make an oath according to Islam.

I was very polite and respectful.

"I don't need to take the oath," I said. "I will speak the truth under Allah."

They told me how the review would go and asked if I understood. It didn't make sense to me. It seemed like they had already made up their minds about me, and what was I to say? This hearing meant nothing to me.

Then they read what other brothers had said about me during interrogations and things I had said in interrogations under torture. They even talked about all the lies I told interrogators when I was playing the trick that got me blacklisted. They asked if I wanted to say anything about what they read, and I told them I had a statement to read at the end. The review went on for a long time and, finally, I was asked to read my letter.

First, I recited a verse from the Qur'an. Then I read my statement about how the United States was oppressing the world's religions with their criminal acts. I read that they preached democracy and human rights and justice for all, but these were just fabrications to hide all their vicious killing and torture. I told them I was a jihadist—that it was my duty to continue in the way of jihad until the very end. I even praised the attacks on America as opening the door to jihad.

They listened, clearly surprised at what I said. It was apparently the most forceful statement any brother had presented. When I was done, they asked me a few more questions that were just like the questions they had asked me over and over again in interrogations—was I an al Qaeda leader? Did I go to Afghanistan to wage jihad?—questions that told me they still didn't understand Muslims and didn't care to.

I told them again that I was not al Qaeda, but after what they had done to me, done to us, I would join if they would have me. I told them I was an enemy of the United States and its allies and that I would fight them if they released me.

I was angry. I was hurt. I said things that I didn't mean, but I was in a deep, dark hole. I wanted to make them mad. I had lost three brothers, murdered by the torturers who took my life away. I felt that no matter what I said, they wouldn't release me or believe me. I wanted to teach them a lesson. I wanted to teach them that they couldn't kill us and torture us and expect us to love them for it. No. I wanted them to see what they had created.

- SEVENTEEN -

I knew Ahmed wouldn't actually escape when I saw him walk past my cell door free and alone, completely confident in where he was headed. He was an Algerian brother, well educated, a doctor who spoke four languages. I'd never seen a brother walking through Camp V without shackles and guards. I'd never seen the block without guards in the hallway either, but we were at Guantánamo and hardly anything shocked me anymore.

"Where are you going?" I called to him.

"Out!" He hurried to the gate.

"Control," he said in a perfect American accent. "Open Alpha Block upper gate." The gate opened and he disappeared off the block.

About ten minutes later, alarms screamed and guards ran through the block. I saw Ahmed run past the gate again, followed a few seconds later by about twenty guards. That was it. He was gone and so were the guards.

I saw him again weeks later in the rec yard and asked what had happened.

"I went to take a shower," he said. "And I had one of those nasty army guards. When he put me in the shower, he didn't lock the door. So I took a chance and just walked out. I wanted to get him in trouble and give them all some extra work."

We laughed about it, then we both fell quiet for a minute. If we escaped, where would we even go? Doors were always left open by mistake. We just closed them or asked the guards to call Control to secure them.

Maybe it was time to start acting differently though. I had been at Guantánamo for six years, long enough to know that I wouldn't leave here anytime soon. I'd been told after my tribunal that I would not be released, as I still posed a significant threat to the United States. Okay, I said to myself. I stopped thinking about the future and lived only in the moment. I submitted to Allah's wisdom and plan, knowing that when He gave His permission, I would leave. We all believed this and it kept hope alive that we would eventually be released. But *eventually* was a long way off, and living in the moment seemed to slow the passage of time and made it less painful, if not less relevant.

WHEN WE WERE first brought to Guantánamo, we tried to count the hours using meals, or we wet toilet paper and stuck it to the wall and counted how long it would take to fall. That was too hard, so we tried to count the days by the changing of the guards' shifts, but we stopped that, too. We had all the time in the world, and yet it was too hard to track without clocks or watches or anything to write with. Then we tried to count only the weeks. We stopped that, too, and tried to only count months. But what is an hour, a day, a week, a month when they bleed one into the next and you're still in detention? I never wanted to count the years—it reminded me of how much time I had lost—but the rotation of guards was an inescapable measure of time. The guards served at the camp for around a year, then they rotated out for another mission. We couldn't remember them all, but there were two kinds of guards we never forgot: the very good ones and the very bad.

Some guards rotated back to Guantánamo after serving somewhere else. When we recognized one of them, we'd call them by their nickname and say, "Hey, Sleepy! Are you crazy? Why would you come back to this place?"

I liked to see their reaction when they recognized me. The guards always remembered the detainees who spoke English and the ones who caused trouble.

"Smiley Troublemaker," they'd say. "How in the world do you remember me?"

Some guards said things like, "I liked you so much, I came back just to see you."

"Okay," I'd say. "We have a lot of empty cages. Choose one and we can be neighbors."

With those good guards, we asked about their life and what happened to them while they were gone. Some told us that they went to Iraq or to Afghanistan but couldn't talk about it. Some got married. Some showed us photos of their kids, and we could see the mark of time as their children grew taller and older, photo by photo. Some guards came back clearly very troubled and changed by what they had experienced, like they were living a nightmare.

We always asked the nice guards about the other nice guards who had been to Guantánamo. Some had been killed in battle. Some injured in Iraq or Afghanistan. Some of those guards committed suicide and that made me think about how hard it must be to escape this place, even after you've left, even if you're not one of us. I noticed that when the really bad guards came back, they were the ones who had changed the most. They usually kept to themselves and we didn't bother them. It was clear something had happened to them, and that they weren't like before.

The guards who remembered us always asked about our brothers who had been released. "Did they escape or just get released?" they'd ask, trying to make a joke. They saw the changes in the camp. They saw the same changes in us.

"You're older," they'd say, pointing to my graying hair and beard.

Guantánamo aged, too, and kept growing, even though there were fewer of us here. The mesh blocks of Camp Delta rusted from the moist, salty air. Paint peeled everywhere. The green tarps covering the fences faded. The decay got so bad, they closed Camp Delta and Romeo Block, where I'd been kept until the end of 2006. They moved us all to solitary confinement in either Camp V or the new Camp VI.

Camp VI was an evil design and showed how smart the US government was. It was colder, crueler, and less humane than the other camps. The Geneva Conventions said prisons couldn't be built underground, so the Americans built a concrete bunker aboveground from cement and with no windows. And like Camp V, every block was solitary confinement. They kept Camp 4 open—they had to for media tours, to show the world the softer side of Guantánamo, where the most compliant and cooperative brothers played soccer and shared their meals together. The rest of us, most of us, were hidden away in isolation, kept apart from one another and cut off from the world entirely, including our families.

I had never received a letter from my family and I still didn't know if they knew where I was. We hadn't had contact with our wives, kids, brothers and sisters, and, of course, our mothers and fathers at all since being here. The Americans worried we might reveal things about Guantánamo that would be a threat to their "national security."

In the early days of Guantánamo, back in Camp X-Ray, the Red Cross encouraged us to write letters to our families. How nice of them, we thought. Some brothers did write letters, and of course interrogators read them and used their words against them. Sometimes interrogators even wrote fake letters back to us. We were young then and didn't know much.

By 2007, I was given twenty minutes every week to write letters in my cell. They'd bring me a nubby pen and official Guantánamo paper, and I could write to whomever I wanted and send it one of three ways. There was "detainee mail," which was just military mail, and I knew those letters went straight to the interrogators for translation and analysis. Then there was legal mail, which no one in the camp admin could read but was only for brothers with attorneys. Not many of us had attorneys, though, including me. The last way was through the Red Cross, and we still didn't trust that those letters wouldn't be read by interrogators.

So many of us found creative ways to use that time. Some brothers drew or wrote poetry, but they couldn't keep what they created. I used my twenty minutes to write letters I sent through the military mail, knowing the interrogators would read them. I used my words to test the translators and taunt and tease the interrogators. I wrote a letter to President Bush about Yassir, Mana'a, and Ali's deaths, telling him they weren't suicides and that he should investigate the colonel. I wrote letters to Donald Rumsfeld about my interrogations, noting that I quite enjoyed the screaming vacuums and sleep deprivation. I wrote letters to the United Nations about torture and human rights. I wrote to the king of Jordan about how his interrogators tortured us and claimed they were a delegation from the Arab League—they beat me and told me they would have the women in my family raped by dogs. I wrote a letter to Muammar Gaddafi asking him for a lawyer. I understood he did outrageous things and thought he might actually send me one. I wrote letters to the US Congress telling them that the force-feeding was inhumane and that they should join me sometime for a meal. I wrote a letter to Ali Abdullah Saleh, the president of Yemen, asking him very politely to intervene on my behalf as a brother and fellow Yemeni, and stating that it wasn't kind of him to demand hundreds of millions of dollars from the United States in order to take back Yemeni prisoners. After that, interrogators came to me and wanted to know if I was a part of Saleh's family. The Red Cross, useful as ever, asked me the same thing. I wrote letters to aliens in outer space, warning them that if they came to Guantánamo, they would see the worst side of humans. All the letters came back to me stamped NOT APPROVED.

Still, those twenty minutes every week were the only times I felt like myself. I wrote in Arabic, playing with words and phrases the way I had in my Arabic classes at the Islamic institute. When I told Omar about my letters, he encouraged me to write more and to write about everything we had been through.

"Analysts have to read everything and keep copies," he said. "This is our way of documenting what happens to us so that there will always be a record of it."

And so I wrote an angry but respectful letter, this time addressed to myself, when Abdul Rahman al-Amry, a fellow Redeye, was found dead in his cell like Yassir and the camp admin said it was another suicide. I wrote about how it would have been impossible for him to hang himself, bound the way they said he was with his hands behind his back and a cloth in his mouth, and because there was nothing to hang from. I wrote that he'd had a reservation with his interrogators that day, which they said had been canceled. There was no way for us to know if he went or not, but what did they expect us to think by saying it had been canceled?

I wrote a letter to myself about the black line that was painted on our cell floors and how guards wouldn't give us our meals unless we stood with our toes on the line, and how some guards used it to humiliate us and harass us. I wrote a typical scene of a guard yelling at me to inch my toes closer then farther away from the black line before refusing to give me my meal because I wouldn't stand on the black line exactly as he instructed. I wrote about how Adnan had figured out a way to erase his black line and that the watch commander didn't know what to do without it. I wrote about how I was given five months in solitary confinement as punishment for accidentally stepping on a guard's shoes while passing him in a crowded walkway on my way back from interrogation.

I wrote many letters to my mother and to my brothers and sisters in Yemen. I never got a single letter from them. I only received my own letters back, stamped NOT APPROVED.

Years passed like this and most of us never received anything from our families or loved ones. Nothing except fake letters written by interrogators. We got no sign that the ones we loved knew where we were, that they were thinking of us, that they knew what we were going through . . . nothing. Not even the smallest indication that they knew we were alive.

Some families did send letters through the Red Cross, but they all ended up detained like us, kidnapped, given ID numbers, exposed to many humiliations while they were searched in the worst ways and examined by translators, experts in poisoning and code-breaking, military analysts, and only Allah knows what else. Eventually, some of those letters got out. That may sound like good news. But those letters were released to interrogators, who controlled everything. Even brothers whose families sent letters often didn't have the necessary privileges to receive them or to read them. Here is where the interrogators played their game.

Interrogators would call a brother for a reservation and say something like, "We have something for you, and it's your choice whether you get it or don't."

"What do you have for me?" a brother would say.

The interrogator would take out a letter or even a pile of letters and show him.

"Look for yourself," they would say. "Cooperate with us and help yourself. Here is news from your family. You decide."

It wasn't really a choice. If we wanted to free those poor letters, we had to talk, and not just any talk. We had to give them valuable information.

Some brothers received letters regularly, every time the Red Cross visited the camp. That was also part of the game. When you are totally disconnected from everything—your family, the outside world, news—you might give your left eye for any words from your loved ones. Seeing other brothers get regular letters caused great pain. At one point, we told the Red Cross to stop visiting us because we knew they were cooperating with the Americans. I even wrote an official letter signed by the detainees to the Red Cross asking them to leave the camp and explaining that their presence gave legitimacy to everything the US government did to us. That letter was NOT APPROVED.

After we asked the Red Cross to stop coming, some brothers started to receive their letters. Not new letters—just the old letters, dated from years ago. Most of the letters were blacked out so that you couldn't make any sense of them. Imagine you are a husband and you get your first letter from your wife, your only letter in years, and it reads:

I watched brothers spend days and weeks reading them over and over, trying to figure out something, anything. Interrogators even blacked out the faces on photographs families sent, or they gave brothers a black-and-white photocopy that was so dark, you could only see a silhouette. The Red Cross said it was for security reasons.

Some brothers said that getting those blacked-out letters was even worse than not getting them at all. I don't know about that. Brothers who got any kind of letters—it was like life had been breathed back into them, even if only for a little while.

When I was kidnapped, I disappeared. The United States wasn't going to contact Mansoor Adayfi's family when they were insisting I was someone else. It killed me every day to think that my family didn't know where I was or what had happened to me.

At the end of 2007, after six years of total darkness, I got my first letter from home. A Yemeni brother was released back to Yemen earlier that year. In Sana'a, he visited my cousins and told them what had happened to me and that I was being held at Guantánamo. My mother wrote to me, very carefully writing only what I had instructed via the Yemeni brother, so that the interrogators couldn't find them. Interrogators used everything against us, even our families.

She wrote that she cried when she found out I was alive—she thought I was dead. My interrogators gave me a copy of the letter with lots of words blacked out. Getting that letter made me feel connected to the outside world for the first time. It didn't matter what she wrote. I knew that she was alive and that she knew I was alive—that was more than enough. A very small part of me had been found and I felt alive again. They let me have the letter for two hours and then came and took it away. Then an interrogator told me he would give me the entire letter if I started talking to them again. Seven years I had been there and they still thought I had valuable intelligence I wasn't telling them. I didn't need to talk to them, and wouldn't. I just wanted to know that my family was alive and that they knew that I was, too—that was enough.

As MORE YEARS passed, more brothers were released. Yousif, the boy who inspired me to go on my first hunger strike at Camp X-Ray, went back to Saudi Arabia. Then my Yemeni brother Salim was released.

"Mansoor!" Salim cried as he left the block. "They're releasing me! Mansoor, I'm going home." He laughed wildly. We had joked that he would be released before me, even though he was Osama bin Laden's driver.

"Salim!" I yelled back. "Tell them I am his other driver! Tell them I am his bodyguard or his cook. Tell them I know Osama!"

I was joking but I was serious. It seemed like anyone who knew Osama bin Laden was getting released.

Rumors of new releases spread throughout the camps every couple of weeks. I'd hear through DNN that a lawyer said that a group of twenty was approved for release. I thought the interrogators usually started those rumors to study our reaction and to prevent us from going on hunger strike again, to give us a little sense of false hope.

Omar said that those rumors were our heroin and that we couldn't live without them. I thought there was some truth to that. Those rumors helped keep hope alive when it was always on the verge of death. Sometimes I helped spread those rumors, knowing they weren't true. I knew some brothers were looking over the edge of hope to despair and they needed something to pull them back. That line between having faith and believing rumors was difficult to walk. If we believed too many of those rumors and nothing ever happened, we could really fall into despair.

Even when the rumors were true and brothers were approved for release, interrogators came up with new games to humiliate them and strip them of hope before they went home. Days before Hamam left, he came back from his final interrogation with tears running down his cheeks.

"What's wrong?" we asked. "Did they tell you that you aren't leaving?"

"No," Hamam said. He could barely talk he was so upset. "When I was brought into the interrogation room, they gave me all the letters my family had sent to me over the years. The interrogator told me I could read them if I wanted, then he left the room." Hamam cried now. "Nothing was blacked out. I found out that my mother died two years ago. My father said that her last words were, 'I wish to see Hamam one last time.'"

Interrogators tried the same thing when Majid was released. At an interrogation on his final day, there was a stack of letters on the table. When interrogators told him he could read them before leaving, he said, "Soon, I will be with my family, and you will stay here talking to non-talking brothers. Please send these letters to the White House and that idiot George Bush. Please tell him to stick these papers in his ass. Keep some for yourself and stick them in your asses, too."

It was hard to keep up such a strong front for so many years. While some brothers were released, others like me knew that day wasn't coming, and we risked losing ourselves to the darkness. We stopped talking to each other through the walls—it was too difficult with the ventilation system, the fans, and the vacuums. To talk we needed to lie on our stomachs and shout under the door and then only one of us could talk at a time. Sometimes other brothers were sleeping and got mad when we talked. It was easier now to just withdraw into ourselves and concentrate on our work.

Life at Guantánamo had become a job for all of us—the interrogators' job was to torture us; the guards' job was to kick our asses every day; and a brother's job was to fight back and give the guards as much work as possible. It was like a factory job for us, doing the same thing every day. Day after day. We woke, we prayed, we were tortured, we ate, we fought, we slept, and then we started the cycle all over again. Some of us had suffered serious injuries that never fully healed. Guards had broken my ankle, my wrist, my fingers, and my nose several times. It was the same for other brothers—some had their backs broken by IRF teams, their teeth knocked out, and even worse. The pain became routine, but that didn't lessen the pain.

For years this went on, and then finally the pressure of isolation and the daily fight was too much and we started calling out to each other again about a hunger strike. It had been more than a year. I was very happy to hear that. Time was slipping away before my eyes and I felt like if we didn't take action soon, our lives would slip away, too, and we would be forgotten forever.

MONTHS INTO THE new strike and weeks after they started force-feeding us, guards tied me and Adnan and a few other brothers tightly to our feeding chairs, restraining our heads, shoulders, hands, waist, and feet so tightly we couldn't move. All we could do was breathe. Then nurses tried to break us the way they had in 2005, with fat feeding tubes that ripped apart our noses and throats.

My whole face burned. One brother fainted from the pain. Another brother was taken to the intensive care unit after the tube did so much damage to his throat. We all bled badly and still they couldn't force those tubes down our throats, so they brought out a smaller size and tried again. When the tubes were finally in and our feeding bags full of Ensure, the nurses left us alone, something they should never have done.

"The worst is over," Adnan said. "Now let us get to work."

We didn't have a plan, but we were all Redeyes and we improvised. While one of our brothers distracted the guards, the rest of us wiggled our shoulders to get the tubes from our noses into our mouths, and then we chewed through them and swallowed chunks of tube. Ensure spilled everywhere and pooled on the floor beneath us. We really liked seeing that new mess.

The nurses came running, shocked at how quickly we'd messed things up.

"What did you do with the tubes?" they asked.

"I don't know," I said. "Adnan, where'd they go?"

The nurses needed to account for every inch of tubing. The camp admin worried that any missing lengths could be used to hang ourselves.

A little later, the doctor in charge of force-feedings came looking for the tubes. If we didn't admit that we'd eaten them, they would have to search all our cells, then take us to the medical clinic for X-rays. The nurses were in trouble now.

I asked to talk to the new colonel, but he refused. Instead, the senior medical officer came to talk to us, an African American lieutenant colonel who wasn't such a bad guy.

"Look," I said. "You're crazy if you think you can break our hunger strike with the same tactics Colonel Bumgarner used in 2005. Don't punish us for making a peaceful protest. You don't want three more deaths, do you?" The lieutenant's eyes popped. "Our demands are the same," I said. "So sit with us and try to see things eye to eye."

"Okay," he said. "I hear you. Just confirm for me—did you swallow those tubes?"

I did, and he came back a little later and asked if we would go to the hospital voluntarily to have the tubes extracted from our stomachs. After the procedure, he sat with me, eye to eye.

"Why'd you eat those tubes?" he said.

"Because the nurses were abusing us," I said. "Let me ask you. What if we switched roles? What would you do if you were me . . . if you were held for this long and treated like we're treated?" I had started asking nurses and doctors and guards this question regularly.

It was my test to see if they actually saw me, if they were capable of experiencing even one moment of empathy.

The SMO was silent for a long time and then he just shrugged his shoulders in a way that said he didn't have a good answer. He was like us, trapped in this place, forced to play his role, and all he wanted to do was survive long enough to escape.

"My job is to keep you alive," he said. "Not put myself in your shoes."

He didn't care about us. He needed something for his report, something that wouldn't give him more work. Nothing else. Their indifference really hurt. We tried hard to be seen as human, and the doctors or nurses or whomever we were dealing with just weren't interested.

"We chewed those tubes to make you work harder," I said. "To show you that we're still alive and fighting to get out of this place alive."

The next day, we were back in our force-feeding chairs again, but this time with the usual smaller tubes. We got new nurses, too, who treated us nicely. We knew that wouldn't last for long. The camp admin was always up to something.

AS MORE BROTHERS joined the hunger strike, they moved me and some of the other leaders to Camp Delta, which had been closed for a long time. The walkways and yards were overgrown, and families of banana rats occupied cells that were once ours. I didn't recognize the quiet. No fans or generators. No brothers talking and shouting and singing to each other. No rattle of chains or clanking cages. No sound of brothers fighting with guards. I felt a heavy pain of sadness and broke down in tears as guards escorted me past Alpha Block, where Yassir, Mana'a, and Ali had died. The entrance was still blocked off with yellow tape.

They brought me to Lima Block in Camp 2, now quiet without the wild Afghans. The only clue that men, and not animals, had lived in these cages were the names and dates brothers had scratched into the dull green paint. I remembered the female interrogator who on her first day walked down the block meowing like a wild cat hunting mice, trying her best to intimidate and scare the men she would question. I remembered pulling thread from my shorts and tying it to packs of salt to throw across the walkway to my brother Dan, who loved salt more than money. But the memories couldn't keep me company forever and soon I was really all alone. I wasn't allowed to do anything or have anything in my cage. When I protested anything, they moved me to the closed cells of Oscar or November Block for a couple of weeks where I was even more isolated. The loneliness and boredom were like mountains crushing me.

"How do you do it?" one of the nicer guards asked me one day through the interpreter. "How do you not lose your mind with loneliness? How do you starve yourself? How do you survive without wanting to die?"

"Allah," I said and then tried to explain to him about my faith and the belief that all of this was Allah's wish.

For years, the interrogators, Miller, the revolving door of colonels had desensitized us to the violence of our daily lives. They hit us so much that we no longer felt the pain of the punch. There was something bigger at work protecting us, something beyond our capabilities, and that kept us alive without our losing our minds. This was Allah's mercy, and we all felt it there. We couldn't survive without Allah's help.

It was true that our faith led us through the darkest times and gave us hope that we would be released one day, but that didn't mean we had to sit by and wait until it happened. We would rather die than do nothing. And our hunger strike was a dagger we held to our own hearts knowing that it was the only weapon we had. It was the only thing that had ever made life better for us. By isolating me and other hunger strikers in the abandoned blocks of Camp Delta, the camp admin was trying to take away my dagger, the only thing I owned. I wouldn't let go.

The new colonel would visit me sometimes in the isolation of Delta Block. Colonel Vargo was solid and stocky with the pitted face of a fighter. He said what he thought, and he thought Guantánamo was just another front of the war on terror, misunderstanding us as soldiers to fight. His visits were always casual, like he was walking the blocks and just happened to run into us, but we all knew this was his way of meeting with us unofficially. We always went in circles. One day he stopped by, asking me why we were still hunger-striking.

"We want to be treated as humans," I said.

"By waging jihad?" he said. "That's not my idea of humane. I need to keep you isolated so you don't inspire your brothers to join you."

"This is a hunger strike to protest our years of detention, not jihad," I said.

"I see you talking to my guards about your faith," he said. "You're trying to bring your jihad to America."

"Do I have guns?" I said. "Do I have an army? Look at where I am. We are detained and tortured."

"Look," he said. "There are three kinds of people in the US government. Those who want to kill you, those who want to keep you locked up forever, and those who want to release you. My job isn't to decide which one of them is right or wrong or what we should do with you. My job is to keep you alive until *they* decide."

"Pretend you are me," I said, throwing him my easy empathy test. "All you have is your body to make a peaceful protest for change. What would you do?"

He looked at the interpreter like I was a wiseass trying to outsmart him.

"If we can't feed you from your nose or mouth," he said, "we'll feed you in your ass."

"I'm not negotiating with you," I said. "Either treat us the way you tell the media you're treating us or let us die!"

"We're not negotiating," he said. "Remember—this is just a friendly visit. I'm here to tell you that we won't let you die."

"Then treat me like a human."

He had no response to that, but his silence was loud enough to hear.

In all those casual visits, he never once asked what makes men do things they could never have imagined doing before. The answer was right in front of him. It wasn't holy jihad. It was hopelessness, despair, humiliation.

As the hunger strike dragged on, a brother said to me, "All we have left is our humiliation. So we will use our humiliation against them."

Some brothers started throwing feces all over their cages. If death couldn't get the camp admin's attention, maybe this would.

"Please stay out of it," those brothers told the guards. "Our problem isn't with you. Our problem is with the medical team and the camp admin who won't treat us humanely."

When that didn't make things better, those brothers came up with something new and even nastier. They put feces all over their clothes when they went to their force-feeding.

"Why this?" I asked. This was too much even for me.

"We've been here for six years and still we don't know when or if we will ever leave," one brother said to me. "What do they want from us? They won't let us live like human beings. They won't let us die in peace. How do we make them listen?"

I didn't have the answer. I'd been circling around the same question for years, trying everything I could think of to find the answer. Block riots and violence. Boycotting interrogations. Writing letters.

Declaring war on the United States during my tribunal. After all of that time, here I was stuck in the endless routine of fighting with guards. I thought the hunger strike might be the answer. We had been on hunger strike a while now, maybe more than a year, and like fighting with the guards, it had become a routine, too. My brother asked, *How do we make them listen?* Maybe a better question was, *How do we make them see us?* I didn't know that answer either. But when I saw myself in the mirror, I saw a man with a graying beard and hair, and the scars of torture all over my body. The man I saw wasn't the same boy who was brought to Guantánamo so many years ago. I wasn't sure who I was anymore.

- EIGHTEEN -

As the hunger strike dragged into 2008 with no end in sight, something unexpected shook the camp and inflamed wild debates. The hot topic that occupied us all was the American presidential election.

We lived in solitary confinement, locked away in our cells twenty-four hours a day. We had force-feedings twice a day in our block walkways. And once a day, if we were lucky, we had one hour in the rec yard, sometimes with another brother in the cage next to us. Every chance we got, we talked about the election. When guards turned off the fans, we called to each other under the doors. We hated the killer George Bush, so we wished the Black guy Obama would win.

We didn't have TVs or any other news, but we had our DNN and that's how we heard that Obama promised to close Guantánamo. Some of us also liked him because he was African American. I'm sorry to say this, but our hearts were not full of warmth for most of the white guards. It wasn't because they were white, but because they were racists and didn't think of us as humans. Generally speaking, Muslims are forbidden from treating people differently based on color or any another reason. All people are the creation of Allah and should be treated equally. But the Americans were really good at their racism and brought it to new heights. *N***er! Sandn***er! Towel head! Haji!* They had so many names for us and it always hurt. They called Black guards and brown guards the same names and worse.

Now when we had a problem with a white guard, we could say something like, "Just wait and see. Your next boss is going to be a Black man." Saying this to some of the guards was worse than splashing.

I was on force-feeding one day with several brothers and we went straight to our favorite topic.

"Personally," I said, "I wanted Hillary to win the primary." I was trying to turn up the heat on the conversation.

"If Obama wins the election," Adnan said to the nurse, "I'll stop my hunger strike."

We asked some of the guards and other medical staff whom they wanted to win. All of the Black guards supported Obama, and it was clear that a lot of the white guards didn't want him to win.

Magid, who was really educated, turned to me and said, "If Obama wins the election, it will be one of the most important events in US history."

I knew nothing about American history. I didn't know if either of them would change anything. I'd wanted Hillary to win because I liked the idea of a woman president and I thought she would be more reasonable about our situation here.

I was very surprised when an older brother told me that he had sent a letter to Obama in 2006 telling him that he would be the next president. This brother had lived in the United States for many years and was very educated in politics. He believed that Obama would win and close the camp.

"He could do it with one stroke of his pen," Magid said. "It's called an 'executive order.'" We had many debates about this point. Could it be that easy to close Guantánamo? I had my doubts. It seemed too good to be true.

Tensions rose all over the camp the closer we got to the election, until it turned into an election war between us and the camp. The guards and the admin really didn't like Obama. They were afraid of him. Maybe because he was Black. Maybe because his name sounded

Muslim. Maybe because if he won, it would be like saying there was something wrong with Guantánamo and that would make the guards and camp staff feel like they had been part of something really bad.

For years, guards and camp staff had made our lives miserable. Now it was our turn.

We were determined to know who won right away, as soon as the announcement was made on TV. If it was Obama, we wanted to celebrate and make the guards feel worse. We became obsessed with this. We wanted to send a message to the interrogators that no matter how hard they tried to cut us off from the world or from each other, we still got news and could spread it quickly. That would really piss them off. We were practicing the fine art of confusion and chaos.

Some brothers decided they weren't going to sleep on election night until they knew who won. San, a Yemeni brother a little older than me, really wanted to make a big party if Obama won. San had gone to Pakistan to get treatment for a head injury and was sold to the CIA. He wasn't a Redeye or even a brother who fought that much with the camp admin. But he had been imprisoned for seven years without any reason and wanted Obama to win and close the camp. He swore that if Obama won, he would wake up the entire camp and get Colonel Vargo out of bed.

On the big night, San stood at his door hunting for any guard he could ask about the election. He finally spotted one of the Black guards coming back from a meal break.

"Hey!" San called out.

The guard didn't say a word; he just smiled from east to west and touched his own skin.

"OBAMA WON!" San screamed. "IT'S THE BLACK HOUSE NOW!" He banged and kicked his door and called out to guards. "It's the Black House! It's the Black House! Who's your boss now? It's the Black House!" He woke everyone up on the block.

We all laughed. He was so excited; it was like he had seen his mom dancing down the block.

When San calmed down, a brother called out to him. "How are you so sure Obama won?"

"I swear by Allah," San called back, "that guard's face lit up like the moon, he was so happy. He didn't have to say a single word."

On another block, brothers asked a white guard who didn't like Obama the same question.

"Hey, man!" Hamzah called out. "How do you like your new boss?"

"I don't care, man!" the guard cried out. Hamzah said he looked really upset.

Before the big night, San had spread word through DNN that if Obama won, he would get guards to call a Code Yellow.

On every block, guards were assigned to an IRF team, and one guard from each block's IRF team was assigned to the camp-wide QRF riot team. When big emergencies were called, the QRF guards came running from every block, banging doors, stomping up stairs, making so much noise that everyone in the camp knew what was going on.

As soon as San learned about Obama's win, he covered the window of his cell door with a towel.

When the guard asked San to take the towel down, he didn't. And when the guard called to him to answer, San stayed silent. This was a big deal. Ever since our three brothers had died, we weren't allowed to cover our windows, so that guards could see that we were alive.

"Code Yellow!" the guard called. "Code Yellow, Alpha Block!"

Soon, guards in riot gear came stomping from every block, making so much noise that brothers everywhere woke up.

"Allahu Akbar!" brothers yelled out in celebration. It was chaos.

When the QRF team gathered at San's cage to go in, he uncovered the window.

"I want to talk to the watch commander," San said. "And the camp officer!"

The watch commander came and so did a medic with the suicide emergency gear. The watch commander refused to call the camp officer, so San covered his window again.

Every time the watch commander called to have San's cell door opened, he pulled the towel off the window. SOPs said that guards couldn't go into his cell if the window wasn't covered.

"I will play with you all night long," San called. "I won't stop until the camp officer comes."

In a few minutes, the camp officer was standing in front of San's cage.

"Now that you are here," San said, "I have a message for the chicken colonel. Please tell him, THERE IS NO MORE WHITE HOUSE! It's the Black House now!" San laughed and laughed. He was crazy with laughter.

It was after midnight and brothers in every block were talking to guards, either congratulating the Black guards or making fun of the white ones.

"How did you all know who won?" guards asked.

"Obama called me himself!" one brother said.

"I just came back from the Black House," another said.

Many of us simply said, "It's classified."

But one brother joked, "We have a radio."

Not even an hour later, dozens of guards stormed into the camp. Day shift, night shift, guards we had never seen before. They came with civilians and cameras and many high-ranking officers. The last time we saw the camp admin send in so many guards and officers was when our three brothers died in 2006. At first, we thought one of our brothers had died.

Guards searched every cage in every block in every camp and we thought we were being punished because Obama had won. That wasn't it. The camp admin was shocked that we seemed to know that Obama had won the election, all at the same time, even before some of the guards. It didn't make sense to them. None of the guards had told us—that would have been a security breach. And they thought it was impossible for us to communicate from block to block and camp to camp so quickly. When our brother had joked that we had a radio, they'd thought he was serious.

One thing we had learned about the Americans was that they were really good at overthinking everything. Instead of believing that we were telling the truth all these years, they believed we were trained in special counter-interrogation techniques. Instead of thinking about how the Code Yellow woke up the entire camp, they believed we had somehow built a radio network. Imagine the logic.

It didn't matter that night. The Americans had a new president, one who promised to close Guantánamo, and we all wondered if the time had finally come for change.

CAMP VI

Maximum security used as
solitary confinement until 2010

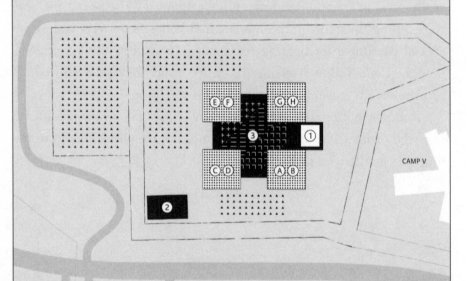

CAMP V

CAMP ECHO

BUILDINGS AND STRUCTURES

Ⓐ Alpha
Ⓑ Bravo
Ⓒ Charlie
Ⓓ Delta
Ⓔ Echo
Ⓕ Foxtrot
Ⓖ Golf
Ⓗ Hotel
① Gate
② Classrooms
③ Control

USES

▦ Administration
▦ Communal Living
✚ Medical
▦ Meeting Rooms
▲ Recreation

– PART 4 –

DEPARTURE

- NINETEEN -

I last saw Waddah alive around the time Obama became president and signed the executive order to close Guantánamo within a year. As I watched guards escort Waddah from Camp V, I thought I'd see him again in a couple of weeks when they rotated him back, or maybe at a force-feeding. The way I felt now about Redeyes like Waddah was how I felt about my tribe—they were in my blood; they were a part of me no matter where they were. We'd suffered together and sacrificed ourselves for each other in our resistance to interrogators and the camp admin. It was more than shared pain, though, more than torture and isolation and hunger. We also shared small moments of stolen joy in the jokes we played, the songs we sang, the little news we got from our families, especially when we learned of a marriage or a new baby. Cut off from our families for so long, we found a new brotherhood in all this darkness.

The day Obama signed the executive order to close Guantánamo, we all shared a sense of hope we'd never felt. The news spread quickly.

Cries of "Allahu Akbar!" rang out across the blocks.

Everyone was talking about leaving—camp officials, guards, camp staff, lawyers, the Red Cross, and even the iguanas, cats, and banana rats. I really hoped it would be true. Obama was better than that idiot George Bush, but I had my doubts that Guantánamo could close so quickly. It took more than four years and a hunger strike just to get salt included with our meals, and Obama thought he was going to close the camp in one? Nothing at Guantánamo happened that fast.

The first thing Obama did was send a delegation to Guantánamo to evaluate the situation.

We might never have another opportunity like this, so I thought it was time to plan a massive hunger strike to get more attention and help Obama close this place. About fifty of us had been on hunger strike since 2007, and many of us had been moved to Camp V Echo, a new detached solitary confinement block where they kept what Colonel Vargo called troublemakers, instigators, and leaders segregated from the other prisoners. I was still mostly with brothers like Waddah, Hamzah, and Adnan—the same brothers I'd been with for years. Most of us were on hunger strike or keeping our weight just above one hundred pounds, which was when they started force-feeding us. Being isolated in Echo made it hard to convince more brothers to join us. It took weeks to talk to brothers who weren't on our blocks. And even when we did, many of them doubted a hunger strike would do anything.

It was hard to organize with the camp listening in all the time. They had cameras in most of the blocks and heard everything we said. They'd even moved Omar to Camp VI, knowing he was one of the brothers who could bring us all together. But we got started anyway. The first thing we did was ask brothers, "What can you do?" Not all brothers could hunger-strike or wanted to, and that was okay. I understood. It was hard on your body, and there were other ways to join the new resistance. Some brothers said they could splash guards who harassed us. Some said they could begin refusing to leave their cells, which would cause all kinds of problems with IRF teams.

We had learned from the 2005 hunger strike that not all brothers could withstand the pain and health problems that came with not eating for long periods of time, especially those with diabetes or other medical problems. So we decided to gradually build the strike over time. First would be the brothers who were strong enough to strike for months or longer and could handle force-feeding. After that, every couple of weeks the brothers who were a little weaker would join the strike until we had everyone.

I volunteered to continue my hunger strike, to be the tip of the spear for this greater effort.

One day Colonel Vargo came to us when we were force-feeding.

"What in the world are you planning?" the colonel said through his interpreter. "You know you're leaving soon, right? There's no need to instigate a big hunger strike."

"If I am here just one hour," I said, "I'll protest for better conditions."

"What more do you want?" Colonel Vargo asked.

"You should talk to 078," I said. That was Waddah's ISN. He wasn't on force-feeding yet; he was in his cell, down the block.

"I'll talk to him," the colonel said. "But I know you can't bend that one."

We'd asked Waddah to represent us if the camp admin came to us to negotiate. Waddah was patient and measured and firm when he talked to the colonel, but more important, we knew he would always have all our interests in mind and not just his own. He would never bend.

"We want you to respect us like human beings," Waddah told the colonel. "Let's start with that. Come talk to me when you can do that."

A few days later when I was on force-feeding, escorts came for Waddah.

"Where are they taking you?" I called to him.

"You know, brother!" he called back. "They're taking me to the BHU."

This is what they did—as soon as they understood we were organizing, they broke us up. I still have nightmares about the BHU, about being strapped to the metal bed, paralyzed, and the constant harassment. I still remember the cries of brothers fighting and in pain. It was far away from Camp V, which meant once you were there, you were really cut off from everything else in the camp that could give you strength, even from DNN.

Waddah was thin but strong the last time I saw him. He smiled defiantly when he left the block. All the wheels were in motion. Brothers had already started smaller protests, like boycotting appointments and refusing to leave their cells. More brothers were skipping meals and eating less. We had started to break the camp's circle of control. We were organized and I had hope; I never imagined that would be the last time I would see Waddah alive.

After Waddah was escorted away, I refused to leave my feeding chair in protest. So did all the other brothers on force-feeding that day. Our bodies had aged and become more fragile with time and we were too weak to resist like we did in the days when we fought guards every day, but we could still make the guards work. This was a lot of work: They had to pick us up and put us on our stomachs, restrain us, then pick us up again and carry us back to our cells. Then we refused to get up for each feeding after that. We refused to come back from the rec yard. We refused to come back from the showers. With each passing year the fight got harder, but we couldn't stop, especially not with hope on the horizon.

A COUPLE OF weeks later I was told that, for the first time, I had been assigned an attorney. This was seven years after I was kidnapped in Afghanistan. Seven years and they'd never once charged me with a crime or told me what crime they thought I'd committed. They'd accused me of being this Adel and then Alex, both al Qaeda leaders, but these were only games they played with me. They had never shown me any evidence, any documents, any photos that connected me to these men. And now they wanted to give me an attorney? It was suspicious. I couldn't figure out why some brothers had lawyers and others didn't—there didn't seem to be any logic behind it. Some brothers had military-appointed lawyers. Some brothers from wealthy families had lawyers. Some Saudis and Kuwaitis had lawyers.

Why all of a sudden would the US government give me a lawyer? I didn't know what to do. What was the point if Obama was going to close Guantánamo? I'd learned that the Americans couldn't be trusted, so why should I trust them now?

I was still on hunger strike in Camp V Echo. I asked Fouzi, a Kuwaiti brother in the cell next to me, what I should do. He'd had his attorney for a long time and liked him.

"Mansoor," he said, "what do you have to lose? Go and meet this attorney. Be yourself. If he's nice, you can have him be your attorney. If he's not, then don't accept him." He thought about it again. "Just go!" Fouzi was very wise and smart.

I thought a lot about it that night. I thought about the life I had imagined for myself before Guantánamo and how I'd been so close to going to university in one of the Gulf States. Where would I be now if none of this had happened? I would be in Qatar, maybe, where jobs were good. I would be married and have children of my own. What kind of man had I become? Seven years was a long time to be fighting. What kind of man did I want to be? I could continue fighting and hunger-striking, lost in this vicious cycle, or I could try to find a way to live up to the man I thought I would be when I was younger. Who would I be next week or next year? Who would I be in another seven years?

Was this the man I wanted to be when I died?

No. I agreed to meet with this attorney.

I was at force-feeding when they came to get me for my first attorney appointment. Two years of hunger-striking had withered my body and I weighed only about one hundred pounds. After I finished the Ensure, guards escorted me to a small meeting room in Camp V. There were metal chairs, but no table. They chained me to the floor and to the chair and left me by myself, and all of a sudden, doubt raged inside me and I didn't want to be there anymore.

Then this huge Irish guy walked in. He had sharp eyes like a tiger and really broad shoulders. He was over six feet tall and made the guards and interpreter look so small. His hands probably could have squashed me with just one squeeze, yet the way he looked at me, wide-eyed with shock, I thought he was more afraid of me. This was Andy Hart, my attorney.

I stood up to greet him. I was very shy and nervous, but polite.

"Assalamu alaikum," this giant said.

He was with another attorney, Emily, and a male interpreter. They both looked terrified, too.

"Wa alaikum Assalam," I said back.

Andy looked really confused.

"Detainee 441?" he said.

"Yes," I replied.

He turned to Emily, who was visibly shaking, and to the guard. There was lots of whispering between them and flipping through their files like something was wrong.

"This is really 441?" Andy said to the guard, like maybe he was in the wrong room or with the wrong detainee.

"Just relax," I said in my best English. That made him smile.

"You're so . . . small," he said. "The guards . . . You're just not at all what I expected."

"Nothing makes sense here," I said through the interpreter.

Andy laughed and we all sat down, each of us nervous for our own reasons. Andy explained that he was a public defender who worked for the Ohio federal defender's office and he was here to help me if I wanted him to.

"Have you ever had representation?" he asked.

"No," I said. I explained to him how the private attorney I'd asked to defend me earlier had refused because they said I was al Qaeda. I told him about how I was classified as an enemy combatant and how I'd presented myself at my tribunal. Then I asked him, "Why give me an attorney now? I've been here for seven years."

He had calmed a lot by now. So had Emily. I saw real sympathy in his eyes as I told my story. With every word I spoke, they both seemed to relax more.

"You were included in a mass habeas corpus filing in 2005," Andy said. "And the Supreme Court ruled recently that even though you're here in Guantánamo, you have a constitutional right to challenge your detention." He explained how the government responded to that habeas corpus petition and Andy's office in Ohio picked up my case. "I'm here to help you."

It still didn't make a lot of sense to me, and I wasn't sure if I could trust these lawyers who wanted to represent me.

"If you convince me that as my lawyer, you can help me," I said, "then fine—you can be my lawyer." I was polite but very direct. Although Andy was nice, nothing at Guantánamo told me I could trust the Americans. "If you can't convince me," I said, "you can still represent me, but I won't come to these meetings. I won't talk to you about my case. And no matter what, I won't answer the same questions about al Qaeda. I don't want to be manipulated or feel like I'm being interrogated. I don't want to have any false hope."

Andy listened to me carefully, and then we had a long and serious conversation. I told him about all the guys who had been released without lawyers—many of them had been accused of being al Qaeda and Taliban leaders—while the camp kept others, like me, who had protested our detention and fought against torture. I told him about our treatment and the thirteen-page letter I read at my tribunal. And how they had changed their accusations over and over again, always telling me they wanted me to confess to being someone I wasn't. Always demanding that I confess to being al Qaeda or Taliban.

"Your statement didn't help," Andy said.

"I didn't come here like this," I said. "They made me."

We talked like this for hours. He explained to me that he couldn't tell me exactly why the Americans still held me—it was classified—but that he knew the details of my case and that we would have to build my defense without me ever knowing what the government knew or thought they knew about me. As the meeting came to an end, he became very quiet, like he was trying to decide if he was going to say something.

"I thought we had the wrong room when we came in," Andy said. "The guards who brought me here warned me that you were a hardened terrorist, and that you would cut my throat if you had the chance. I was told all kinds of things by the camp staff here. They even said you were the leader of a terrorist cell here." He studied my file for a minute while the interpreter finished. "And to be honest, I was really scared to meet you. I was terrified! I've worked in American prisons and defended murderers and criminals and the worst racists—really big and bad guys. But I was more terrified to meet you than anyone else in my life."

Emily let out a nervous laugh and smiled.

He told me that there were three categories of detainees: low, medium, and high risk. The high-risk ones were too dangerous to ever be released. They called these men Forever Detainees. Not only was I categorized as the highest risk of Forever Detainee, I was classified as *the* worst of the worst—the one they used as an example.

"Really!" I was surprised.

"They made an example out of the statement you read at the Administrative Review Board in 2006," he said, "when you declared that you were an enemy of the US. Some of your statement was published in newspapers."

"I was hurt and angry and confused when I wrote that," I explained. "I didn't have an attorney and it seemed like they had already made up their minds about me. It was a bad time here. Three brothers had died."

"I thought I was going to meet a monster today," Andy said. "Instead, I met you. Thank you for agreeing to meet with us. I will do whatever I can to help you."

When the guard came to get me, he was a real asshole. He yanked my chain and was rough with me. Andy told him to stop. Before I left, Andy extended his hand, confident and friendly, as if he'd known me for a long time. He was maybe the first person to see me at Guantánamo as who I thought I was and not as an animal. Me, Mansoor. Not the al Qaeda leader they said I was. Not 441. Not Smiley Troublemaker. Just me. He also crushed my hand.

"I think we're going to be good friends," Andy said.

WHILE WE WAITED for news that the camp would close, Obama's Guantánamo delegation began making recommendations to improve conditions. The camp admin resisted. They had been here too long and couldn't change the way they saw things. To them, we were at war and Guantánamo was a battleground, not a prison that needed better conditions.

Colonel Vargo came to me again one day while I was tied up and force-feeding.

"What are you still protesting for?" he said. "You're leaving!"

"You believe that?" I laughed at him. "You will see."

Brothers like me had come of age in this place and we didn't have the best view of America. The Americans knew we wouldn't have anything good to say, and worse, they were afraid we would join some battle against them if we were released. So why would they let us go?

I told Andy Hart this during one of our meetings. After just a few meetings, I came to like Andy a lot and felt I could talk to him about anything. With him, I finally felt like I was connected to the outside world and something other than Guantánamo.

"You're talking like you're the president of the United States," Andy said. "How can you be so sure?"

"Let us wait and see," I said. "You'll see. I'll be right. And we'll have to protest for better treatment."

The camp did start to change a little. They stopped searching our genitals, and we even got more time in the rec yard every day. More of us were allowed to have books and magazines. But the biggest change was that we finally got to have a call with our families.

I couldn't sleep at all the night before my call. I worried they wouldn't recognize my voice or that I'd forget the names of family members they'd talk about. Brothers and sisters had grown up. My parents had grown older and I worried about getting bad news. I'd heard stories of brothers learning on their call that their parents had died. But when I heard their voices on the other end, I felt the weight of a mountain lift off my chest. My parents were both alive and healthy! My older brother was still teaching at the same school, and two of my sisters had moved to Sana'a, where they were teaching. I cried knowing that everyone was still alive, still there, and that life hadn't stopped without me. I cried knowing that they remembered those parts of my life I had pushed away and forgotten, and now I wanted them back.

The next call didn't go as well. There were so many restrictions on both ends of our calls. We weren't allowed to tell our families anything about the camp or what we were doing. We couldn't say much more than "I'm fine." If we said anything restricted, the call was terminated. And that's what happened to me when I told my mother that "I am healthy, even though I am on hunger strike." Instantly, the call terminated. My mother was old and had traveled over six hundred miles to Sana'a to the Red Cross office. I turned crazy. But before I did anything, I calmly explained to the guards that I didn't mean to say anything about the strike, I just wanted my mother to know that I was okay. They didn't want to listen, so I activated that beast within me, 441. I hadn't seen him in a long time. I broke everything I could get my hands on: the table, chairs, the computer monitor. I pulled all the cables out. I even broke two cameras. I did all this with my legs chained to the ground.

"Don't come in!" I yelled when they came for me. "I'll hurt anyone who comes in." I did what I did because the camp admin had stopped other brothers' calls, too. Because they always found ways to use anything good to hurt us the most.

The guards came and kicked my ass and brought me back to my cell. The camp admin never forgot what I did. They couldn't believe what I did with my bare hands. They classified me as "very dangerous" after that.

THEY THOUGHT WADDAH was dangerous, too. We hadn't had any news about him since he'd disappeared to the BHU months ago except that he was on hunger strike. I didn't worry about that; I worried about how long they had kept him in the BHU. It wasn't normal to keep brothers there for so long. And then we got news from one of the nice nurses in the BHU that an IRF team had broken Waddah's back while they were restraining him to go to force-feeding. This had happened to many brothers before. When guards put us on our stomachs to be restrained, they always knelt on our backs, grinding their knees into our spines. This had happened to me and I still suffered from bad back pain. After we heard about Waddah's back, the camp admin announced that they had changed the SOPs to reduce IRFs and forced cell extractions.

I heard from a brother who had been at the BHU that Waddah was in really bad shape and had lost a lot of weight. He said that the psychologist, a really evil guy, had ordered Waddah's clothes taken away. He said Waddah couldn't walk anymore without using crutches and that he was always in a lot of pain.

I wrote letters that week to Colonel Vargo and the camp commander asking them to move Waddah back to our block so that we could take care of him. This would have been the humane thing to do. I knew what it was like to be in the BHU with no brothers around for support and that it would be hard for Waddah to recover in isolation like that. I never got a response.

The next week, I was on force-feeding when the senior medical officer pulled up a chair and sat right in front of me, very serious. He took off his hat and put it in his lap and started to ask me about how I was feeling being on hunger strike and if I'd had any thoughts about hurting myself. They did this sometimes when we were hunger-striking. They didn't really care—they just needed to pretend like they did. For some reason I can't explain, I knew something was wrong with Waddah.

I interrupted him. "Is 078 okay?" I asked. "Is there something wrong with him?"

Wa Allahi, all the blood in the SMO's face drained. He got up without finishing his questions and hurried away. I knew right then something bad had happened to Waddah. I knew.

Back at the block, I saw Fouzi at the rec yard and told him about my meeting with the SMO.

"They're not telling us something," Fouzi said.

Two days later, a camp officer came to Camp V Echo with an Arabic interpreter and told us that our brother Waddah had died in the BHU.

I had known Waddah since the very beginning of Guantánamo, when he had always passed at least one of his meals to brothers he thought needed the food more than he did. Waddah stood up for anyone, whether he knew them or not. Brothers loved him, even brothers who didn't know him well. He had fought the camp and the interrogators with us. He had honor and integrity and kept his word. He didn't deserve to die at Guantánamo just as things were starting to improve. He didn't deserve to die at all.

I dropped to my knees and cried. All of us on the block cried out for Waddah. We were consumed with sadness for days, and then we vowed to continue our hunger strike to honor Waddah.

The camp admin said that Waddah had committed suicide by hanging himself with his underwear. It didn't make any sense. The BHU had cameras in every cell, and Waddah was under something called "Direct Line Watch," which meant that a guard stood stationed at his door looking at him every minute of every day. Waddah was a fighter and he never would have taken his life like that just as we were organizing what could be the most important hunger strike yet. I didn't believe this lie any more than the same lie they told about Ali, Mana'a, and Yassir.

I was so mad. We all were. But I knew the best way to honor Waddah was for us to stay strong and united. For months, the camp admin tried to end the hunger strike and other forms of resistance by playing games with us, moving us around and hiding us. Yet every month, more brothers joined the hunger strike and more brothers were put on force-feeding. No matter where they moved us and no matter what they did, the camp couldn't stop the hunger strike from spreading.

By the beginning of 2010, Guantánamo was still open and there were no signs of it closing anytime soon. I didn't want to be right about Guantánamo not closing, but I knew I was. I started to see fear and disappointment on my brothers' faces that Obama wouldn't fulfill his promise. It was around this time that Colonel Vargo was replaced by the new colonel, Donnie Thomas, a tall Black man we called Obama.

The new colonel right away began to negotiate an end to the hunger strike. We knew we had to play it right this time, and our plan was simple. We told the new colonel that the only brother who represented all of us was Omar. We had trusted Omar for years and he had looked out for us more than any of the other brothers who wanted to speak on our behalf. The camp admin trusted him, too, because he was calm and always kept his word. I'm not exaggerating when I say he saved a few lives in the camp. He was charming and charismatic and humble. He knew how to see everyone's humanity and use it to solve problems.

Omar knew very well that closing Guantánamo wasn't going to happen, so he'd been trying to negotiate with the camp admin to improve life for us while we were there. He made the same demands of the new colonel that he'd been making all along. He wanted to end solitary confinement and get us all into communal living, like Camp 4. He wanted to end interrogations and all the hideous punishments we had suffered for years to get us to talk. He wanted to get us the proper medical treatments we needed and for the psychologists to stop punishing us in the BHU. He wanted to open up communication with our families with more phone calls and letters that didn't go through the interrogators. He wanted us to have access to TVs, newspapers, and books. He wanted us to have better food and clothes. He wanted us to be able to take classes, get an education, and begin to prepare for the day when we would be released. He wanted the guards to treat us better. None of these things were unreasonable.

We had to be strict with our brothers about the negotiation and insisted that no one else except Omar talk to the camp admin on our behalf. No one. If the new colonel or other camp admin tried to talk to anyone, the brothers had to refer them to Omar. There was one group of brothers who thought that any improvements in our daily lives would distract us from the real goal, which was to be released. Of course we wanted the camp to close, too. But that wasn't happening soon and we wanted better lives while we waited. It was complicated, and there was a real risk of brothers becoming divided about what we needed to achieve and when. I was afraid the camp admin wanted to break us apart to make it easier to give us nothing. We couldn't afford to repeat the same mistakes we'd made in 2005.

First, we insisted that Zak, the Jordanian cultural adviser who was really a torture adviser, not be included in the negotiations. Zak said he represented us, but things always came out worse when he was involved. All we had to do was count the number of brothers who had died since Zak arrived, now at five.

Omar asked that hunger strikers be treated for medical conditions that came with hunger-striking, not just fed and thrown back in isolation cells. The camp staff was really angry about that. They thought that any new privilege, even medical treatment, was like giving up ground to the enemy. They never agreed to the change.

Then Omar focused on improving living conditions. The new colonel moved fast and turned two blocks into communal living, but only for four hours a day. They did what they always did—they tried to give us the very least they could get away with. We had learned a lot during our eight years at Guantánamo; we knew how the camp admin thought better than they did, and none of the brothers agreed to move to those communal blocks. Why would we? Omar argued that everyone should be moved to communal blocks, and those blocks should be like Camp 4, where brothers had access to common space twenty hours a day.

It was a big deal when Omar came to our block to talk to us. When I saw him escorted in, I knew we would be ending our hunger strike and that things would change. He had good news: he had negotiated to convert Camp VI into communal living. If we ended our hunger strike and agreed to be compliant to the camp rules, we could join him.

I had mixed feelings. I had spent more than eight years fighting for better treatment, had even lost good friends like Waddah in the struggle, and now there was a real possibility that it would happen.

I was happy. I tried to imagine what life would be like if Omar was able to negotiate all the things he had asked for, like classes and books and news from the outside world. But would they actually categorize me as compliant if I stopped the hunger strike? If they did, would I really be able to read and study again the way I wanted? I had never been categorized as compliant and I worried what that would mean for me. Would better living conditions just distract us from fighting for what we really wanted, which was to be released? And without fighting and resisting the camp admin, would I really be able to focus on myself the way I wanted to? I worried that maybe I had changed too much at Guantánamo and lost that Mansoor who had dreamed of going to university one day.

- TWENTY -

I was ready to leave the dark ages of punishment and solitary confinement behind me, but I waited to transfer to Camp VI's communal living until all the other brothers were moved and I knew that Colonel Thomas and the new camp commander would keep their word about improving conditions. I stayed in Camp V Echo, where we had stopped fighting with the guards the way we had before. The days became longer as we waited, and we were bored, all of us—guards and brothers.

Camp V Echo was made out of shipping containers just like Oscar Block—with solid metal walls—but we had glass doors. It was also one of the only blocks in Camp V that didn't have cameras, probably so that they couldn't document abuse and inhumane conditions. Without cameras, the guards could sleep, read, play games—we even joked around sometimes with the friendly guards.

Our jokes were almost always on new guards. When new guards arrived, they were so young and fresh, and all of them had been told terrible things about us. That was where the fun began.

On the outside of each cage was a detainee card with all our information. Next to the card was a white card where guards could write notes for other guards, like restrictions, critical medical conditions and medications, punishments, and warnings.

Sometimes, working with the block sergeant and older guards, we left the new guards strange new instructions. My favorite was "bedtime stories."

One day we asked the nice female block sergeant to write BEDTIME STORY on a few of our white cards. After the last meal and prayer, she called the new guards and told them to see how many detainees needed stories.

"I counted three, sir!" one of the new guards said.

"Okay," the block sergeant said. "Let's divide up. Who wants to read stories?"

"You can't be serious," another new guard said.

"They can't sleep until someone reads them a story," the block sergeant said, "or tells them one. It's up to you."

"What kind of story do we tell them?"

"Just read to them from the books they have."

"Story time, please!" Abdul called out. "I'm tired."

Three new guards took chairs and each of them sat in front of a cage. They all looked really confused. Hamzah lay down on his bed and asked the guard to start reading from a specific page in the copy of *Men Are from Mars, Women Are from Venus* he had on top of his cage. Khalid did the same. The third guard found a *National Geographic* and started reading an article about saving energy. Everyone laughed quietly while they read, and the brothers fell asleep. When the guards were done, we all called out for more stories.

"Read me a story, please!" we called out.

Sometimes the block sergeant wrote things like HAND EATER or FLAME THROWER on our cards and made up crazy stories about how a brother had eaten guards' hands or could breathe fire. Once, the old guards told the incoming guards they needed to collect our number two before each meal. Brothers had a lot of fun with these jokes. The new guards would believe anything after what they had been told about us during their training. Usually, they figured things out in a couple days, and by the time they rotated out, they were joking around with us and planning pranks on the new rotation of young guards.

We also played jokes on brothers who were moved to Camp V Echo from Camp 4, where the living was much easier. Some of these brothers had never been to this block and knew nothing about the hard life in solitary confinement. On our block, we were only allowed to have a blanket for around seven hours a night, between 11 p.m. and 5:30 a.m. We asked the night shift block sergeant to tell one of our new brothers that the block rules said he had to give up all his clothes at 11 p.m. and sleep naked. It was a mean joke to show him what our lives had been like, but it was also our way of welcoming him to our block of the worst of the worst.

At 11 p.m., the guards went to this brother's cage.

"Hey, man," the guard said, "I need your clothes."

"What?" the brother cried out. We all heard him yelling.

"It's for your own safety," the guard said. "So you can't kill yourself. It's block rules, man."

This brother panicked. He was used to the comforts of Camp 4. He called out to us for help.

"This is solitary confinement," Hamzah called back. "It's different from where you lived."

We did this with several brothers. They always said the same things.

"I promise I won't kill myself!" he begged. Then he was reasonable. "The cell is really cold, and I can't sleep like that." Then he was nice. "Please . . . can't you make an exception?"

This guard played his role well. "Hey, man," he said, "I hear you. I do. But these are the rules for new detainees. You'll get your clothes back before morning prayer. It's only for the first week."

That new brother was silent for a while. Then the guard said, "Hey, man, if you refuse, I've gotta call the IRF team. They're gonna come and take your clothes anyway."

Some brothers would call to us again and ask us to intervene on their behalf. We had a reputation for intervening.

"We're sorry, brother," we'd call back. "If we do that, we're afraid they'll take all our clothes."

We let the guard take his shirt, flip-flops, towel, everything in his cell, and when the guard had taken everything, he said, "Please, I need your pants now." This was the cruelest part of the joke. Most brothers refused and the guard would offer a blanket in exchange for their pants. Sometimes the brother would refuse again and ask for an Arabic interpreter and the watch commander. Some got angry and shouted and cursed at the guard. That's what happened this night and we couldn't hold it in any longer. We started laughing.

The guard returned the new brother's stuff. "These guys were just messing around with you," he said.

"Animals!" this brother screamed at us. "You're all just a bunch of criminals and animals!"

That just made us laugh even more.

"Welcome, brother!" we called to him.

They couldn't stay mad at us for long. Soon there would be another new brother and they'd be in on the joke, too. A lot of the time, the jokes we played on each other played off our worst fears. Somehow these jokes helped us see each other for who we really were—just guys trying to survive. The new guards would get to know us during their rotation, and many of them realized that what they had been told about us didn't match the reality. Maybe our jokes allowed us to see the humanity in each other's fears.

TWENTY-ONE

I was still in Camp V Echo the day the Camp VI escorts came to move me. They were nice, and this surprised me. In Camp VI, I was taken to a special room normally used for meetings with attorneys and with the Red Cross. The Camp VI commander was already there with three other camp officers and an interpreter. I'd been through a lot of commanders by now and could tell almost instantly what kind of commander they would be from their body language and the way they looked at me.

"How are you doing?" each one asked, putting out their hands for a handshake.

"Welcome to Camp VI," the commander said. I think he meant it. He was a short guy, a lieutenant colonel with a kind smile. I knew right away that life under this commander would be different.

"So that's what it feels like to shake the Americans' hands!" I said to the interpreter. "It's against SOPs, you know. Where's the IRF team to welcome me?" They all laughed. "Do you know that I once got two months' punishment in isolation for shaking a man's hand?" I wasn't joking about that, but I was smiling.

"It's a new era," the commander said. "Everything's changed."

"You mean we're all new commanders here!" I said, and we all laughed.

"It's a new period for us," the commander said. "We hope you'll help us keep the peace."

"And please understand we've been living in hell for the last eight years," I said. "We have fought hard for this. We've been burned before and need to heal and maybe learn to trust you. Give us some time to adjust."

"I understand," the commander said. "Our guards need time to adjust, too."

"Look," I said, "tell your guards we're not fighting jihad. We just want to be in peace. Please promise us that when we have problems, you'll listen to us and not just come with IRF teams and pepper spray."

He nodded.

We both agreed that we were interested in everyone's safety—the brothers and the guards. The camp commander went over some of the rules and SOPs, and then he stopped suddenly. He smiled like we were maybe just wasting time.

"I get the sense that you already know the drill," he said. "Let's get you in there."

Camp VI was built as a maximum security prison, complete with communal living areas, like a real American prison. But since it opened in 2006, it had been used for solitary confinement. The communal areas intended for prisoners had instead been used as a place for guards to hang out while on duty. I couldn't imagine what communal living would be like. I was excited but cautious—nothing ever ended up being what we thought it would be and I'd learned it was safer to be prepared for the worst.

When we got to Camp VI's Echo Block, where I'd be living, the guard called Control.

"Control, this is Echo," he said into the radio. "Control, please open Echo gate for Smiley Troublemaker."

Like magic, the gate slid open. The guards gently removed my shackles.

"Fly free, Smiley!" The camp commander patted my back and I walked in.

I couldn't believe what I saw. The communal area, a place we were never allowed to be before, had several metal tables. Now brothers in tan clothes—not orange—sat around talking, eating, drinking coffee! They were smiling and laughing—just relaxing and being happy. Past the communal tables, I saw cell doors wide open. Brothers walked around freely with no shackles. I was still in my orange clothes, a color I'd been wearing for eight years and that meant I was in solitary confinement. I stuck out like a burning flame.

Brothers rushed to me and circled around, each one hugging me, welcoming me, singing to me—we were crazy with happiness. Omar, Hamzah, and Salim brought me to my cell. They had already cleaned it and set it up for me. I felt lost and confused. I couldn't hold my tears back seeing all this . . . seeing my brothers happy and not suffering. *Am I in a dream?* No, this was what we'd fought so hard to achieve, and it was real.

Brothers brought me new clothes, tan like theirs, and a special meal they had prepared from earlier meals. I sat at those tables in the hall and ate my meal freely with my brothers.

After eating, we walked around the block and the recreation area together. Everything looked very different. Everything felt different. Brothers lounged casually in their cells eating food, not worrying about guards punishing them for eating twenty minutes after mealtime. At the showers, brothers bathed with the doors closed, no guards standing outside timing them. They sang as the water flowed forever, steam rising above.

Brothers walked out to an actual recreation yard whenever they wanted, without having to wait or endure searches and chains. They exercised freely and some played soccer, laughing and happy.

I didn't know what to do, what to say, or where to go, overwhelmed by all the space and choices. I walked up and down the block, looking into cells where every door was open. Even the cells looked different now. They were still white with metal beds and no window to the outside world, but the fact that they were open and had mattresses and sheets, not just ISO mats, made them seem friendlier now.

I made my way outside to join my brothers in the rec yard. *Oh Allah!* I let my eyes travel up to the open sky and my mind relaxed taking in the vastness of all that blue. I had never seen such a beautiful sky. The tiny rec yards in solitary confinement had always been covered with green tarp. I thought about all the people outside of Guantánamo who looked up every day without realizing how precious that was, how most probably never stopped for even a second to look and explore that great expanse. I felt the sky welcome me. I felt a strong bond with it that I had never felt before. Tears ran down my cheeks again. That mountain that sat on my chest for so many years had lifted a little and the weight of it all became less. I walked around the rec yard, looking out over the fence to the small hill covered with grass and trees. I couldn't remember the last time I had looked so freely at nature. The brothers watched as my mind flew to the sky, to the hill, to nowhere and to everywhere. They all knew how it felt: every brother had the same experience when they moved to the communal blocks.

The rec yard was only a hundred feet by thirty feet, but it seemed huge to me. I felt like my legs had forgotten how to walk normally without chains, without guards, without a big canister of pepper spray in my face. It was like learning to walk for the first time. I worried that this freedom would end at any minute.

I stayed outside all day, just watching the sky. For years inside, we didn't know how to distinguish night from day. All we had were the bright lights that never went off. Even when we had rec at night, the lights washed out the sky.

At dinner, I received my food in the common area with all the other brothers, not alone in my cell, standing behind the black line with guards harassing me or watching me eat. But I had no appetite. After so many years of hunger strike and force-feeding, food wasn't that big a deal anymore. But the way we all sat together, sharing our meal, talking, laughing—it reminded me of my family and the life I'd lost.

After dinner, I lay down on the ground in the rec yard and watched blue sky turn so many colors while the sun set, before turning a beautiful black. I spent many hours by myself looking at the stars and the moon, thinking and talking to them. I told them all the things I had wanted to tell them for so long. The main lights went off at 10 p.m., leaving only a few small lights burning dimly in the block. When I came in from the rec yard to go to my cell, my eyes relaxed under the softer light. After so many years living under very bright lights, any light felt like thousands of small pins sticking into my eyes. At last, that feeling started to go away.

GUANTÁNAMO WAS LIKE a small piece of fabric woven together with threads from all over the world. We came from different backgrounds, but together we made something unique, a rare opportunity to encounter so many different experiences and perspectives. Living with the others for the first time, I wanted to learn more than how to endure the physical pain of hunger strikes, strategies to fend off an IRF team, and tactics to survive hours of stress positions.

Naturally, I spent a lot of time out in the rec yard, and one day soon after I'd moved, I heard a brother call my name from the neighboring yard.

"Hey, buddy!" Dan called to me in English. "What's up?" He had changed. His hair and beard were trimmed neat. He walked to the fence with a swagger and confidence I'd never seen on any of the other brothers.

"What happened to you?" I yelled.

I hadn't seen Dan in years, since he'd moved to Camp 4 with the compliant brothers. He was Yemeni and from a good family, his father a military general and his mother a doctor. He'd been swept up with a bunch of other Arab brothers in Pakistan and sold to the CIA just after the Americans invaded. He was about my age and had the greenest eyes I'd ever seen. He was very handsome but also very short. I think his size just made his personality bigger.

We talked through the fence. He told me how he learned English from other brothers and from the guards in Camp 4. The way he talked about English it was more than just a language, it was a part of his life now. He'd learned how to rap in Arabic and could recite poems in English. He told me how he spent those years in Camp 4 reading books in English, watching movies, and talking to the African American guards.

"At first, I just wanted to be able to talk to the female guards," he said. I remembered how he was always trying to flirt with the female guards in the open cages of Camp Delta.

One of the Camp VI guards came up to Dan.

"Yo, the King!" the guard said. They slapped hands in a complicated handshake and then did the most incredible thing—they sang a quick rap together.

I couldn't help laughing. I'd heard there was a Yemeni brother who rapped and danced like an American, but I never imagined it was Dan—I mean, the King. This was the same brother we gave a hard time for not joining our hunger strikes because it made his stomach hurt. I was still the same Smiley Troublemaker who would send him my food anyway, but he was something new.

The way he talked about music and movies and the American guards he called friends, I realized that he'd done so much more than just learn English. The way he walked, smiled . . . He was full of confidence and a style that was all his own.

Learning English had created a bridge to another world that was full of life and love and even hope for Dan, one where guards could see him and talk to him not as a detainee or a suspected terrorist, but as the King. I think the King was who Dan would have been outside of Guantánamo—he was himself. Speaking English had empowered him to do that here.

I knew a lot of English by that point. When I met with Andy, I could understand what he said most of the time. Same with the guards and officers. But I couldn't speak the language. I couldn't hold a conversation and express myself, and I felt trapped because of it. In those first days in communal living, I decided the most important thing I needed to do was to learn English.

I didn't want a kingdom like Dan's. I wanted to learn English so I could be Mansoor.

OMAR WAS NEGOTIATING with the camp commander and Colonel Thomas to get classes for us, but this was still Guantánamo, and even though things were changing, they resisted anything that would help us make our lives much better. Omar was always reading and writing and encouraging the younger brothers like me to make the most of our time here, so while we waited for classes, he encouraged me to learn English on my own. In the beginning, I didn't have anything to help me out—no books or pens or even paper. So I started with what I could get. I borrowed *Around the World in Eighty Days* from the library and read it line by line, translating each word and sentence until I understood everything. I practiced what I learned reading *USA Today* with any guards willing to spend the two minutes that SOPs allowed them to talk to detainees. I hunted for vocabulary words and definitions in anything I could get my hands on, like *Men's Health* and *National Geographic*. It was a slow and long journey.

While I learned English, life in Camp VI continued to improve. We got TVs, more magazines, better medical treatment, and better food. The new rotation of navy guards was friendlier with us, too, and I think that came from the new colonel. I was now working with Omar and Khalid in pushing the camp admin to deliver on their promises to bring classes to Camp VI—English classes, art classes, and even computer classes. We wanted to prepare for our release and try to catch up after years of isolation. Classes weren't a priority for everyone, but they were for Omar and me. Every week, we met with the camp commander and sometimes with Colonel Thomas to review our progress and go over issues we wanted addressed.

You might think all these improvements were a good thing. They were, and they weren't. By now, the US government knew that they couldn't close the camp, so they made just enough improvements to distract us from demanding our freedom. Our bodies were very weak from so many years of protests and fighting, and our health had gotten worse. Some of us had diabetes now, or heart conditions, high blood pressure, or kidney problems. With so much change and better conditions, it was hard to keep on top of camp admin the way we used to. They still only wanted to do the minimum. But we tried to keep up the pressure in our weekly meetings and I wrote letters.

Some brothers didn't want to fight anymore. They told me, "Look, Mansoor! We're tired and we need to relax. Please, let us just wait for our day in peace." I could see in their eyes they were happy with the new peace and wanted just to *be* for a little while. In this way, the US government succeeded in quieting us, at least for a little while.

I was tired, too. Life in detention wasn't easy, and it took me a long time to calm myself in communal living. The harshness of nine years of solitary confinement and fighting had obvious and lasting effects on me. Why did it take me so long to read *Around the World in Eighty Days*? I couldn't focus. I had terrible headaches and eye aches. It was hard to read and keep my thoughts together.

We also had entirely new issues to contend with in communal living, ones that would have been unthinkable in the past. Now we had to argue about things like what we could watch on TV and if we should have video games. When the camp admin brought Game Boys

to the block, a few of the older brothers appointed themselves cultural advisers and asked the guards to take them away before anyone
could even turn them on. Most of the brothers on the block wanted
to avoid any conflict, and even though they wanted to play the Game
Boys, they let the guards take them away. I didn't care about confron-
tation, and I went straight to the guards and told them to bring the
games back.

"But your brothers told us . . ." the guards started.

"They aren't the bosses," I said. "There is no boss here."

The guards were actually very nice and just trying to avoid conflict, too. They gave me the Game Boys, even though I had no idea
what to do with them. I'd never even heard of Nintendo.

"How do I turn it on?" I asked.

In just ten minutes, I learned everything about the Game Boy and
Mario Bros. and handed them over to those brothers who wanted to
play.

When one of the older brothers saw what I'd done, he came yelling, "No Nine Tendos!"

This really upset me. We had spent so many years having every
minute of our lives controlled by interrogators and guards, and now
this brother wanted to control us when we had just a little bit of
freedom?

"Who gave you the right to take them away?" I said.

"You want people around the world to see us playing Nine Tendos?" he said. "Shame on you."

"People all over the world don't give a shit about us!" I said.
"That's why we're still here."

When we all calmed down, we had a long and serious conversation about the Game Boys. Some brothers were concerned someone
could watch porn on them. I understood they were trying to protect
us, and I wanted them to understand I didn't want someone just
telling us what we could and couldn't do. I asked the guards if you

could watch pornography on the Game Boys. That made them laugh and they said you couldn't. But their word wasn't good enough for the self-appointed cultural advisers, so I called one of the camp officers and an Arabic interpreter. I really just wanted these brothers to understand that the Game Boys couldn't be used for porn, that they were just games. I wanted us to work it out so that we were all okay with the games.

"Please," I said. "I don't want you to laugh. This is a serious problem. Can you explain to these brothers that you can't watch porn movies on the Game Boys?" The camp officer thought this was really funny, too.

"Are you serious?"

"I am deadly serious," I said.

I finally talked those brothers into keeping the Game Boys. For just a little while, as we settled into our new lives in communal living, I became the advocate for things like video games and the TV. The world had left us behind and I wanted to catch up. Some brothers had never seen TVs or watched movies before. They didn't know what to do with them. We had one TV in the block and sometimes one person wanted to watch the news while another wanted to watch the Arsenal soccer game. I helped create a schedule so that brothers could sign up to watch their programs. Managing our brothers' issues was at times harder than dealing with the camp administration. It was political.

Brothers went crazy for *Mario Bros.* They called Mario "Mario the Terrorist." We took turns and played day and night for weeks. One brother used his entire body to control Mario, as if Mario was controlling him, not the other way around. I loved watching my brothers play. I loved seeing them happy. In just a few weeks, those brothers who were so opposed to the Game Boys were asking for their share of game time, too. I knew exactly what we needed. We all needed to live in our daydreams for a little while, and that's where Mario transported us. To his magical kingdom in the clouds.

FOR NINE YEARS, I had lived in solitary confinement, fighting constantly with camp admin and interrogators to improve conditions in the camp. For nine years, we had lived our lives blacked out from the world. Nine years of computers and technology had happened in the world while we fought guards with our bare hands and bodies. When we came out of isolation, we found ourselves behind the whole world.

Some of those who claimed to be our leaders had been treated well in Camp 4 and other special blocks. They had read books, watched TV and movies, and kept up on what was happening in the world. News and technology didn't pass them by. They got mostly whatever they asked for. I wasn't jealous. I didn't blame those brothers who lived there, even though everyone knew that Camp 4 was used for American propaganda to cover up the real torture. We were all free to make our own decisions. They made theirs and I made mine. I chose to spend those years fighting for others; now I wanted to focus on myself and see who I could become. I wanted to master English and learn about computers, picking up my education where it left off before Guantánamo.

Everyone knew I was reading *Around the World in Eighty Days*, and that it was taking me a long time to read. Guards stopped by my cell and cracked jokes.

"Are you living the journey day by day?" They'd laugh.

"I haven't found my sweetheart yet," I'd say. "When I find her, then my journey will end."

We had only one Arabic-English dictionary on the block and the library had limited dictionaries. Someone was always using them.

One day I was reading a *USA Today* in the yard and one of the navy guards stopped to take a look at what I was doing. He was a nice African American guy I liked to talk to. He saw how many marks I'd made in the newspaper.

"What's all that?" he said.

"Those are all the words I don't know," I said.

"Why don't you look them up in the dictionary?"

I explained my dictionary problem and he helped me go through the words I didn't understand. Then a couple of days later, that guard came to see me in my block.

"I got something for you," he said.

"Food?" I said. "Candy?" Navy guards often brought in stuff like that for other brothers.

He laughed. "It's better than all of that." He handed me an English-language Merriam-Webster dictionary. I was really surprised. "It's not Arabic-English, but this way you'll be able to look up words in English and learn even more words."

This really touched me. He had thought about something that I needed, something that would help me, and he got it for me as a gift. This was friendship, and I appreciated it.

Reading words in the dictionary wouldn't be enough, though, and I knew I needed to take classes and really study English the way I had studied Arabic. Finally, after months of negotiations, the camp admin agreed to begin offering a limited number of classes for English, "life skills," computers, and art.

Predictably, the classes were more lessons in humiliation than anything else. Just to get to the classes, which were in another now-empty block, I had to be searched three times: once when I left the block, again when I got to class, and a third time before I was allowed into the class. And even that wasn't enough—they brought in full-body scanners like in the airport to search us whenever we left our blocks. What did they think we were hiding? Once in the class, guards shackled me to the desk and to the floor. I think it was the camp admin's way of making something better yet still punishing us. It's no wonder only three other brothers showed up.

While we waited for the English teacher to arrive, the Camp VI commander came in. I called him over.

"What brings you here, 441?" he said.

"I want to master English," I said.

He looked at me like I was crazy. "Smiley," he said, "I think we hear enough from you as it is. What are you going to do when you master English?"

"I will run the camp, of course," I said. "And let you rest."

He laughed hard at that.

When the English teacher arrived, he handed out a single paper to each student and then sat down and didn't say anything. I called him over to my table and introduced myself. I reached out to shake his hand, but he wouldn't take it.

"I'm not allowed to," he said. That's when I knew for sure that the camp admin was intentionally ruining the classes.

I asked him how he was going to teach us English.

"I can bring you stories to read on one piece of paper," he said. "And you ask me questions if you have trouble understanding them."

"Aren't there any books?" I said. "Any lessons? Vocabulary? Verb conjugations?"

"Nope," he said. He wasn't trying to be difficult and neither was I. He kept his eye on the guards to see if they were watching him. I understood he was nervous talking to me.

"How can I learn English if I don't have books?" I said.

"This is what they told me to do," he said. "I'm not even supposed to talk to you like this." He looked to the guards again. "You should talk to the camp admin."

I called the watch commander with the Arabic interpreter and told him how crazy it was to call this a class.

"I understand," he said. "You need to speak with the Officer in Command." That was the Camp VI commander I talked to earlier. I told him I would be sure to bring it up in our next weekly meeting.

The other brothers in the class thanked me for speaking up and trying to make things better. They didn't understand the stories either. It was my first day of English class and I hadn't learned any English. But I thought we'd made some progress, and sometimes that's all you can do.

My first computer class was even worse. It was full of brothers and everyone had his own agenda. Some wanted to learn English, some wanted to learn how to type, some wanted to learn how to use a computer, and some just wanted to get off their block and chat. I was serious about class. I was supposed to study computers when I went to university. I'd even taken DOS classes in Yemen, but I'd never used the internet and I wanted to catch up.

I was really late to my first class because of all the body searches, and the only computer left was a half-broken laptop nobody wanted to use. The teacher just gave it to me and didn't show me how to turn it on or anything. Because we only had an hour—often less—and everyone wanted to learn something different, the teacher divided his time, which meant each of us got about five minutes of instruction.

I turned to my neighbor, Amr, for help. He was a Saudi brother who had lived in Camp 4 and was very good with computers.

"No, I won't help you!" he said. "I know you're going to use the computer for forbidden things, like watching movies or listening to music."

I was shocked. He was one of those brothers blinded by self-righteousness.

After class, I talked to Omar about what happened.

"Mansoor," he said, "you will be fine without his help. Focus on you, not him."

The next time I went to computer class, I called one of the navy guards to my table while the teacher was helping others.

"Do you have a minute to help?" I asked. "I don't know anything about this. I don't even know how to turn it on."

This navy guard was very nice and patient. He started from the very beginning and taught me how to plug in the laptop, turn it on and boot it up, log in, open programs, shut it off. I wrote everything down and drew icons. In just one hour, I learned a great deal.

Amr was so mad that I was talking to a guard.

"You're a guard, not a teacher!" he yelled. Then he demanded to talk to the camp commander. He mistook me for a brother who would tolerate his nonsense.

I turned to Amr. "And who gives you the right to tell him what his job is? When guards talk to me, it's better to keep your mouth shut and mind your own business!"

"Don't talk to guards!" he yelled at me. "I won't allow it."

Here we were in classes for the first time in nine years and he was trying to control what I could learn. Hadn't we had enough of that?

I stayed in the room after class was over and refused to leave. The teacher stayed with me.

"Thank you for what you said," the teacher said. "This guy drives us crazy. He wants to run the class."

In the next weekly meeting with the camp commander, I told him that the classes were a disgrace.

"I'm serious about learning English," I said. "That's not teaching. That's a new form of torture. That's depriving us of knowledge."

"You're already making policies," the camp commander joked. But he understood. I think he really wanted to help. Of course, he had no control over the classes, but he said he would arrange for me to meet with Colonel Thomas. I wrote up all the things we needed for the English class, and I asked the teacher to make a curriculum so we could request the necessary books, CDs, and anything else he needed to teach. The camp commander said he would write up a report documenting all my issues and suggestions. With the curriculum and the report and the list, we could talk to the camp admin and the Red Cross to push the camp to get us what we needed. Andy could help, too. And other lawyers. I continued writing official letters to Colonel Thomas with my requests.

Despite the issues, I kept attending classes and learning on my own. I wasn't shy about getting help from guards whenever I needed to. I took meticulous notes on everything in computer classes and studied on my own in my cell so that during class I could practice my typing.

Eventually, we got an Iraqi teacher named Jamal, who was very nice and well educated.

"Don't worry," he said on his very first day, "I will teach you all about a PC until you know how to do everything—even fix technical problems."

I was so happy, but he didn't last long. The next class, he told us he was leaving.

"I'm not allowed to teach you what you should know," he said. "The camp admin gave me very firm restrictions. I can't stay in a place like this, where they won't even let me teach you what kids in first grade know."

I begged him to stay and do his best. He agreed, but he only lasted another month. By that time, though, Andy had brought me English grammar books and books about Windows Vista and Microsoft Office.

Now I was learning English and Microsoft at the same time. I didn't get a lot of time with the laptop, so I read a lot in my cell to make the most of my time. In just a couple of months, I had learned a great deal—I knew the ins and outs of Windows Vista and could create any kind of document with Microsoft Office. My English was even better. I was still just learning the basics, but for me, it was a big deal, and for the first time, I was starting to imagine what a life could be like after Guantánamo.

DIFFICULT AS IT was for me, Andy was always thinking about the future and had it in his mind that when I could read and write well enough in English, he would help me get into an American college so I could begin working toward a degree. Andy came about every three months, and with every visit, we became closer. Whenever he visited, he always brought me coffee from McDonald's and tuna fish sandwiches from Subway. It was hard to get halal food in the camp, and I missed having any kind of seafood. If I was really lucky, he'd bring my favorite treat, salted almonds.

After our first meeting, I'd told Andy that if the US government wouldn't tell me why they were holding me and what evidence they had against me, there was no sense in us talking about my case. He was okay with that. He laughed sometimes, thinking aloud about the things he'd read in my file, like that one reason I was considered a threat was because I was smart and capable of leading people. He couldn't tell me why, but he was confident that based on the documents he'd seen, I had a strong habeas corpus case.

So instead of talking about my case, I told Andy about life at Guantánamo. In one meeting, I sang for him a funny song one of the brothers made up in the early years of General Miller and Camp Delta, when things were really bad and brothers were splashing guards. We'd sing this song just to the nasty guards, like the ones in the 9/4.

I have no money! I have no job! I have no food! I have no clothes! I have no freedom! I have no appointments! I have only shit to do.

Some guards and camp staff loved that song, but not the 9/4. They knew that when we sang it, they would have a bad night.

Andy laughed hard when I sang it for him.

"You need to write these stories down!" he said.

"I'll write a book," I said. "And I'll write about all the moments from Guantánamo that no one knows about."

Andy listened and laughed—he had the biggest laugh. It felt good to tell my stories and see his eyes grow big at some of the things I'd say. I told him about Nono, who was the first brother to splash

General Miller with shit, and how a guard brought him chocolate afterward as a secret thank-you, since most of the guards hated Miller just as much as we did. I told Andy how one of the guards said that Miller hated the song we sang together when brothers were taken to interrogation, and that he had nightmares where he woke up singing that song himself. I sang it for Andy: *"Go with peace, go with peace, may Allah grant you ever more peace and ever more safety. Go with peace, go with peace."* I told him to imagine forty-eight guys all singing that together in a metal shipping container.

It was strange to hear myself tell these stories and to remember everything we had been through. It was like reliving another man's nightmare. Sometimes I didn't recognize myself in those stories, like the wild twenty-year-old painting his cell with his own blood. Andy got really upset when I told him some of the worst stories, and he told me he felt ashamed that his government could do such things.

"It's more complicated than that," I said. "Guantánamo is made up of people who were ordered to do things they didn't believe in. There were always some good people, even some of the interrogators. But this place chewed them up, too." I told him about the young female guard who refused direct orders to drag me to interrogation, and about Captain Yee, the Muslim chaplain who was arrested for espionage trying to make our lives better. But the stories I liked to tell the most were about those small moments that made me laugh. Like when General Miller introduced a new rule that we had to stand in front of our cell door before guards gave us food, and my neighbor, the shortest guy at Guantánamo, got into an argument with the guard about whether or not he was standing. Talking to Andy helped me begin to understand what had happened to us and what we had lost of ourselves as we struggled to survive.

My favorite part of our meetings was hearing Andy talk about his family. After shaking hands and getting settled, he always said something like, "My family says hello and sends their kindest regards." After more than a year talking to Andy like this, I felt like I'd come to know his family, and I wished one day I would meet them. Andy was a father, and the way he talked about his family brought sunshine into the room. The love he had for them made me miss my sisters and family even more. Andy and his family brought me hope that one day I would get out of Guantánamo, start my own family, and fill a room with sunshine talking about my own children with Andy.

When we said goodbye at the end of our time together, we always shook hands, and I'd say, "Please, Andy. Give your family my kindest regards."

ANDY'S IDEA OF applying to colleges made me really want to learn to speak and write English perfectly. I'd heard about a brother who lived in Camp 4, Saifullah Paracha, a Pakistani businessman who was one of the most educated men at Guantánamo and had taught many brothers English. He had become like a father to everyone in his camp. We called him Shasha. I was so happy when he moved to Camp VI. We were in different blocks, but I saw him in the main rec yard and immediately went over and welcomed him. Right away, I understood why all the brothers and guards liked and respected him. He was gentle and sociable and didn't mind all the questions I asked him, so I asked if he would teach me English. He didn't even think about it. He simply said yes, then told me we would start the next day. No questions. There were problems though. We were in different blocks, so we could only meet at certain times and would have to talk to each other through fences, with a walkway between us. He didn't care.

The first day, I told him how I had taught myself English and what I had learned. He didn't care about any of that either. He said to me, very serious and strict, "I'm the teacher now. You will do as I say." He looked at my handwriting in English and he told me that we were going to start by learning how to write every letter in the alphabet in cursive, neatly and correctly.

"No one uses cursive," I said. Even I knew that.

"You will," he said, and that was the final word.

He told me to write ten pages of letters, which I did, but he didn't like them. He went over every single letter I wrote. There was no room for mistakes or jokes, and I learned a lot in the first couple of weeks working like this.

He wasn't just teaching me. Every day he taught from 8 a.m. to 10 p.m. He had eight groups and wanted me to move to his block, Delta, to make it easier on both of us. It was hard to move blocks, but eventually I did and joined a class with three other brothers who were better than me in reading and writing, so I had to catch up.

One of the first things we did when I changed blocks was to prepare a classroom so that Shasha had a place to teach. Cell 105 was empty, but all we had was a single chair. No table. No shelves. No chairs for students. I went to my friend Moath for help. Moath was learning how to build furniture and shelves from the recycled cardboard the camp admin threw out. He drew up plans for a table made out of cardboard, and chairs for Shasha and the students. He drew up plans for bookshelves and everything else we would need to create a real classroom.

Our brothers in Delta Block all came together and helped make everything we needed from cardboard and other recycled materials. Brothers donated books and other supplies. When we were done, we had brought Moath's vision to life. We had a bookshelf with Arabic and English dictionaries, framed instructions and classroom rules, a clock, and a table in the center.

Brothers, guards, and camp officers from all over Camp VI came to see our classroom. No one could believe what a few determined brothers had created. When we sat in that classroom, we weren't prisoners in Guantánamo anymore. We were transported away and became students.

We had physically transformed the cell into a classroom, but Shasha alone made it a space for learning. He was always pushing us to learn more, and one day in English class, he asked me and my three classmates very seriously what we would do when we left Guantánamo. For years, we couldn't think past surviving each day, let alone leaving. We had no answer, and that scared us.

"I'm going to teach you business," he said. "So that when you leave here, you can start your own business and be your own boss."

"But we're learning English," I said.

"Now you will learn English *and* business," Shasha said.

It was hard at first, and a lot of work, but it was interesting, and we were learning a lot. He gave me a notebook and instructed me to take "meeting minutes" during every class. After class, I had to write up a report of our class-turned-meeting and present it at the next meeting for him to review and sign. Shasha made us study management, self-sufficient and sustainable communities, and other business topics I had never imagined learning about. He made us write papers in English, which he examined very carefully and then had us discuss those papers in class. After about three months, he came to class one day with a new question for us.

"Do you think you could put everything we've studied into a book?"

"No!" the four of us all said at the same time. He gave us a really scary look, and we knew what was coming.

"Let me put it a different way," he said. "How long would you need to put together a book about what you've learned?"

"Three months," Khalid said.

"Two months?" I said. I knew Shasha was pushing us and I didn't want to disappoint him.

"I'll give you a month," Shasha said.

We looked at each other like he was crazy. But we got started anyway. We had to create a business, and our idea was to create one that could be self-sustaining and good for the community and the people who worked there. After going through many ideas, we settled on one that meant a lot to all four of us. We were going to create a feasibility study and business plan for the Yemen Milk and Honey Cooperative Farm. Our farm would be energy independent and offer housing for workers and schools for their children. And it would be owned and operated by the workers for the workers. We didn't have access to lots of information or sources you would normally need for a project like this. But we made do with what we had. We read whatever business books we could get our hands on. We followed business news on TV. We asked our lawyers for articles and information. We asked brothers for advice, and some of them laughed at us and made fun of what we were doing. It didn't matter. We looked for help wherever we could find it, and by the end of the month, our first draft was ready.

Shasha examined it and gave us some notes and more time to work on it. He wanted two copies this time, one in Arabic and one in English, both handwritten with graphs, pictures, and notes. When we handed it in, our boss wasn't satisfied and he ordered us to redo it all. For the third draft, instead of photographs, we hired artists to il-lustrate everything. We revised and revised until we finally got every piece of artwork perfect. Finally, our project was up to his standards, and now he ordered us to organize an official presentation of our book and findings to the public.

Some brothers in other blocks wanted to read it, but neither the camp admin nor the interrogators would make copies for us. In fact, the interrogators threatened to confiscate it. So I asked the psychol-ogist, a nice guy who was amazed at what we had written. He made copies for us.

We were really proud of what we had accomplished. We had learned English and business and how to work as a team. Shasha was even more proud of our work.

For the opening ceremony and presentation, we invited brothers from two blocks plus camp staff and guards. We had sweets and refreshments. And the psychologist brought twelve copies of the book for us. Each of us had to present a section of our work to the audience. I introduced the project and talked about our plans to generate electricity to be energy independent. At the end, Shasha delivered a speech about the importance of education and knowing business and encouraged other brothers to learn business and other useful skills before leaving. Then we handed out copies of the book to other blocks. Those brothers who'd made fun of us early on were the first ones to request books.

Everyone was surprised by how professional we were and how much we knew about business. Just a couple months before, we had no idea what we were going to do, and that day we presented ourselves as real experts and businessmen.

Our book became a hot topic all over Guantánamo. We sent a copy to the colonel and to the camp, telling them this is what we could do with good classes. I sent a copy to Andy to use for my college applications.

It even made it into the news when the *Miami Herald* published an article about us headlined "Gitmo Inc.: 5 'Forever Prisoners' Have Business Plan for When They're Free Again." We were entering a new golden age at Guantánamo, and we were all starting to look forward to our futures.

I HADN'T SEEN Andy in months, since I'd started studying English with Shasha, and I was excited to hear what he thought about the Yemen Milk and Honey Co-op. Andy arrived this day with coffee from McDonald's and a clamshell of Yemeni food and no interpreter. Right away I got so lost in the fragrance of cumin, coriander,

cardamom, and cinnamon that filled the room—a smell that transported me back home—I didn't notice he didn't have an interpreter.

Andy put his things down, shook my hand, and sat. "My parents
send you their kindest regards," he said. "I'm sorry I couldn't arrange
an interpreter."

"Just relax," I said. "You know my father used to make lamb mandi.
You bake it in the ground for hours and hours in a pit covered with hot
coals and sand."

Andy looked at me with wide eyes and the biggest smile I'd ever
seen.

"Your English!" he cried.

"Yes," I said. "It's okay? Good enough that we don't need that
interpreter?"

Andy jumped up and shook my hand again with both of his. He
just stared at me like he couldn't believe his eyes. He looked at me
really proudly, like a father.

We sat down and he slid the clamshell over to me, still smiling
about my English.

"It's meat and rice, just like you asked," he said.

I pushed the box back. "Please," I said, "you must eat with me."

"I brought it for you," he said. "That's a gift."

"The gift is eating together," I said. "It's our custom. Do you want
to shame me?" I was joking, but serious. He didn't have a spoon or
fork because of the camp security, so I showed him how we eat in
Yemen, scooping some rice and meat in your fingers like they're a
spoon. Andy struggled and I could tell it was his first time. It meant
a lot to me to share a meal like this.

He never got the business plan I sent him, so I told him all about
Shasha and my business class with Khalid. I was talking fast, the way
I always do. Andy interrupted.

"Hold your horses!" he said. "Whoa."

"What does this mean?" I asked. I'd never heard this phrase before. "We don't have horses in the mountains. We have only donkeys."

Andy laughed so hard he fell back in his chair. "It means slow down," he said.

"Okay," I said. "I'll switch to donkey speed."

I talked and talked and finally, when our meal was over and hours had passed and I still had more stories to tell him, he had to go.

He decided that day that he would start applying to colleges for me. He'd done some research and had found programs that offered remote learning for guys who were in prison. Before he left, he got serious with me.

"Please write your stories down," Andy said. "Write them in English and send them to me. There's just too much to talk about when we're together and they're important stories to tell."

ONE OF THE letters I wrote to Andy right away was about the animals at Guantánamo, how they always brought us a sense of comfort and good feelings, and how they always found ways to get to us. I wrote that when we fed the animals, whether banana rats, cats, or iguanas like Princess, we felt love and happiness in our hearts. We felt connected to the animals, connected in our souls, actually. We loved them all, except the woodpecker who hammered day and night on the ventilation shafts, making more noise than even the vacuums. We joked that that woodpecker was sent by the interrogators to torture us even in our cages.

In Camp VI, we managed to bring a couple cats into the rec yard, and soon they had kittens. We treated them like family. We fed them milk and rice, and sometimes tuna fish from our meetings with lawyers. We gave them showers and washed them with the shampoo our lawyers gave us. Our cats were very clean and smelled nice. We had a feeding schedule and shared cleaning up after them. When brothers forgot to feed the cats or they got angry, the cats peed and pooped in the common area or in front of our cells. When they were really mad at us, they pooped on the tables where we ate.

When one of the mom cats had kittens, we all got very excited but worried. Mom cat went into one of the drainpipes where it was safe and that's where she gave birth.

We played with those lovely kitties until they were too tired to play. They grew up quickly and soon they were having kitties of their own. Even at Guantánamo, life continued.

There was one male kitten who grew up and didn't know how to breed. This became a big topic on the block.

"I think we should call a nurse and see if his equipment works," Hamzah said.

"Maybe our little friend has a psychological problem," Khalid said. "Maybe we should call the psychologist and she can ask him if he wants to hurt himself."

We all laughed at that.

"No," Omar said. "She'll want to take him to the BHU and we know what happens there. We want to keep him safe."

"Maybe he needs a sex education class," Omar said. "Mansoor can write a letter to the camp commander."

We laughed hard. We were just a bunch of brothers sitting around the communal tables sharing coffee. These were the best moments, just being with friends and joking.

Joking around like this might seem like a simple thing, but it was a big deal for us. We had been in communal living for less than a year and we were adjusting. Sitting around talking together without vacuums and fans or guards harassing us really changed our lives. We had been friends and brothers for years—since the very beginning. We had forged deep bonds fighting and resisting the camp admin and interrogators. But we had still experienced the worst of Guantánamo alone, in our cages or in interrogations. In these casual conversations, where we sat around drinking coffee, we processed what we had been through, and that somehow made us feel like we hadn't been alone. We remembered together our experiences: First being brought to Guantánamo, the first time we saw an iguana or banana rat. The fights we had. The bad guards—those who'd broken my ankle, those who'd taken Omar's prosthetic leg—and the good, like the one who'd given Khalid a slice of bread when he was on food punishment. The worst interrogators and the kind nurses who treated us humanely. We remembered the brothers we lost: Yassir, Mana'a, Ali, Waddah, al-Amri, Hajji Nassim (Inayatullah), and Awal Gul. And our remembering together made our losses and those solitary experiences real and a part of all our memories. It validated them and reminded us that, even though we were in solitary confinement or isolation or thousands of miles from the ones we loved, we had never been completely alone. It reminded us how we had grown older together and how we had become our own kind of family. A family with cats.

- TWENTY-TWO -

We were at the peak of the golden age when Moath made his own windows. One opened east to Makkah and the sun rising over a vast blue sea dotted with ships and palm trees swaying gently in the morning light. The other window opened west to the most beautiful sunset, palm trees so close you could touch them, birds flying freely, and the sea a deep and mysterious blue. People came from all over to enjoy those windows and his other work. No one was jealous, except maybe some of the guards. The camp admin didn't know how to feel about them.

It wasn't easy making windows. But Moath could make anything once he set his mind to it. He made AC vent covers out of boxes. The levers were controlled by a string hanging above his bed. He could turn the air on and off or change the breeze's direction. There was a little compartment in the box controlled by another string where he could put a piece of scented paper (usually a cologne sample from *Men's Health*) to make the air smell nice.

Camp VI was a terrible place. No windows. Solid concrete walls. Steel cells on the inside. Two stories that made any sound echo and boom all over the block. Once inside, we couldn't tell if it was day or night. If we were lucky, our block had a window in the common hall ceiling, but it was hard to know what kind of light it was—daylight or fake. The guards called it "maximum security." We called it many things. A black hole. Maximum control. The cemetery. Hell. And since moving into communal living, we'd spent a lot of time and energy trying to change it from the inside, to make it more livable and humane. We had gotten the camp admin to hang sound-absorbing banners in the common area to help soften the echo. And now we were chipping away at the prison's bleak interior with our own beautiful artwork that showed who we were.

I had a lot of bad memories of a hard life in these cells, and even with the golden age, it wasn't easy to make our prison a happy place. Those same bare cells where we once lived in complete isolation twenty-four hours a day were now open twenty hours a day, and we could walk freely anywhere in the block or recreation yard, even to other blocks. How does one adjust to such a life when every inch of that space is a reminder of the years spent isolated? We tested our freedom daily, pushed it forward little by little, and started to reclaim ourselves.

MOATH WAS INSTALLING curtains over his windows when the camp commander stopped by his cell and looked in. He had gone a long way in relaxing the rules since the beginning of communal living and I felt like he had come to respect us.

"You're not allowed to have a mopstick on the block," he said. We weren't allowed to have anything that could be used as a weapon. This also included paintbrushes, needles, and scissors. At least we had nail clippers. It's amazing what you can do with a pair of nail clippers. You could build a ship.

"It's not a mopstick," Moath said. "Everything you see is made of nothing." He pulled down the curtain rod Velcroed to the wall and showed him.

The commander laughed. "Plastic bottles?"

Moath saved plastic bottles, stacked and glued them together, then wrapped them in white paper so that they looked like a real pole that was perfectly straight and strong. Nothing went to waste.

"Wow!" The commander laughed. "Smart!" He joked with us all the time, especially when Moath made something new. "If you managed to make all this with nothing, what the hell would you do if you had actual stuff?"

"We would build a helicopter and fly away." We all laughed hard. It was the truth.

Over the years, we had learned to make use of everything we had. We had so little that small things we once took for granted could change our lives. Take for example a piece of clear plastic that usually covered our meals. The air conditioning was always on and our cells were always cold. Sometimes we didn't have clothes or blankets. Before 2010, covering the vents could get us sent to solitary confinement, or worse. But if the guards forgot to collect that clear plastic with our meal trash, we put a little soap around the edges and glued it over the vent. The guards couldn't see it and that thin skin of plastic stopped the flow of cold air from freezing our cells.

Our work was more than practical. From the beginning of Camp X-Ray, we had been creating, and those small acts were our escape. Some of us wrote on Styrofoam cups and plates. We used spoons or twisted the tiny stems off apples to write poems or draw flowers, hearts, the moon. We made flowers out of stickers we found on fruit. These were tiny expressions of our former selves breaking through, resisting the identities imprinted on us. These simple expressions were as necessary as food and water, and they were always punished. Even an etching of a flower was not a flower; it was a message to Osama bin Laden and a national security threat. For years, it was a game we played with the camp admin. We took nothing and made something, and what is more human than that? In turn, they took whatever we made and punished us to prove that we weren't.

We continued to push our boundaries when the Arab Spring finally arrived at Guantánamo. Some brothers marched through our blocks chanting slogans for change. We threw out our block leaders and elected new ones. We protested the camp again and demanded reforms and better living conditions. We protested for better classes. Guantánamo Spring wasn't violent—there was no blood or killing or beating, but no one knew about it but us.

By now, it was clear that Obama wasn't going to close Guantánamo. With a new law passed by Congress, he wasn't even releasing brothers anymore, even ones who had been approved to be released. Instead, they made our detention more bearable and humane. The camp admin under Colonel Thomas had relaxed the rules even more than we expected. We got new health care, better food, video calls with families, uncensored letters, books, CDs, newspapers, magazines, and even PlayStation 3s. We got a refrigerator and microwave. I had never seen or even heard about a microwave before Guantánamo. Shah liked to use it to dry his fancy boxer shorts. For eight years it was against SOPs for detainees to have cold water. Then one day we were able to put a cup of water in a refrigerator.

Instead of battling navy guards, we became friends with them. The navy, which had been in charge of Guantánamo since 2005, had one year left under its command and that made for a unique situation with the guards—they stopped caring about punishing us and enforcing SOPs that made no sense. Now they gave us all sorts of contraband, like watches, DVD players, sunglasses, and even sewing needles. The camp administration knew about everything but watched us from a distance. They were testing us to see if we would fight less with fewer rules and less interaction with the guards. It worked. They left us alone for the most part, and though they conducted block searches every now and then, they barely ever confiscated any of our contraband. It was a game we played: How much could we get away with? One of the guards told me, "Be careful with that stuff. The administration writes reports about everything, and one day they'll use those reports as an excuse to lock down the camp."

We'd learned to be skeptical, but for now, we couldn't help taking advantage of our new freedom.

More important than the things they gave us was the freedom we had over our lives and our contact with the world. It might sound simple, but just being able to have a pen and paper in my cell changed my life. I could write whenever I wanted. Being able to have a clock and a watch gave me power over my life I hadn't had in years. I created a daily regimen to make the most out of every day. I'd wake up and pray, do some exercise in the rec yard, and then read before breakfast. I had time scheduled for classes with Shasha, reading, and tutoring brothers in Arabic and English. Every day I set aside time to walk around the rec yard with Adnan and Omar to talk to brothers and collect stories for my two books.

The first book evolved out of the stories I had collected for Andy. I called it "Moments from Guantánamo," and it was just that—a big collection of small moments from our daily lives that captured the conflicts and friendships I didn't want lost forever to this place. I always had a notebook and pen in my pocket, even when I played soccer in the rec yard. We collected stories about black sites and torture and countries that helped kidnap and sell us to the CIA. We collected stories about sexy late-night pizza parties thrown by female interrogators for detainees who were cooperating with interrogators. As much as we'd seen, we were constantly surprised by the stories brothers had to tell, stories we never could have imagined or made up.

The other book was inspired by our interrogators. For years they had accused us of being al Qaeda and Taliban. When I came to Guantánamo, I didn't know a lot about those groups—I don't think many brothers did. So Adnan and I decided we would learn everything we could about al Qaeda and the Taliban and write a comprehensive history of them and how they related to Guantánamo. We talked to brothers and detainees who knew firsthand stories about bin Laden fighting the Soviets in Afghanistan or his activities in Sudan, guerrilla wars, al Qaeda training camps and ideology, and Taliban history. I even interviewed one of the founders of the Taliban and several of bin Laden's bodyguards. I thought that if I knew everything about al Qaeda and the Taliban, about what the Americans called extremists, then I would be able to understand what they saw in me that justified keeping me for so long. I would learn what crimes I had committed. But I didn't find what I was looking for.

I wrote mostly in Arabic, but practiced writing stories in English for Andy, trying to make each letter a perfect gift for him. I'd write a story and give it to Shasha to read first, and he would give me notes for revising. Sometimes I asked guards to read the stories to see what they thought, and then I made more changes to get the stories just right. Every couple of weeks I sent Andy my stories as letters through legal mail. Working on these books helped me make sense of this place and what had happened to us. It was my way of processing and even reclaiming the power to tell the world who I was in my own words, not the interrogators'. They could control my life, but I wouldn't allow them to define it.

WHILE I WROTE about our lives, other brothers used the art classes to express their experiences in drawings and paintings. Of course, as always, we had to work to get better art classes and supplies.

"We're afraid that some of your brothers will use art materials to make poison and kill themselves," one of the officers said to me.

"Why would we want to kill ourselves in such a caring environment?" I responded.

We protested. We asked for better teachers who were artists. We asked for better materials and more paints. We asked for colors—colored paints, colored paper, color photographs. Eventually, we convinced them that we weren't a threat to ourselves and they let us have colored paints we could use in the classroom. And then Adam came and art at Guantánamo really took off.

Adam was an Iraqi art teacher with a PhD who truly cared about making sure we had the tools and inspiration to dig deep and express ourselves through art. It didn't matter if we were drawing a flower or building a ship out of cardboard like Moath, Adam believed art allowed us to be who we really were. He worked with the camp admin to find brushes and paints that brothers could use in their cells instead of just in the art class. He made sure that each brother in art class had his own box of pastel paints. When I had a class with him, I didn't know what to draw and he told me just to draw something that I loved or missed. I was embarrassed at first, but he knew how to encourage me and I drew a beautiful rose. Too bad the camp admin wouldn't let me keep it. Adam knew how to inspire brothers to look inside themselves for creativity.

By the time art classes got better, the class had been moved to a building outside of the camp—constructed in 2007 but never used. We could just walk through the camp gate, through the rec yard, right to class, but the body searches never stopped—security concerns!—so most brothers didn't want to go. There was one brother, Sabri, one of the camp's best artists, who always went. Art was so important to him; he would put up with any humiliation just to have access to paints and a canvas. In this hell, being able to create art transported him away.

In art classes, we could draw whatever we wanted from photographs, books, magazines, or our memories, so long as it wasn't about being at Guantánamo or being tortured and didn't show guards or the military or anything political that would make the camp mad or embarrass America. But we had to finish our drawings in one class, and we couldn't take them back to our cells or blocks. With much protest and some patience, even that changed.

Little by little we were allowed to put up artwork in our cells. The first piece that went up was a ship Sabri drew before art classes began. Sabri used to use his letter-writing time with the Red Cross to draw instead of write letters. A brother who was in love with the sea had asked him to draw a ship. With just a short little Red Cross pen and legal paper, Sabri drew a beautiful ship over four feet long covering eight separate sheets of paper. The details were beautiful. Now the brother hung it up in his cell using soap. Everyone admired that drawing, even the guards.

One of the most important developments was when the camp admin allowed the Red Cross to bring us photos that we could keep in our cells. Photos of animals, cars, motorcycles, the sky, the sea, oceans, trees, and flowers, my favorite. We had spent years with no color in our lives except for the orange of our clothes, the green tarps covering all the fences, the gray of raw concrete, and the dull green paint on our cell walls. Those photos brought *color* into the block and into our lives again.

We couldn't have real flowers or trees, but we could make them, and that's what we did. Most of our early creations began in art class with a simple outline drawn on cardboard, like a flower. If we were making a flower, we gathered photos of flowers from magazines. We couldn't use scissors—a security risk—so we asked the guards to cut those flowers for us or we tore them ourselves. Then we glued them to the cardboard cutout in the shape of a flower, making a beautiful collage. I loved flowers and missed them so much. When I'd made a bunch of flowers, I created a cardboard vase for them. Eventually, I grew a large collection of many different flowers in beautiful colors. Creating these pieces was teamwork. Some guards had blisters on their fingers and joked, "I found my new career: cutting cardboard."

I made many of those vases and gave them to friends—guards, nurses, and some camp staff. I was good friends with an Italian navy guard who helped me practice English. He told me one day that he was going home to visit his mother and that she worried about him working at Guantánamo. I saw how much he loved her, and that made me miss my mother even more. Before he went home, I gave him a vase with cut flowers I had made. Guards weren't allowed to accept gifts from us—according to SOPs, they weren't even allowed to talk to us!—but just like he broke the rules to talk to me, he also broke them to accept my gift for his mother.

"Please, send my best regards to her," I said. "Tell her this gift is from 441."

He smiled and I could tell it was a happy smile. When he came back from his holiday, he came to visit me on the block.

"When I told my mom who made those flowers, her jaw dropped to the floor," he said. "She asked me a lot of questions about you. She doesn't worry about me now." This warmed my soul. "She says thank you and sends you her best regards back."

She was a complete stranger to me, but knowing that his mother had sent me her regards—that still warms me to this day. We started to feel like humans again. I had missed that part of my life very much. I wanted to be seen as a normal person again, not as a terrorist. *Oh Allah.* How I missed that part of my life.

MOATH'S WINDOWS DIDN'T just appear; they evolved over time. We lived in windowless cells and Moath asked himself, *How can I open a window?* At first, he took photographs from magazines and pasted them on his wall with soap. He had trees and mountains, but they were just photographs on a wall. Then he thought of something else—a windmill. Wouldn't it be amazing to have a windmill in his cell? So he made one out of Styrofoam cups and hung it in front of the AC vent. The guards didn't make him take it down. They liked it, and he asked himself, *What else can I build?*

I was like Moath's assistant and helped him with all his big projects. For the windows, we started with a simple shelf for his cell. We melted soap in water for a few days until it was softer than dough. Next, we ripped up a lot of recycled paper and soaked it with the soap. Then we shaped it into pieces that would fit into the corner. We used more melted soap to glue the pieces to the wall and we had to stand there holding them securely until they dried. It took hours, and sometimes we took turns holding that shelf up until the soap dried. When it was dry, it was so securely attached to the wall, it could actually hold books. We waited to see how the camp administration would react. They didn't say anything, so we made more. This single invention allowed us to keep and organize things in our cells. This is how we created the desks and shelves for Shasha's classroom.

Then Moath built a small model ship with masts, sails, and rigging. He built it from cardboard, mop string, cups, and shampoo bottles, cutting all the pieces with nail clippers. It was incredible. It looked like it was made of wood. Word spread, and Colonel Thomas and the general requested to see it. The camp administration took it and brought it back after a few days. After that, the Camp VI commander said guards could cut cardboard for whatever we needed.

And so began the cardboard industry at Guantánamo. We discovered that soap could also glue together larger cardboard pieces from the boxes used to bring our meals. Moath and other artists would draw up plans for something they wanted to make, breaking it down into parts that could be constructed from cardboard. Guards became a very important part of our work, cutting the shapes we needed. Without rulers or tape measures to measure accurately, we made our own from sheets and towels. Before gluing, we used the concrete floor to sand the edges smooth so that each piece fit perfectly together. That was the hardest part—the cement was smooth, so it took a lot of work. Assembling the first joint in a new piece of furniture could take an entire day or two to dry, and someone had to hold it in place the whole time. We took turns. The act of creation took teamwork and patience—supplies abundant at Guantánamo. We started with more shelves, but moved on to desks, storage boxes, side tables, dressers and cabinets for clothes, toilet covers, Qur'an stands, chairs, picture frames . . . if we could imagine it, we created it.

Most blocks had cells they turned into workshops. Some brothers hoarded cardboard so they could build desks or dressers, which required lots of boxes and took months to save. Moath and other craftsmen supervised and gave instructions, and when everything was ready, they would go to the cell to install the pieces together. I wasn't a craftsman, but I was always helping Moath, especially when he built his ships.

When we were gluing a mast one day on a ship Moath was building, he turned to me with the most serene look on his face. "When I'm working on my ships," he said, "it's like I'm out at sea, free from this place."

Keeping busy kept our minds calm and distracted from where we were.

Supplies were limited and the only place to get colored paints, glue, and nice paper was in art class. Going to art class still meant going through body searches, so many brothers didn't go. We asked the camp admin to let us have art materials on the block. It was too hard to change SOPs, but the camp commander told guards to let us have supplies in our cells.

"Not a lot," he said. "Just a reasonable amount."

In time, Adam, the art teacher, got us glue, acrylic paints, and other materials to use outside of class to make our work better. He was very popular among our brothers for his kindness and support. He had trouble getting brushes for the paint, but after a long discussion we managed to get brushes with soft plastic handles instead of wood.

With paint and clean paper we crafted real furniture—chairs you could sit in, desks you could write on—that looked like it was made from wood. The camp administration also agreed to let us have more glue, tape, Velcro, and markers. They saw the value in keeping us busy. If you wanted to make something, you had to collect cardboard, glue, paint, paper, bottle caps, and other things. We started a market, selling to one another. You might pay thirty pieces of cardboard and ten bottles of glue for a used cabinet. Even more for a new one. Sometimes we used real US dollars to buy from each other, or guards would take our money and buy us supplies, which required trust and secrecy on both sides.

We didn't stop with furniture. We made things we weren't allowed to have or even to see. We made trees—yes, trees!—that stood six feet tall, full of beautiful green leaves, fruit, and birds. You would never believe they weren't real. We made jambiya, Yemeni ceremonial daggers, and dallah, long-spouted Arabic coffeepots. We made model cars, motorcycles, and even the mosques of Makkah and Jerusalem. One brother saved ice-cream sticks for months and made a palace with a beautiful garden. It took him over a year to finish. He was always asking other blocks for their ice-cream sticks. One of the most beautiful pieces was an ornate lantern made by a Bedouin brother. When we had blackouts in the camp, our brothers called out, "Bring the lantern!"

Moath made his windows this way. He built the frames from cardboard with hinged shutters he could close. Inside, he made a sculpture with trees and birds, and behind them a painting of the sea and beautiful skies. This was his window to the outside world and the home he dreamed of having one day. They weren't just his windows; they were ours, and that included the navy guards who helped cut the cardboard.

The most important piece we created was the communal library Moath designed. It took us six months to build. When it was finished, it was six feet tall, with shelves for books, magazines, and CDs. Underneath the shelves were rows of drawers that opened with handles made of shampoo-bottle caps. Below the drawers were cabinets with beautifully painted doors. We had an indexing system with cards so we could find what we wanted easily. We had nothing, and from that nothing we created life and order.

As I ASSISTED Moath and worked on my books, I learned that to be an artist you must harness your fear to take risks, question rules, and dare to cross boundaries. For years, our brothers in Camp 4 had all the privileges while we suffered, and they hadn't created anything. No art. No furniture. Fear of losing their privileges had chained them. While there were some wonderful poets among the compliant brothers, few wrote anything down. The brothers like me who had resisted the camp admin with our bodies and had lived in isolation for years were now the ones most dedicated to creating art. At first, I just thought that we were hungry to claw back any part of ourselves we had lost during those nine years and art was our way of doing that. But I also wondered if maybe we had been artists all along, that self-expression was a part of us, and that our resistance was our way of expressing our humanity and showing the world a raw part of ourselves.

As we had spread resistance, now we helped spread art-making. Art eventually came to every block in Camp VI, even to those who didn't want to go through body searches to get to art class. Adam gave supplies to anyone who wanted to create art in the block, and talented artists like Sabri, Rabbani, and Moath gave lessons. Most brothers wanted to create art that told the stories of their survival in this place. This defined us as artists: we found beauty where there was none and communicated our experiences to others.

The sea was prominent in a lot of artwork. Though we still couldn't see the ocean, brothers had held on to those images from the hurricane. The ships sailing the open waters connected us to our freedom. But the vessels were always empty, ghost ships sailing an in-finite sea. It wasn't all about freedom though. Brothers created paintings with chains, tall fences, hooded men in orange jumpsuits, Statues of Liberty, and other symbols that told our painful collective story. For some reason the camp admin didn't take them away.

We put beauty in everything, even in the communal hall where we hung signs drawn in ornate Arabic calligraphy. We had signs there with schedules for cleaning, TV time, sleep, soccer matches, and a big sign with prayer times in Arabic and in English to avoid any misunderstandings. The kitchen had signs with rules everywhere, some painted specifically for brothers who were messy or never followed the rules. One brother had a sweet tooth and always ate the desserts we saved from our meals. We had to put signs on our food, like DON'T EAT MY CAKE! We had a sign with rules written in Arabic and in English—agreed upon, of course, with the camp officer—that had a man dressed half in orange and half in a military uniform to represent how the rules were for both brothers and guards. Our monochrome world of gray exploded with color and life.

Our cells became outward reflections of ourselves. The best cells belonged to the artists—Moath, Sabri, and Rabbani—and looked like museums. Of course, we had to fight to get the privilege to keep artwork in the block instead of just in art class. In my cell I had a cardboard desk and chair, where I wrote early drafts of what would become this book. A curtain separated my toilet from the rest of the room, and I had shelves by the sink to hold my toiletries. Bookshelves held my books: *Longman Dictionary of Contemporary English*, *Around the World in Eighty Days*, *The Hunger Games*, and *Harry Potter and the Sorcerer's Stone*. Above my desk was a flowered picture frame I had made and inside was the photograph a friend had given me of his daughter, the most important object I owned. It reminded me of the life I dreamed of having. On another wall was a sign a friend had made for me with the words TIME IS LIFE written in beautiful Arabic calligraphy. Those were my words, and they inspired me every day to make the most of my life by learning and being kind.

At night, I caught guards walking around the block taking in all we had created. They'd stop and examine a new book in our library or stare at a painting Sabri had just finished. They admired our trees, our signs, and maybe most of all Moath's windows looking out to a better world.

WE WERE LEARNING, transforming our world, and there was still so much we didn't know. We'd taught each other plenty of classes over the years, trying to keep our minds busy imagining what we would do when we were finally released. A journalist from Al Jazeera had taught a good course about journalism. A brother in the Mafia had taught a class on stealing cars—which we would never do, but it was good knowledge to have. A former chef had taught a cooking class. Of course, we couldn't cook on our block, so we had to imagine everything. He walked us through the market in our minds, picking out chicken, picking up vegetables, feeling them, smelling them. Then we cooked. "Now, I will add the onion to the hot oil—*shhhh shhhh*." He imitated the sound of onions frying because of course we had no onions or oil or stoves. He joked, asking us to please taste the dishes to test for salt, and even to imagine getting burned. I didn't like that class.

One topic we were all starving to know more about was marriage. There were only about 160 of us left at Guantánamo, and many of us were young and single and had become men in this place. We were starved for any information about what life would be like when we got out and could start families of our own. Younger brothers were always showering the older married brothers with questions about love and marriage. When a brother told a story about a woman or love, we listened very carefully, taking in every word. Kareem, an older married brother, saw how hungry we were, and he decided to teach us about married life so that we would be prepared when we left this place. He called it "marriage class." It was my favorite.

Until I was twelve, I thought I had been born from my mother's knee. I learned in school where babies really came from, but my knowledge remained theoretical. The same was true for most of us.

Even so, women were one of our favorite topics of conversation. Not in a bad way; as Muslims, we're forbidden to talk about women in a bad way. But we talked about women because it relaxed us. While we were surrounded by men, we imagined loving women.

On our first day of marriage class, Kareem began by asking us each to say what we thought about how men should treat women. We agreed that men should have absolute respect for women, but many of the students said men always were, and always would be, superior to women.

Then he asked, "If you were a woman, how would you answer my question? How would you want men to treat you?"

At first, we started laughing, imagining each other as women.

"Look at Mansoor with hair all over his body," one brother shouted at me. "You would scare all the men."

"If I were a woman," another said, "I would make you all dream, cry, and spend all your money—but none of your ugly faces would touch a single hair of mine."

Kareem let us joke for a while but then said, "Answer my question, ladies!"

I said that if I were going to choose someone to accompany me for the rest of my life, I would want a wife who was better than me.

One of the students tried to embarrass me by saying, "So will you let your wife be in charge? Should men just be like donkeys, serving women?"

"This is where the problem is," I said. I argued that men have considered themselves superior throughout history but look where we are now. War follows war without end. Men never give birth to a single soul. They only harvest lives.

I said that all of us, guilty or innocent, were sitting around Guantánamo talking about marriage instead of experiencing it because of what men had done. I finished by pointing out that we all knew that when there was a female commander in charge of our guards, we lived more peaceful lives.

"Mansoor is biased toward women," one brother said with a laugh.

"No!" I said. "It's simple. Women give love and life. What do we as men give? I think every man should ask himself that question."

"I can give some love!" the King said. "I just need a woman. I'm tired of looking at your hairy faces." The King could always break the tension in class with a joke.

We passed many classes debating like that and took our debates about women with us to the rec yard. I think we all started to think differently. The moments I remember most were when we talked about love and what it felt like. Very few of us had felt the sweetness of love and we had a lot of questions. The idea of love that we talked about in class would help us overcome all the pain we felt. Love was the foundation for everything in marriage and family life—not just love, mutual love.

When I thought of my life after Guantánamo and imagined getting married and one day having kids, I was warmed by love and that gave me hope.

As we kept meeting for marriage class, Kareem taught us about loving and being loved. He described what it would feel like when we saw and talked to the woman we loved. He told us how we would act on our engagement day.

Our final class was dedicated to the biggest day in our lives, the marriage day. We pretended that Khalid was getting married and planned a traditional Yemeni wedding celebration. We wrapped a sheet around him and put another on his head like a Yemeni wedding outfit.

"Today we are going to have a wedding party!" Kareem announced like he was welcoming his guests.

"Who's the bride?" Zakaria asked.

"The Wrestler!" Hamzah joked.

"Noooooooooo!" Khalid cried. "Not her!"

We sang and danced all night as if it were a real marriage. We began with Yemeni dancing, moved to Afghani, back to Pakistani, back to Saudi dancing . . . we learned the dances of all our brothers' homes and then we ended with our own new dance that brought them all together. We called it the Guantánamo dance.

It was a lovely time that returned us to our homes and families, if only for one night. We lived in a golden age, but it was still a hell. Even in that hell, we created small, beautiful moments that made us feel alive again.

The next morning, we asked our brother how his first night was with his new bride, the Wrestler. But we didn't talk about the first night of marriage in class. It was too embarrassing for all of us, so we talked about it in private with Kareem.

I had never been in love, but now I felt its sweetness and knew what I had missed out on. My twenties ended in this place, and even though I was preparing myself for the day I would get out, I didn't know when that would be or how I would find a wife. Sometimes I would just sit by myself, away from everyone, and live in my own secret world where I had a wife and two daughters who loved me very much. I would escape to my cell and just lie on my bed and beam myself to that warm world where I loved my beautiful wife in a way that no one else could. We were best friends. We loved each other. We talked, fought, made up, laughed . . . just lived our lives together. My secret world brought peace and tranquility to my heart.

One day, I was lying on my bed in my cell, my eyes closed, a big smile on my face, when Moath came in.

"Mansoor!" he called. He had been trying to get my attention for some time. I finally opened my eyes. "Where were you?" he asked.

"I was with my wife and my daughter, Amal," I said.

"Brother," he said very seriously. "I think you're turning crazy."

Yes, I was going crazy, but in my own way. In my reality, I didn't know what it meant to have a woman in my life, but in my dreams, I could live the life they took from me, the life I hoped might still be out there. If such sweetness could take me away from the hell I lived in, how much sweeter would it be in real life? I dreamed about the day I would find out.

Since living together in Camp VI, we had become like a big happy family, and we looked out for each other the way a family should. It was nice to have this break. Yes, we had fought with the guards for years, but the past was the past and we were in a new time at Guantánamo. I saw the guards as men and women with their own lives and problems, not just as soldiers. I liked those young guards. I spent a lot of time talking to them, advising them to leave the military. I stuck up for them sometimes when I thought the camp commander or colonel was treating them unfairly, like when I wrote letters to the camp admin to get tents for the rec yard so guards could have some shade. I think I connected with those guards because they were the same age I was when I was taken to Guantánamo. I was thirty years old now, and even though I was the age of a man who would be married with children, I felt like I had missed an important period of my life, one lost forever. I felt that void, and talking to the younger guards helped fill it. I think I was trying to recapture my youth, hoping it wasn't too late.

The golden age allowed us all to look at who we could be if the camp let us be ourselves. Writing, painting, learning, building our little piece of cardboard heaven helped connect us all while maintaining a rare calm across the camp. The guards behaved and so did we. I looked around at the calmness and thought, *What would the camp admin lose if they just left us alone until they started the Review Boards again and gave us our freedom?*

- TWENTY-THREE -

Obama made life better at Guantánamo instead of closing it. We all knew this, but we didn't know what that meant for our freedom. We were afraid to lose the little hope we had. So we kept our minds busy as the navy transitioned control of Camp VI to the army. Because Guantánamo was run by a joint task force, commanders and control of the camps rotated between the army and navy. We had been under control of the army before, and we had a very bad history with them. The army considered Guantánamo a war zone, and we were the front line. Making matters worse, fewer than two dozen brothers had been released in the past two years. The hearings had stopped and even our attorneys felt like nothing was happening.

Some army officers didn't like the golden age we had created under the navy. They thought we had taken too much. To them, we weren't artisans and students, we were terrorists, and they wanted to see us suffer the way we did before 2010. One of those men was the officer who'd written the Camp VI SOPs in 2006. He'd become a facilities inspector after leaving Guantánamo, and when he returned at the end of 2011 to inspect Camp VI, he was really pissed off at what he found.

"Smiley Troublemaker!" he laughed when we met again. "You're not on hunger strike anymore—I see how it is now."

"I don't need to be on hunger strike anymore," I said. "After you left, everything went just fine." I spoke English very well by this time and that surprised him. "You're a lieutenant colonel? How did that happen?"

I don't know what he wrote in his inspection report or what he recommended for the incoming army colonel replacing Colonel Thomas, but in 2012 things started to change quickly. Colonel Bogdan had spent years in Iraq and saw us only as a threat to be contained. While Colonel Thomas ran the camp thinking that less interaction with guards and more freedom would make for less tension, the new colonel believed that tougher rules enforced strictly would eliminate the security conditions for tension. The first thing he did was tighten all the rules the navy had relaxed. The camp admin stopped bringing us recycled cardboard. Then Velcro, then markers, and then paint.

It wasn't just the art supplies. They changed the SOPs and started to take away privileges. A new rotation of nasty army guards started harassing us again with cell searches and body searches. We were all on edge, waiting for the next hammer to fall. None of us wanted to go back to the way things were, and every day brought more fear and anxiety that things would change.

Then they took Adnan away to the BHU, and we felt like the message was clear. The army wanted to provoke us, harass us, punish us, and send the camp back to the way it was even before 2005.

"The camp rules must be followed," Colonel Bogdan said to me the first time we met.

"I think you should review the camp's history," I said. "Most of us spent more than eight years in solitary confinement, always fighting with the camp admin. The life you see now is peaceful."

"We have security and safety concerns," he said. "And my job is to keep everyone safe."

"Your government says we are 'the worst of the worst,' but tell me please, how many guards have been hurt? How many have died? How many have been threatened? How many times have block doors been accidentally left open? How many times have your guards lost their keys and we returned them?"

He looked at me, surprised.

"For two years we've lived in peace and calm, and you want to change that over cardboard you throw away? That trash kept us busy, so let us be busy. Let us escape the feeling of being in prison instead of trying to escape."

"Okay," he said. "I'll try to regulate what we give. Don't take a lot of stuff. We'll keep it for you in an empty block, and when you need it, you ask the guards to bring it."

But just like always, he didn't keep his word and the peace didn't last long. Omar tried to secure another deal with camp admin and that didn't work either. The army enforced the new SOPs. They stopped giving us supplies, and life went back to darkness. Then we heard that Adnan had been moved to an isolation cell in Camp V. I wrote letters about the conditions and about Adnan to Colonel Bogdan and to the admiral in charge of the entire base, but the admiral never came to the camp. No one seemed to care.

It wasn't long after that that we heard Adnan had died. They said it was another suicide but we had our doubts. I wrote letters to the White House, to Congress, to the United Nations, to the Red Cross, and to aliens in space but nothing happened. Nothing. It's like we had been forgotten again. We had only one choice—we would prepare to go on hunger strike. This was the only peaceful protest that could get their attention.

One day, I saw Colonel Bogdan escorting a group of high-ranking military personnel through Camp VI. One officer was taking notes and I could tell they were up to something. I got as close to them as I could.

"Don't you think you've done enough to us by holding us here for so many years?" I called out. Brothers in the block gathered around to listen. One of the high-ranking army officers came over to me.

"Excuse me," he said, "but you chose to be here."

"And how is that?" I said.

"You chose to be in Afghanistan."

"So, you Americans kidnap people from all over the world and then tell them, 'You chose to be here'?" I said. "I was in Afghanistan. Yes, this is my fault. That doesn't give you the right to hold me forever without any rights or justice. To just forget about me. What about those men who were kidnapped from different countries and brought here? What do you tell them? What if some government kidnapped your son and held him without charges and no rights? What would you say to that?" I looked around at our block. "Is this what American greatness is about?"

His group called to him. Before he left, he looked at me and said, "You'll make a great lawyer."

"Exactly," I said.

I hadn't changed anything, but at least I felt like he had heard me. That's what speaking English did for me now.

I overheard officers talking as they left. They were already planning to take away our privileges. They talked about locking down the blocks, shutting down communal living, and opening them up again as solitary confinement with stricter rules and no privileges. They didn't see the world we had created and how it had brought calm and peace to the camp. They didn't want to. They only saw terrorists who needed to be detained.

THEY STARTED HARASSING us, especially my block where many of the artists and old troublemakers lived. They targeted us with more frequent and invasive block searches and took from us things that we had had for years, like our paints and brushes and DVD players. They took belongings our attorneys had given us, our families had sent us, even things guards and interrogators had given us as incentives. It didn't matter what they took—books, CDs, clothes—they just wanted to punish us. They made new rules that restricted what we could do and what we could have. They stopped classes. They even took away medical care. It was obvious that all the harassment was intended to provoke us into fighting with the guards again to prove we were just jihadists ready for battle. When they didn't get the reaction they wanted, they sent their worst officer to search us.

It had been years since we had negotiated with the camp admin to stop guards and camp staff from touching or searching our Qur'ans. Anyone who had spent time here knew this was just common sense. So many of our fights with guards had been over our Qur'ans. We had agreed that instead of guards or camp staff searching our Qur'ans, the block leader would collect them from brothers and go through them in front of the guards to show that we weren't hiding anything in them.

This army officer went to the one block in Camp VI that was mostly Afghani brothers who just wanted to be left alone. The communal camp had had so many arguments and so many troubles over what games to play, what TV shows to watch, what to eat, and these brothers just wanted a simple life. So they'd moved to one block together. They listened to the radio. They read. They prayed. They didn't have a TV so that they wouldn't argue over what channel to watch. They just wanted to be. When the block leader collected the Qur'ans, this army officer insisted on searching the Qur'ans himself. Remember, the Afghans were very protective of their Qur'ans. It was clear the camp admin wanted to provoke a reaction.

"You're not allowed to do that," the block leader said.

"I don't give a damn," the officer said. He was arrogant and careless. He grabbed the Qur'ans and searched them himself. It was like declaring war.

The next day, that officer went to another block to search, and they refused the search. Everything escalated after that. The camp admin said that we could be hiding weapons in our blocks if we were refusing searches. We covered the cameras in our blocks so they couldn't see us and brothers started going on hunger strike.

Block leaders tried to negotiate a deal with the camp admin over the Qur'an searches, but they sent the same officer who'd initially searched the Qur'ans, and that made us even more determined to continue until they agreed to stop Qur'an searches. They refused that one point—one we had dealt with so many lifetimes ago—and that's why all negotiations failed.

Over the last two years, we had pushed beneath the surface questions about when we would be released, too afraid to face the possible answers. Now those unspoken questions rose to the surface again and we had no choice but to address them. Going on strike wasn't just about the Qur'ans or losing privileges; it was about our future. The beginning was difficult, but soon it was like Mr. Hunger Strike had never left my side.

Because many of us had attorneys, our stories started to get out to the world. The camp admin didn't like that we were getting media attention and showing the world that conditions had gotten worse, not better. It was embarrassing for them, but it didn't have to be.

We didn't have a plan, but sometimes the best plan is to not have a plan at all. That is what made the hunger strike so powerful.

The camp admin tried to use time against us. They thought we wouldn't last long this time. We didn't plan to take the hunger strike far; we started off just making a point about the Qur'an searches. We just waited. Most of us didn't expect the camp admin to actually shut down communal living.

But Zak, the cultural adviser, had gotten involved with the colonel. They were together all the time and Zak was advising him to take control of us. I don't know why, but he hated us.

Within twenty-five days of the Qur'an search, Camp VI had turned into a death camp. Almost everyone was on strike. We survived on water, salt, sugar, and coffee. We lost a lot of weight. Some of us fainted all the time. We were all traveling to death together, on a slow and painful journey. We lay in our cells with empty stomachs and worn-down bodies, in pain, too hungry to sleep. Our dreams were all about food.

It wasn't the first time we became skeletons. And unlike all the previous hunger strikes, we weren't locked in isolation cells. But we were too weak to even talk or move around. Walking down the stairs for prayer was like walking a million miles. We prayed three times a day instead of five because we didn't have the energy. The few brothers who were still going to art classes stopped. Soccer stopped. Even our poor cats had to stop eating and go on hunger strike with us. I was so ashamed we had no food or milk to give them, but we were now all in this together. Life stopped. The camp became a morgue.

Of course, the psychologists never stopped coming. They sent their assistants to ask us the regular questions: Are you eating well? Do you sleep well? Do you have any dreams? Do you want to hurt yourself? Do you want to kill yourself?

We stopped talking to them. We refused to leave our block, even for medical checks. The guards watched us through the cameras. They told us that they couldn't even recognize some of us—that we looked like we had risen from the dead. We hoped the media would push the camp admin to stop their new policies. But nothing changed.

On the fortieth day, the administration declared war.

It's difficult to sleep when your body is feeding on itself. You feel every nibble of muscle. Some of us slept outside in the recreation yard to keep our minds clear. The weather was nice at night, and it was delicious to taste the freedom of escaping our freezing cells.

I heard the first shot just after two in the morning. I thought it was a dream, and then I heard our brother scream in pain. Soldiers lined the outside of the fence and one had shot a brother at close range with rubber bullets.

I ran to help him, but soldiers shot at me, too. I turned and walked back toward the block and was met by a hundred guards in body armor, shields, and dogs. Outside the block, more soldiers surrounded us with armored cars and heavy guns.

"Get inside!" the guards shouted. It was chaos straight from *The Hunger Games.*

I smiled. I don't why. Maybe because I couldn't believe what I saw. Maybe because I knew all along that this is where we would end up. Maybe because we had fooled ourselves falling asleep in this dream that was still Guantánamo and always would be. Maybe because I was just too weak to do anything else.

I heard more gunshots and saw another brother hit.

"THIS IS A LOCKDOWN!" an interpreter repeated in Arabic over a loudspeaker.

There were fewer than a hundred men living between seven blocks in all of Camp VI. Some blocks had fewer than ten detainees living in them. My block had fifteen. Maybe the Pentagon didn't understand that or made a mistake or got confused. We were half-dead on hunger strike and they sent an army to deal with our corpses. I hadn't seen so many soldiers since we destroyed Oscar Block.

We didn't resist. We couldn't even walk. Still, they shot us with rubber bullets, tear gas, pepper spray. They beat us and set their dogs on us.

They rounded us up and locked us in our cells, and that was the end of Phase I of their crackdown.

Phase II began with the guards' chaplain dancing into our block, guards laughing behind him. He danced straight to our lovely library, the one we'd spent six months building. As he danced, he kicked it as hard as he could. First the doors, then the drawers. The guards joined him like a pack of hyenas. The library didn't stand a chance. They didn't stop until it had been beaten to death and packed into trash bags.

Then they set out in pairs and tore down shelves, paintings, signs, everything we had made. Some of my brothers shouted. Some cried. Some called the guards savages. The cardboard furniture didn't break easily. We were good craftsmen. The guards kicked and punched and worked themselves up into a sweat.

Once the common areas had been stripped, the guards came to our cells in teams of six wearing body armor and riot gear, just like the days of IRFs.

"Look at these cells!"

"This is fucking better than my room."

They beat us, shackled us, pushed us hard against the walls, and searched our genitals like they used to, in the worst way possible. They took our clothes, the clothes we had made or altered or colored, and gave us orange shirts and pants—the uniforms we hadn't worn in years. They sat us outside our cells and then went in and got started on their real work.

"Looks like a fucking hotel in here."

"Not for long!" They stripped everything off the walls and broke it all—desks, picture frames, shelves, artwork—they spared nothing.

Then they returned us back to those empty cells.

We listened for hours as they went from cell to cell.

"Hey, guys, watch this shit!" a guard yelled. Then he threw the Popsicle-stick palace with the garden over the second-floor railing. When it hit the ground, it shattered into a thousand pieces.

"Awesome, man!"

"More! More! More!" guards chanted and laughed.

Our beautiful trees? Over the railing.

When they found paintings, they critiqued them first.

"This is pretty enough to clean your nasty ass with," a guard snickered.

Or they pretended to be one of us.

"Look at my beautiful painting! I used my dick to paint it."

If we tried to reason with them, they mocked us.

"Why?" They laughed. "No!" they screamed like they were children. "Can't you see that I'm an artist?"

If we asked them to please save a painting, they taunted us.

"You mean this?" a guard said while ripping the painting he was holding.

If any of us protested, pepper spray.

We'd built our own worlds in those cells, where we were allowed to be human again. Where we dared to reveal who we really were. Determined not to let the guards strip him of everything, one of our brothers called the guards over to his cell. He tore down his paintings. He tore down his shelves. "We are better than this," he said, handing everything through his bean hole. "We aren't the savages." They tore it all to pieces.

They saved Moath's cell—the best—for last. They tore down his shelves, his curtains with the most perfect curtain rod, the AC vent box, and the windmill, the first piece he'd created. Then they took down his windows. The windows he had created for all of us to look out onto a better world and the dream of freedom and one day home. The guards stomped those windows with their boots. They kicked them. They tore the shutters off their hinges and shredded the palm trees. Just like that, our cardboard heaven was gone.

When the guards finished picking the block clean of everything that had given us life, that proved we were alive, we stood at our cell windows and watched them stuff the remains into trash bags. The colonel and a group of officers inspected the empty block. Their mission was a success. They had shown us.

We'd created a small, simple life from scraps. We had connected with each other, with guards, and with the world beyond our cells through the simple act of opening ourselves up and expressing ourselves. If that was so threatening, nothing would change their minds. But it didn't matter what they saw in us. We had regained ourselves, something they couldn't take away from us ever again. And we were determined to fight for it.

THE CAMP ADMIN closed communal living the way they had planned to all along, and now they treated us worse than the first days of Camp X-Ray. What they didn't understand was that the hunger strike wasn't about art or contraband or even living conditions—it was about life. Our lives.

It was clear now that there was no end in sight to our indefinite detention. This really scared us and made us realize we had nothing to lose and everything to gain.

The lockdown didn't stop the hunger strike. Instead, it inspired more brothers to join, and within days our numbers spiked to include everyone in Camp VI except two brothers who had serious medical conditions. The camp admin had spent years keeping hunger strikers separated from each other in solitary confinement blocks or spread out between all the camps. But now we were all together, mostly in Camp VI, and we united.

We knew how they were going to try to stop the strike before they did. I knew the drill. First, they put me and all the other hunger strikers back in the orange outfits of noncompliant detainees and locked us in our empty cells. They took away our toothbrushes, toothpaste, soap, blankets, books, letters—everything except ISO mats—and once again we were in our colorless world where we had nothing. They put us back on a program of sleep deprivation and harassment. Guards woke us up every twenty minutes to make sure we were "still alive." They started IRFs again and the use of pepper spray. If I didn't show guards that I was awake and alive when they banged on my cell door, guards called an IRF team. I think we know what happened then. Pepper spray. Five well-fed guards slamming into me. Me on my stomach, my arms and legs tied behind my back. And, of course, their favorite humiliation: pulling down my pants and searching my genitals in the worst possible way. Yes, they even started routine genital searches again.

If guards weren't waking us up or searching our asses, they were busy making as much noise as possible. We'd been through this before, but we didn't have the energy to resist anymore. All I could do was refuse to leave my cell and continue the hunger strike. That's what we all did.

Others joined us from outside of Guantánamo, and it felt like finally the world had found us again after we had been lost for so many years. Families in Yemen and in countries around the world organized protests demanding our release. Andy and dozens of other attorneys signed a letter to Secretary of Defense Chuck Hagel detailing how bad conditions were in the camp under the new command.

While our voices grew stronger with the help of our supporters, the camp admin tried the same tactics they had used for years to undermine our simple demands—they told the world that we were terrorists and jihadists and that our hunger strike was our way of waging war in prison. Through DNN, we heard that Colonel Bogdan held a press conference to show all the weapons they'd confiscated during the crackdown. He had a table spread with curtain rods made from bottle caps and weights fashioned out of water bottles and broomsticks that the camp admin had allowed us to use instead of metal weights, which were a security risk. When asked the number of detainees on hunger strike, Zak downplayed how many of us were on strike and instead told reporters that a hard-core cell of extremists was determined to hunger-strike until many of us died, as if we had made a suicide pact.

I didn't want to die, but I also didn't want to spend the rest of my life in this place for something I didn't do. There were no easy choices, but I chose my path. We all did. I spent fifty-seven days without food, surviving on just water, the longest I'd ever gone before being forced into force-feeding. I lost more than sixty pounds in that time, and I was so tired and exhausted that I prayed to Allah to take my soul. Just months earlier, I had been working out in the rec yard, and now I could barely hold my head up. Some brothers weighed only eighty-five pounds. One brother was in a coma in the intensive care unit. I had never felt closer to death, and that's when the camp admin moved me to the BHU, where I began to get IV infusions. They were separating leaders and instigators, hoping it would stop the strike. I couldn't help thinking about Waddah and how he died there years ago. I wondered if I would be next.

In the BHU, my body started to shut down, even with the infusions. My mouth was dry all the time and I was thirsty. I couldn't sleep, even though I was exhausted. I couldn't hear well, and my vision was getting blurry. I could barely stand up or walk, so I just lay on my mattress. I really thought I might die, and I tried to find peace within myself. It wasn't what I wanted. I wanted a life on the outside. I wanted a wife and a family. I wanted to see my parents one last time. But if Allah wished it, I would let it be.

One night, after I finished my last prayer, I lay down and fell into a deep, deep sleep where I dreamed that I was resting beside a small stream of water. In this dream, I could barely keep my eyes open as I struggled between life and death. Above me, at my head, stood a woman weeping, her hands raised in prayer to Allah. I watched her tears drop into the water, and then I leaned over to drink from the stream. As soon as the water touched my lips, I was jolted awake.

I hadn't been asleep for long, only five minutes maybe. But I felt a deep sense of peace and tranquility in my heart. I had never felt that way before. All the pain and tiredness and exhaustion, all the hunger and thirst I had felt for weeks was gone. As I remembered my dream, I recognized the woman as Maryam, *peace be upon her*, the mother of the prophet Jesus, *peace be upon him*. I cried but I was also elated. I knew that Maryam was praying for me. I knew that I drank from her tears. May Allah grant her the highest level in paradise. With that dream, I knew I would have the strength to continue my hunger strike until the end. I knew I wouldn't die. I knew I would survive Guantánamo.

The days after that melted into weeks at the BHU and my world blurred again. I remember certain moments clearly as if they just happened to me yesterday. I remember they started force-feedings again, twice a day as they had before. I remember the sting of the tube when it first entered my nose and the explosion in my sinuses that made me cry. I remember the kind nurse we called Katniss talking about how there were so many brothers in bad shape that the camp admin had set up force-feedings in Camp VI, Camp V, the BHU, Camp Echo, and the hospital.

"It's a big mess," she said.

I remember the kindness and sympathy in her green eyes when she said she understood why we were on strike. "I would do the same thing if I was in your shoes."

I remember asking Katniss to please do my feeding instead of a male nurse who was always rough with me. He always put the tube in without enough lubricant.

"You mean the guy training from Israel?" she said. I remember how casually she said it then went on to tell me how the camp admin brought in teams from other countries to help out with the feedings and to train on live patients. I had been through so much, but I could still be shocked at what the camp did.

I remember writing letters to Andy giving him updates about what had happened to me and asking when he would visit again. I even asked him to bring me Yemeni food—I said that if he did, I would suspend my hunger strike for that one day just to taste the comfort of home again.

I remember the blinding pain of kidney stones and the doctors telling me they wanted to do a procedure to help me, and I remember writing to Andy and asking him to give me advice on what I should do because I didn't trust the doctors at Guantánamo.

I remember I had one phone call and that it was with my sister calling from Sana'a with my cousin, and I didn't say anything about the hunger strike or how I was in the BHU or what happened during the lockdown. I was so happy to hear their voices but sad and confused that my mother wasn't on the call. My sister talked a lot and avoided the questions I asked about my youngest brother and my younger sister, who still hadn't been on a call with me. I was weak, but I still pressed my sister until she told me that my youngest brother had died of cancer and my sister had drowned swimming in a mountain spring. This was the same sister I had always herded goats with. They had kept the news from me for years, worried that it would make me too sad. Every time I'd talked to my family, I'd asked about them and why they weren't on the call—my mother was very good at making up excuses. My brother was only six years old when I left home for Sana'a. He was so young. I had missed seeing him grow up. I couldn't believe that he had died. My sister had been my best friend.

I remember wanting so desperately to be with my mother, to see her, to feel her touch, to hear her voice tell me that everything would be okay. I was so sad for her having to suffer tragedy and protect me all that time. She knew how much I loved them. I loved them so much. I was devastated. I had been through so much those past twelve years but nothing compared to the pain in my heart from this loss in my life. What really hurt the most was that I didn't get to see them one last time, and now I worried I would never see any of my family again.

I remember soon after that call I was moved to the detainees' hospital to remove the kidney stones. I was lying in bed after the procedure, still heartbroken and trying to escape the feeling of being alive, when my cell door opened and someone came in. Who would dare come into my cell without first restraining me? I opened my eyes and saw a male nurse in his thirties standing at my side. He had such a kind face with soft eyes that put me at ease. He brought a chair close to my bed and sat down next to me. He put his hand on my shoulder.

"Be strong, my friend," he said. He talked to me for a while, trying to give me some hope and strength that life would get better, something to help me keep going. "One step at a time," he said. "That's all we can do. Put one foot in front of the other and keep moving forward." His sympathy touched my heart and gave me hope. I heard later that he was one of the nurses who had refused to force-feed us while we were on the hunger strike.

I remember around the time of Ramadan, the colonel negotiated a compromise with brothers still living in Camp VI to reopen the communal living, but this time with strict restrictions and only for twelve hours a day. The colonel also said that guards wouldn't search Qur'ans any longer, the same promise they'd made for years and always broke. It didn't matter anymore. None of us wanted to move back there after what had happened. More important were the rumors that the hunger strike forced Obama to wake up and refocus his attention on Guantánamo. It had been two years since Congress stopped the release of detainees to countries they considered too dangerous or that had hosted terrorists. Yemen was one of those countries and there were more than eighty Yemenis still at Guantánamo. Obama was going to lift that ban and he appointed someone to negotiate detainee transfers. There was talk of hearings, something called Periodic Review Board hearings that would determine whether or not we were national security threats or could be released. There was even talk again of closing Guantánamo.

Like many brothers, I decided to stop my hunger strike with the beginning of Ramadan. I had lost so much over the past year. I lost the freedom of Camp VI and communal living. I lost my friend Adnan, and I had lost my brother and sister. I almost lost my will to live. But we had to lose everything before we could finally win. We lost our golden age, but we won a hard-earned, real hope that we would be released and that there was finally an end in sight to our detention.

- TWENTY-FOUR -

Soon after Eid al-Fitr, the holy day that celebrates the end of Ramadan, we began to see the fruits of our hunger strike when two brothers were released—the first in more than two years. This felt like a good sign, that after more than ten years of fighting, we had finally brought about real change. I stayed in the BHU for several months afterward, recovering from the hunger strike and building up my strength again. Most brothers began to end their hunger strikes with Eid al-Fitr, but some continued on through the summer to see if the changes announced were just temporary and if the Periodic Review Board hearings would really begin. There were a lot of conversations about the PRBs and I wanted to talk to Andy. I knew he wouldn't be able to represent me—for some reason, no federal defenders could—but he'd encouraged me earlier to take any review boards seriously if they started again.

I hadn't heard from Andy in months though. At first, I thought he was just busy and that I'd eventually hear from him. But other brothers he represented hadn't heard from him either. I started to get upset and worried. I knew other brothers whose attorneys had dropped their cases and just disappeared. What had I done to make him stop writing to me like that?

WHEN I STARTED gaining weight again, they moved me to Camp Echo. They were splitting us up between camps so we couldn't lead more protests. I was fine with that. Camp Echo was where they kept some high-value detainees and those who were leaving. It was all free-standing cottages, and each cottage was divided up into two cells. It was comfortable with showers and a meeting cage, but they were still cages. Shasha was close by, too. He thought that maybe they'd moved him there to keep him from having a heart attack, but the camp admin never did anything out of kindness, and I wondered what they wanted from us.

Soon after I arrived, I was told I had an appointment with the FBI about the books I'd written while I was in Camp VI. They'd taken my only drafts and I worried I wouldn't get them back. I'd poured my life into collecting those stories. They were like my children, and the camp admin just kidnapped them and took them away. It killed me. I'd written letters to the colonel and the camp admin every week asking to have them returned, but I never got an answer.

When I met with the FBI, they told me that interpreters had read my books and passed them on to analysts and the FBI and that they had a lot of questions. I had my own questions, like *Where are my books?*

I met with two officers, maybe in their thirties, one a couple years older than the other. They seemed like they were new at this.

"I have one question for you," the younger agent said. He was a nice guy and hadn't been rough with me at all. "How did you manage to gather all this information?"

"I have no idea what you're talking about," I said.

He laughed.

"No, really," his partner said. "I understand you talked to a lot of guys to put these books together. Why would they talk to you? Why would they tell you all this stuff—all these stories?"

The other cut in on him. "We want to know who these guys are you're talking about. There's a lot we don't understand. Like, what dialect did you write in?"

I laughed. "I wrote in my tribe's dialect," I said. "You don't understand my Arabic? Shame on you. You should study harder." I'd also used symbols, initials, and numbers for the names of brothers and detainees in my stories and in my al Qaeda history. I didn't want to get anyone in trouble. And I'd promised all the brothers I talked to that I wouldn't use their names. Besides, I didn't think I'd written anything that those brothers hadn't said in interrogations.

"We know you're smart, 441," the older agent said. "But we're always smarter."

"If you're Mr. Smart," I said, "then why are you asking me about this stuff now? You've been asking these brothers the same questions I asked. Maybe you weren't listening. Or maybe you aren't as smart as you think you are."

"This guy is really something," the younger one said.

"So, are you going to let me have my books back?" I said. "Even if just for a couple days so I can read them one more time?"

They all laughed.

"What books?" the older FBI agent said. "Were we talking about books? Did you lose something?" He was trying to be funny about it, I think, like we were all playing a game. But this was plain cruel.

So this was why they moved me to Camp Echo.

I thought that after our meeting, I would be moved back to Camp V, but I wasn't. For some reason they left me, and right away I created good relationships with the guards. This is one of my best qualities and what I consider my most important survival skill and secret weapon. I like to talk and I was always asking guards questions about camp affairs, other detainees, stuff like that. I wasn't being nosy or trying to be a snitch, I was just curious. I just liked to talk.

One day, one of the guards I had become friends with asked me one of the strangest questions. He was a really nice Native American guy who wasn't afraid to talk to me. I'd told him all about my village and my tribe and he'd told me about his.

"Smiley," he said, "is it true what's written about you in your files?"

My file was classified. I'd never even seen my file, and Andy told me that I never would. I didn't think guards were allowed to see our files either. I didn't know what he was talking about, but I didn't want him to know that. I'd had more than ten years of interrogation training from some of America's finest, and dumbest, interrogators. I probably could have done their jobs better than most of them by now. I played it cool.

"Tell me which part you want to know is true," I said, "and I promise I'll tell you."

"It says you were the general of the 055 Arab Brigade," he said.

I was shocked. This was the first time I'd heard that. I knew they thought I was some kind of leader, but this was new to me. In all my conversations with brothers about al Qaeda while writing my books, I'd never heard of this brigade. I played along with my guard friend to understand what they were looking for.

"I'm sorry," I said. "But this information is classified."

We laughed and he waited for me to answer and when I didn't, I think he understood that it really was classified and he didn't ask me about it again.

I had an interrogator at the time I called Jason. Yes, after more than twelve years of being in Guantánamo, I was still going to interrogations. I think they were just studying us now, to see how we engaged with each other and adapted to new situations like the crackdown. Jason was a good guy, young and just married. He and his wife were expecting their first baby. At our next meeting, I burst into the interrogation room with a lot of questions.

"I want to know more about this 055 Arab Brigade!" I said.

"That's what we've been trying to get you to tell us all along," he said without even thinking. Jason was young and inexperienced, and he'd broken the most basic rule of interrogations: don't reveal your objective. I talked to him very casually, like I knew everything in my file. I'd learned this technique from *Criminal Minds* and *Lie to Me*. I found out they thought this Adel, the name I was sold under when I was eighteen, was the name of an Egyptian general who commanded an elite Arab fighting force under direct orders of Osama bin Laden. Really!

They believed he planned the embassy bombing in Nairobi and had lived in England. They even believed he had plastic surgery to look young and different, I guess to look like me. I couldn't say how many interrogations and torture sessions I'd suffered through being told I was this guy, this general in bin Laden's army. The Americans thought of us as puzzles to solve. I may have only had a high school education, but I was smart enough to figure this one out: Can an eighteen-year-old Yemeni, with a Yemeni accent, who speaks a specific tribal dialect and doesn't speak English, really be an English-speaking, middle-aged Egyptian general who's also the leader of an experienced Arab army? They tried for years to hammer a square into a circle, but they couldn't. Here was my own puzzle: How could this have been so complicated?

ANDY NEVER ANSWERED my letters, but I finally got a letter from his friend Carlos, another attorney in the northern Ohio federal public defender's office. Carlos requested a call with me so we could talk, but he didn't say why. I was worried.

"I have bad news for you," Carlos said when I got on the phone. "I'm sorry to be the one to tell you this, but your friend Andy Hart died a few months ago."

"I don't understand," I said. "Please, can you say that again?"

He told me again and I just hung up the phone. I couldn't talk. I couldn't move. You think you've been through so much and that nothing can shock you or hurt you anymore . . . but Andy's death was like a dagger in my heart. I thought how Andy had helped breathe hope into my life. I cried thinking about how sad and devastated his parents must be to have lost their son. I cried all the way back to my cell.

One of the nice female guards saw me.

"Hey, are you okay, man?" she said. Another guard gave her a hard time for talking to me, and she stepped away. The cruelty of that place knew no end.

That night, I thought about my first meeting with Andy, when I was hard on him about defending me. I had been so cut off from the world and so hurt, and Andy had helped me heal a little. I was sorry I had been upset with him for not writing back all those months.

I told the other brothers Andy represented that he'd died, and they were deeply sad, too. He was one of the first Americans to treat us as humans and friends. Andy was the best attorney, but I thought of him as more than just a lawyer; he was one of my best friends. I wrote a letter to his parents, telling them how much Andy meant to me and how he was such a kind and wonderful person. I begged the camp admin to give back the dictionary Andy had given me, which they'd taken the night of the lockdown. It was the only thing I had to remember him. It wasn't dangerous or contraband. It was just a dictionary. What could be so dangerous about that? But the camp admin refused.

I HAD LOST more than just my good friend. I had lost my attorney, my adviser, and the one person on the outside who believed in me continuing my education and going to college. Obama had ordered the PRBs to start and everyone was talking about them. This really made me miss Andy. I knew he couldn't have represented me, but he would have been able to advise me and even help me find another attorney to help. After my review hearing in 2006, I didn't believe that

PRBs would actually lead to my release. I'd seen so many detainees released without even a hearing, or a trial, or a review. They were just sent home. I knew brothers who'd been cleared for release in 2006 and 2009 but were still here, with no special privileges, as if they were still considered terrorists.

Shasha insisted I begin preparing for the PRB, even though I didn't have a hearing scheduled. An important part of that preparation was continuing my studies. I started studying to take my GED and began a new class Shasha taught on starting a business. Shasha had me update the business plan for the Yemen Milk and Honey Cooperative again with new artwork and resources. We also worked on a personal statement about what I wanted to do when I was released and how I would live my life after Guantánamo. Shasha was meticulous in his preparations and made me work hard writing and rewriting everything until it was perfect.

Then he insisted I write to his attorney and ask him to represent me. I knew I would need another attorney, but it couldn't be just anyone. Shasha said his attorney was the best attorney working at Guantánamo. I was hesitant, but I wrote the letter anyway, and his attorney agreed to represent me.

We met during his next visit to Guantánamo and it was a difficult meeting. I could tell right away it wasn't going to work. He didn't see me, Mansoor. He saw only 441 and what my file said about me or maybe what other detainees and the camp admin saw in me. After that first meeting, we met a couple more times, only briefly, and I just knew it wasn't going to work out. I was okay with that. I felt like my time was coming and that I would be released, but not with this attorney. I can't explain why I knew that—I just did. I felt it in my heart, but I needed a lawyer who would see me—not an accused al Qaeda general, not an enemy combatant, not a troublemaker fighting the camp admin—just me, the person I had grown up to be.

WHEN I WAS told I had another appointment with the FBI, I thought, *Nothing good can come from this.* I was surprised and scared. They brought me to one of the nice rooms reserved for important meetings. They shackled me to my chair, then two FBI agents came in with several high-ranking military intelligence officers, army officers, and a New York City prosecutor. They also had a very pretty Iraqi interpreter. They were nice but serious about why they had come to see me.

The FBI agents read through my file in front of me. They called me Adel, referring to the Egyptian general, and I thought, *This isn't good.*

I told them I didn't want the interpreter to translate for me, I was okay talking in English. This was an important conversation, and I didn't want anything to get lost in translation.

They took out a pile of photos and asked me to look through them to see if I recognized one man in particular, a man they called Sulaiman Abu Ghaith, who they said became the spokesman for al Qaeda after the attacks of September 11. They had extradited him to New York City for trial and were convinced I knew who he was and could identify him. They talked about me as if I were Adel and said that Abu Ghaith had been at al Farouq and other places in Afghanistan that Adel had been, and if I was Adel, I should know him. But I didn't know him and I told them that. They kept pressing me. They kept talking about all the things interrogators had written about me in my file, trying to intimidate me, and for a while I was worried.

"We want you to testify against him," the prosecutor finally said. Now I understood the real reason I was moved to Camp Echo. They wanted me to say that I knew him and that he was close to Osama bin Laden. They wanted me to be a witness.

I couldn't believe I was going through all this again after so many years. The prosecutor told me that they'd fly me to New York City, where I would appear in court. In exchange for my cooperation, they would relocate me to a Western European country, where I'd get citizenship, a generous house, a college education, a car, and $150,000. They said they would relocate my mother, my father, and my youngest siblings there, too. I would disappear so that no one would ever be able to find me and that I would be safe. I'd heard brothers talk about such deals but I always thought they were fake.

Believe me, I wanted all those things. I wanted to be free and to see my family. I had left my home when I was thirteen so that I could get an education and one day take care of my mother and father when they were older. This was my dream, the dream that had first brought me to Sana'a and then to Afghanistan. And in exchange for all this, all I had to do was identify a man I didn't know.

"I cannot," I said. I couldn't lie. It's forbidden in Islam. It's against everything that I fought for. It's against everything that I am.

I told them again I didn't know the man and that I couldn't identify in court a man I had never met. I looked across the table at my file and all the photos they had, and I remembered the interrogations, the torture, the years of beatings that they put us through trying to get us to name other men, identify people, give them intelligence we didn't have. Now they wanted me to do that for a price. No. I couldn't, not even for everything they offered me.

"You seem like a sophisticated man," the prosecutor said.

"Yes," I said. "That's why I can't do this no matter what you offer me."

I knew I could be punished for refusing to testify, but I couldn't lie about a man and determine his fate.

I went back to my cell, and soon I was visited by a brother I knew and trusted. He was very nice to me and very respectful. The prosecutor and camp admin had sent him to talk to me.

"Mansoor," he said. "You should take the deal. This man's fate is already sealed. He is going to be convicted no matter what, even without your testimony. They will never release him. Ever. You should at least make a right out of a wrong."

I had lost so much at Guantánamo, but in all those years, I prided myself on being honest, never snitching on brothers, never agreeing to lie for interrogators no matter the cost to me. I had made it thirteen years and still had not lost my integrity. Why did they think I would lose it now? I had found myself again and I wouldn't let go.

I stayed in Camp Echo for a few more months with Shasha. I studied hard for my GED and I passed. I finished a good draft of my personal statement with Shasha. During that time, the FBI tried twice more to get me to testify. Each time, I refused.

After that, the colonel tried to move me to Camp VI, but I refused. None of us would go back after what they had destroyed. It would have been too painful remembering what they'd taken away. When he came to talk to me, I told him I'd go on hunger strike again if he made me move there. The colonel was a tough guy. He didn't care about whatever history we had with Camp VI, but he also didn't want trouble with me.

So he moved me to Camp V Delta, where Omar, Khalid, Hamzah, and Zakaria lived on the lower level. I was sorry to have left Shasha at Camp Echo, but I was happy to be back with my brothers in communal living.

- TWENTY-FIVE -

In the early years of our uncertain detention, we teased each other about how long we would be there, imagining the worst. We'd say things like, "I think the Americans will keep us here until we become old men with no teeth." Or, "We should put in requests now for wheelchairs. By the time interrogators and camp admin approve them, we'll need them."

There was almost always a bitter truth to our jokes. After thirteen years, some brothers couldn't walk anymore, and they did need wheelchairs and walkers. Some had lost most of their teeth and now had dentures. I'd had many teeth removed; the years without toothbrushes and toothpaste caught up with me. I had to start wearing glasses—the harsh light from eight years of solitary confinement had damaged my eyes badly. Many of us suffered from high blood pressure, diabetes, and high cholesterol. This scared me.

I wasn't worried just about my body. Life in prison was like having your hard drive slowly erased. The longer you stayed, the more your memories were overwritten with new ones. It was a battle we all fought. I talked to my family every three or four months and that helped me remember. They sent me letters with news and that helped, too. But I looked for something more than I got from the news or phone calls or meetings with attorneys—an emotional bond with the outside world that had been taken away from us. I found that connection in stolen moments with the natural world, like with my dear friend the sea. He had a magic power that healed me and took away some of my sadness. I could tell the sea anything, and he would keep it and carry it away.

We all loved the sea, and catching just a glimpse of our friend made us happy and calm. From the upper level of Camp V Delta, some of my brothers had a view of the sea. Anytime I felt hopeless or lost, I went to one of those brothers and asked to look out their window. I said to the sea, "Nice to see you again, my friend. People change, but you never do." Sometimes I spent an hour or more just staring out at my friend, lost in my memories. It transported me to the beaches in Hudaydah and the carefree happiness I'd felt as a child. In my mind, I could throw myself into the waves and try to wash away the difficult life I'd lived at Guantánamo. It always made me feel better.

I also went for long walks around the rec yard, where we could see the open sky and catch glimpses of the hills beyond the fence. One day, I found myself walking in the yard, completely lost in my own thoughts. This happened to all of us—we called it being in our "nowhere." I was in my nowhere when I heard a dog howl in the distance. That single sound snatched me away from Guantánamo and dropped me on the rocky mountain trails of Raymah, walking through a reclaimed memory. I smelled the coffee plants. I felt the chill of morning frost. I was with my father hunting the fox that had been eating our chickens. Samra, our dog, was ahead of us—she had something to prove. My father had accused her of not taking her job seriously, and she felt guilty. We followed the fox's trail of chicken feathers to a gathering of thick bushes. Samra quickly flushed the fox out and cornered her. But my father didn't shoot the fox. He saw that she was pregnant.

"I can't kill a pregnant fox," he said.

I really liked the fox; she looked so innocent and helpless with her big belly.

"It's forbidden to kill a pregnant animal," my father said.

"Papa," I said. "Won't she keep killing our chickens?"

My father scratched his beard. He put his rifle down and went to the frightened fox and held her very tightly. He looked very seriously right into the fox's eyes and yelled, "DON'T COME BACK!" I was afraid of that serious look. Then he set the fox free. "Samra," he said, "get her!" Samra launched after the fox, which ran as hard as she could and disappeared up the mountain. My father called Samra back. The fox had accepted the deal.

"We all want the same thing," my father said. "To live and to survive."

Samra came back to my father, barking and jumping, she was so proud of herself.

The dog was still howling off in the distance when Omar tapped my shoulder and asked if I was okay. My heart ached when I realized where I was again. I stood still, listening as if Samra were off in the distance. My father's words were simple and basic, a reflection of another life and another time. I had carried his words close to my heart for all these years, fighting, protesting, resisting for myself and my brothers so that we could live like humans and survive. We survived, but at what cost? I had spent almost half my life detained for being someone I was not.

The dog's beautiful bark faded into the early evening air. I remembered my father's serious look and how afraid it made me as a child. As a man, I wanted nothing more than to see it once more.

That night I had a dream that I met a woman in a navy uniform in one of the Camp Echo meeting cages. I'd never seen this woman before, but I felt like I knew her in my dream and that she was there to help me. I woke up startled by what I felt and what my dream had told me, that I would get a Periodic Review Board notification soon, and that my personal representative, the person assigned to detainees to prepare for the PRB, would be a woman. If this happened—if I got a female PR—I would get released soon. I just felt it after that dream.

IT WAS SPRING of 2015 and many brothers were getting PRB hearing notifications, and brothers like Hamzah and Sabri, who had been cleared years ago, were released. Everything was moving quickly now. Even the Yemeni brothers who had been approved for release years ago but couldn't be released to Yemen were now meeting with delegations from host countries about relocation. Days after my dream, I was told that I'd been assigned a PR, the first step in getting a PRB hearing. It was hard to balance how I felt. Deep down, I just knew that my time was coming, but all those years at Guantánamo told me to expect the worst. For thirteen years, every time I'd had any hope that things would improve or that we would be released, the camp admin crashed down on me and made our lives miserable.

Guards came for me and escorted me back to Camp Echo, where all the PRB and attorney meetings took place. When guards opened the door and I saw my PR, I stood up laughing, shaking my head. A woman in a navy uniform walked in, just like in my dream. She was a lieutenant colonel and everyone called her Militia. She had short brown hair and eyes that matched and a kindness to her that said she really cared about my hearing.

"I've been expecting you," I said. When she sat down, I told her about my dream and this made her happy.

I'd always had my doubts about hearings, but my meeting with Militia made me feel that the PRB could be different. I still didn't want to get my hopes too high.

Militia explained that she wasn't an attorney and that the PRB wasn't a trial; it was a hearing to determine if I was still a threat to the United States or any of its interests. Unlike the habeas corpus filings, this hearing wasn't about whether or not I had been detained unlawfully or if I'd committed any war crimes or if I was a terrorist.

"You have to make them like you," Militia said. "That's all."

"This sounds a lot like *The Hunger Games*," I said.

She laughed, and I added, "You're like my Haymitch when Katniss got to the Capitol. He told her that she had to make them like her if she wanted to survive in the arena."

Guantánamo was my arena. I had to survive the Americans' game design to get out, which involved being called a "terrorist," "the worst of the worst," a "suspected terrorist," and a "low-level threat." If I passed all these, I could finally just be me again. As Haymitch told Katniss, I had to just go through it to get through it.

We laughed a little about this, but she said that sounded strangely right.

When I thought more about it, I asked myself what had changed to move me from one game to the next. I felt like I was still the same person, but I had survived a lot and now I had different ways to tell the Americans about my frustration and fear. Over the last five years, English had opened up a new world for me that I was glad I experienced. I felt like I knew how to talk the language of the PRB now. I was still the same Mansoor, but I was different. I knew I wasn't a threat to the United States, and now I knew how to show that to them. All I had to do was be myself.

Militia told me that I didn't need a personal attorney to represent me, but that most detainees had them. I still had federal public defenders working on my habeas corpus case, but they couldn't also work on my PRB. I'd never understand Americans. They gave me lawyers, and now, when I really needed them, they weren't allowed to work for me. I wondered what Andy would do if he were still alive. Militia told me she knew of a lawyer who had been representing detainees for years and was supposed to be one of the best working at Guantánamo. Her name was Beth Jacob. I needed a woman as my lawyer, not another man. I'd seen a lot of American men in my fourteen years and learned that American women are more qualified and dedicated than the men. They took things more seriously. And at this point, I needed the best.

The more I asked around about Beth Jacob, the more I liked her. One of the brothers she represented had been cleared for release and was leaving for Oman soon. He said she was one of the kindest and most dedicated attorneys at Guantánamo. Brothers called her *Um Al Muatakaleen,* or Mother of Detainees. Militia wrote to her and then I wrote to her, too, asking if she would represent me. By this time, many of the attorneys who'd represented detainees had stopped. Some gave up, some left, some just stopped responding to their clients' letters. Only a handful still came regularly. A lot of brothers were looking for attorneys to help them with their PRBs.

But Beth responded quickly to my letter—she agreed to represent me and said she'd like to meet me the next time she visited Guantánamo. Only a few weeks after getting Militia as my PR, now I had Beth Jacob. Soon after that, I got my PRB notification for a hearing. For once, everything was coming together.

The first time I met Beth wasn't dramatic like when I met Andy. She was with another attorney from her office and they both came into the room wearing head scarves. Beth had coffee from McDonald's and some candy. I'd learn that she always brought coffee and sweets. I was happy to meet her from the very first minute and not because of the coffee. She was a petite woman, like my mother. And like my mother, she had kind but firm eyes and a fierce presence. She was tough, I could tell. I stood up and welcomed them with my biggest smile.

"Please," I said, "I appreciate you covering your hair, but you don't have to do that on my account. Only wear them if you want to or if they make you more comfortable."

They took off their head scarves and we got to the business of my PRB. I gave Beth the statement I'd written with Shasha; it was long, maybe twenty pages. She said she would help me shorten it. I talked about all the classes I'd taken and how I'd gotten my GED and how Andy had applied to colleges for me but the camp admin wouldn't approve it. She listened carefully, took notes, and I could tell she felt at ease with me.

I had already heard a lot about Beth from other brothers, but I wanted to know why she agreed to represent me and other detainees. She didn't have to think about it at all.

"It's my job!" she said. "As a lawyer, it's my job to defend people regardless of who they are. I take that very seriously. I'm here to defend the rights I think our Founding Fathers wrote into the Constitution, rights I think our country was founded on. Rights that you have and that have been violated by keeping you here." She was firm when she talked and I liked that. I saw that she was a woman of integrity and that she wasn't taking my case to be famous or to say that she was defending detainees at Guantánamo. What she said moved me. She really believed in what she was doing. She really cared. Beth and Militia and all the others working with us saw that Guantánamo was wrong and against the values they thought America was about. They fought to fix the mistakes made by others.

I felt really good about my PRB. "I think I got the best attorney in the world today," I said. I called her Aunt Beth.

Right away Aunt Beth had a strategy. She wanted to show the PRB who I was now and how hard I'd worked to learn English, get an education, and plan for life after Guantánamo. She saw who I was and wanted to show the PRB what kind of life I would have after I was released. We only had two months to prepare.

"We have a lot of work to do," she said.

"Relax," I said. "I know it's my time—I can't explain it, but I just know."

"Nothing is ever certain here," Aunt Beth said.

She was right. Nothing at Guantánamo was ever certain, but I had the perfect PRB team, and they were all women, just like my dream had said.

My attorneys worked hard preparing. Aunt Beth helped me revise my statement down to a few very powerful pages that showed all the classes I had taken, all the subjects I'd learned on my own, the business classes I'd taken with Shasha, the books I'd read, and all the computer programs I'd learned. I wrote about how I taught brothers English, Arabic, math, and all about computers, and that I even translated between guards and detainees. I wrote about my family and how I wanted to be able to take care of my mother and father, and even how I'd read books about raising children so that I could give my sister advice. (I wrote her a sixty-page letter that really opened her eyes.) I talked about how someone in my family tried to arrange a marriage between his daughter and me, but that I declined because I didn't know anything about her or what she thought of me. I wanted to marry and start a family, but I wanted to do it with an educated and lovely woman who could be my friend and partner. Together, we would create a happy family rooted in education. I liked the guy in the statement. I thought Haymitch would be proud.

We collected testimonials from my teachers at Guantánamo. We got a copy of my GED test and my business plan for the Yemen Milk and Honey Cooperative. Even Andy Hart's family wrote a letter on my behalf. They said I had become a model detainee who was curious and kind. Several of the brothers who were suspected of being high-up al Qaeda offered to write letters on my behalf saying that they had never seen me in Afghanistan, they didn't know me before Guantánamo, and they were certain I wasn't al Qaeda.

While we worked on all this, Aunt Beth treated me like family. The more we met and I got to know her, the more I liked and admired her. She visited Guantánamo often because of all her clients, and when she did, she always brought me things I needed or that other brothers requested through me. She was very generous and never said no to anything. She sent me a book on IT and tried to send another book on American history, but the camp admin confiscated it. I guess they didn't want me to know America's secrets. One of my favorite gifts was a CD Aunt Beth brought me of Dr. Martin Luther King Jr.'s speeches. She also sent movies and music that brothers wanted for our library, like Taylor Swift and Shakira. She didn't mind that I was always asking her to send more things like sweets, spices, creamer, and other stuff we didn't have so that I could share it all with the brothers on my block. I knew that she spent a lot of her own money and I really appreciated her kindness. I promised that one day I would pay her back and return the favor. Until then, I made her my special coffee and brought her sweets.

"How did you get coffee through security?" she cried the first time I did it.

"It's classified," I said.

My coffee was the best in the camp. I used the coffee my mother sent me from Yemen and mixed it with cardamom, a little cinnamon, some sugar, and creamer. Just smelling it would make your heart race.

Then one day, Aunt Beth showed up with a special surprise. She turned on the TV and played a video she had brought. Right there in our meeting room was my village in Raymah! My brother had sent her video clips he'd recorded on his phone asking everyone in my village and our tribe to say something about me. There was my elementary school teacher saying how smart I was and how I always got the best marks in class. There was my old neighbor saying that I had always been such a good kid, helping out with the goats. There was an old friend saying how curious I was, and always full of energy. There were my cousins saying how much they missed me . . . There were dozens of people all talking about me, saying hi, sending me their love from thousands of miles away. But the best part was seeing my father talk about me with a powerful sense of pride. I felt my home and their love deep in my chest, and I cried. I couldn't help it. For more than an hour we watched all these people from my life I thought I had lost forever. I couldn't believe everyone remembered me.

"I think this will make a great impression at the PRB," Aunt Beth said. She watched with me and smiled. "We can't use it all, but we'll make a transcript, and we can show the clips you think are the most important."

By the day of my PRB, my overall legal team had grown. I had another PR, a very nice air force colonel who called himself Knight; plus Claire and Cathi, two federal public defenders from Andy's office who wanted to help; and Annie from Aunt Beth's office.

"I dreamed that I only needed one navy woman to win my freedom in the PRB," I said. "Now I have five! I think I've already won."

Only Knight and Aunt Beth went with me into my PRB. We were really prepared and I felt good about my case. We submitted over 180 pages of supporting documents along with a sample of the video clips from my brother. We all knew what we had to do. We all had our prepared statements.

We were led into a large room with a big conference table and fancy chairs for me and my team. On the wall in front of us, between two American flags, was a row of TV screens. Knight, Aunt Beth, and I sat at the table facing the wall of screens. The members of the Periodic Review Board would be attending remotely, from where I didn't know, maybe Washington, DC. The panel would have officials from the Departments of Defense, Homeland Security, Justice, and State; the Joint Chiefs of Staff; and the Office of the Director of National Intelligence. The head of the board for my hearing was a very nice woman.

I took a deep breath—all I had to do was make them like me.

It all went very fast, like a dream or a TV show. Knight made his statement, then Aunt Beth made hers, then I made mine. I looked at the screens when I talked and imagined I was making eye contact with the representatives somewhere on the other side of the camera. They asked me some questions about the early years of Guantánamo, and I admitted that I'd behaved badly. I didn't agree with it, but I knew what I had to do. I was confident being myself. I smiled. I laughed. I charmed them and even made them laugh. I could tell they liked me.

When we were done with the formal presentation and review, I was asked to leave the room so that the panel could speak to my PRs and Aunt Beth alone. I took the opportunity to use the restroom while I waited, and I couldn't believe how nice it was. The restroom was big and clean with no cameras, and even had privacy walls for each of the toilets, which had seats. I wasn't cold or wet, and I didn't have to worry about hiding myself for privacy. It was the nicest restroom I'd seen in almost fifteen years.

When Aunt Beth and my PRs came out of the hearing room, they were smiling.

"Their decision has to be unanimous," Aunt Beth said. "But . . . I feel good."

"I'm sure I convinced them," I said. "It's my magical charm."

Now we had to wait. It would be at least a month before we heard back from the review board. I had fought fourteen years to be released. I could wait one more month.

FOURTEEN YEARS IS a long time to live totally isolated from the world you once knew. While we faced the same routines every day, every month, and every year, the world marched on and got more sophisticated. Smartphones. Social media. Video calling. This world scared me. Would I be able to adjust to a life on the outside when I was released? Would I find a wife? Would Guantánamo follow me wherever I went?

When I looked in the mirror, I couldn't help feeling a little sorry for myself. The hair on my head was graying and so was my beard. I had grown into a man physically, but in some ways, time had frozen for me. I had never felt the sweetness of love or the accomplishment of finishing my studies. This hadn't just happened to me; it happened to all of us, each in our own ways. And then there was the unseen and even unknown damage we suffered from so many years of solitary confinement, bright lights, torture, hunger strikes, and punishment. We had PTSD. We couldn't focus. We got terrible headaches. Our bodies were breaking down. I worried our scars wouldn't heal and go away, even when we were released.

I was watching TV one day and saw a report about women in India who had their faces splashed with acid. My mind went crazy. I called those men every name I could think of. I cried. How could somebody commit such hideous crimes? When I saw Aunt Beth again, I talked about it with her and told her that if I were in power, I would punish those guys by splashing them with acid.

I couldn't stop thinking about it. Then I said to her, "The US government did the same thing to my life. But instead of being physically deformed, it's here." I pointed to my head, then to my heart. "And I'm the only one who can see it."

Like Andy, Aunt Beth encouraged me to write it all down, and that's what I did. While I waited for the PRB decision, I spent my days in the classroom, writing. I'd figured out a way to make my own stationery with an official clearance stamp at the top of the page. I wrote with my legs chained to the floor while blocking what I wrote from the overhead cameras. I kept what I wrote in legal envelopes in a file box so that the camp admin couldn't find it and take it away again. There was a nice female army guard who was new and really liked reading my stories. I made her Yemeni coffee and she brought me pens. And that's how I rewrote the next draft of my book. Every chance I got, I sent big chunks to Aunt Beth through legal mail.

I had lots of new material. In Camp V, Omar and I had decided to rewrite the books the camp admin had taken away from me in the lockdown. I saw the book in my head and just needed to write it down. I wanted to tell more stories this time. I wanted to collect stories from all the brothers who were still here, so I went around begging brothers to tell me about their lives again. I even washed brothers' clothes and cleaned their cells in exchange for stories.

"Mansoor has gone crazy," one brother observed.

Some detainees thought I was working for the CIA. Some of the older brothers made fun of me for thinking that a young guy like me could tell such a complicated story like Guantánamo. I didn't care. Once I set my mind to something, I was like that young Mansoor herding goats with my sister, holding on to the rope and refusing to let go.

"I'm not asking for secrets," I told the detainees who thought I was working for the CIA. "I'm not working for anyone. I'm working for me, for you, and for everyone to write the history of what happened to us here. We're going to leave here one day, and when we leave, I don't know if we'll ever see each other again to talk about these stories. If we don't capture them now, others might try to do it later without us. Why should other people write our history? We must write our history! So let us write it ourselves."

I knew we had to tell these stories. I would make sure they got out of this place, even if we all didn't.

ALMOST EXACTLY ONE month after my PRB, I was called to a meeting in Building 7, where I'd had my hearing. I was brought into a room where Colonel Knight was waiting for me. Militia had been reassigned to someone else. I knew I was going to get good news, but I couldn't escape a little part of me deep down that worried. This was Guantánamo, and nothing was ever certain.

We waited a couple of minutes for Aunt Beth to call in, so that we could all hear the PRB's decision together. These were the longest minutes of my entire life.

Then Aunt Beth got on the call and we were told right away that I'd been cleared for release. Allahu Akbar! I knew it! I'm very

good at interpreting dreams. Thank you, Militia! Thank you, Aunt
Beth! Thank you, Annie and Claire and Cathi! Thank you, women of
America!

Knight read the determination out loud to us: "The Periodic
Review Board, by consensus, determined that continued law of war
detention of the detainee is no longer necessary . . ." He read the
rest of the determination and ended with the PRB's recommenda-
tion that my resettlement location include a special provision for
the opportunity to pursue my higher education.

In that moment, I felt light again, light with hope. I was so happy,
but my mind had already moved on to the next question: Where
would I be placed?

Aunt Beth and Colonel Knight congratulated me and told me I
deserved to be cleared.

I didn't want to boast, but I did.

"See, Aunt Beth," I said. "I knew I would get cleared."

After we got off the phone with Aunt Beth, Colonel Knight left
the room and a navy captain came in. He sat down and congratulated
me and then got very serious. I thought something was wrong.

"The US government will never say what I'm going to say," he
said. "But I feel like you deserve to hear this." He was quiet a minute.
"I'm sorry you were detained like this for so many years. It was a mistake, a pretty clear mistake, that you should never have been here."

I knew it wasn't official, but what that navy captain said to me
meant a lot. Nothing could make up for the years I'd lost and what
had been done to me, but this was a start.

Now the difficult part would begin. I would need to be relocated
and start my life in a new place away from my family in Yemen.

FROM THE VERY beginning, the Yemeni government never cared
that any of its citizens were at Guantánamo. While other governments

had sent delegations to meet their citizens, Yemen didn't until 2003, and when they did come, they didn't even meet with me. They didn't tell our families we were here, and in fact, Ali Abdullah Saleh, the president of Yemen, said he wouldn't take any Yemeni detainees unless the United States gave him $400 million. But now Saleh was gone and there was a civil war in Yemen and it was too dangerous for me to go home. I felt like an orphan left in the street, wailing, looking for a country to adopt me. I didn't know where I would go.

I really wanted to go to Qatar. It was the closest country to Yemen and I had family there. I knew the Qatari people were nice and that they had the best education system out of all the Arab countries. I wanted to go to college, study IT, and start a family, and Qatar was the best place to go. But I wasn't the one to decide.

Host delegations came and went, called brothers to meetings, and then invited them to relocate to their countries. Our lawyers told us that the Guantánamo resettlement program was giving host countries millions of dollars for rehabilitation. Italy, Oman, Ireland, Ghana, Montenegro—they all came and I never got an invitation to meet them. It was 2016 now and I had been cleared for release for months and still I had no idea where I would go.

As brothers left, we followed them on the news when we could and some of us exchanged letters, even though we weren't supposed to. Brothers who were placed in Western European countries or places like Oman were treated well. They were given generous stipends and homes and were able to move on with their lives. But the stories coming from Eastern Europe and the former Soviet Union, places like Slovakia, Albania, and Kazakhstan, scared me. We got news that Hamzah was hospitalized after being beaten badly by counter-terrorist forces who raided his home. Another brother was thrown to the street and didn't have a place to live. In Albania, where Uyghur brothers were sent, the government beat them, forced them to shave their beards, and put them in a refugee camp. They had to protest in front of the US embassy just to improve their situation. Those brothers had no legal status or even IDs of any kind. In Kazakhstan, our brother Asim Thabit al-Khalaqi died after the government refused to give him medical care for a kidney condition. It was like being sent to another Guantánamo, where the United States could turn its back while brothers were beaten or killed. We even heard that brothers who were located in the UAE had disappeared completely with no contact with their lawyers, families, or even the Red Cross.

This scared us all. None of us wanted to end up in prison again. None of us wanted to be tortured again or beaten. None of us wanted to go to countries from the old Communist regime.

I wish I could say that my story at Guantánamo ends with a wonderful placement to Qatar, where I know I'll be given a house and a stipend, and encouraged to get my bachelor's degree in information technology. I wish I could tell you it ends with a smart and lovely wife and a house full of children. But I can't. Allah had another plan for me.

The only delegation the detainee relocation department arranged for me to meet was the Serbians. I refused to meet with them at first, but I was told that if I didn't meet with them, I wouldn't get to meet with anyone else. One of the delegates was a really tall woman who asked me what I knew about Serbia. I was honest.

"I'm afraid I know a lot about your history killing many Muslims," I said. "And that worries me."

She didn't like that. But she said she liked my honesty. She told me about their wars and said it wasn't unlike other countries that had civil wars and that there were still Muslims in Serbia. We only met for about thirty minutes. I told her about my studies and how I planned to finish my college education. I told her I wanted to get married and start a family.

"We have good colleges for computer science, and we can help you finish." She said they would give me an apartment and help me get started. "We aren't going to throw you to the street," she said. "You'll be treated like a Serbian citizen except that you won't be able to vote."

"If I could vote," I said, "I'd elect myself president of Serbia."

She laughed and then talked some more about what life would be like in Serbia, then she said very casually, "If we do host you and you try to leave our country, we will arrest you and put you in prison."

I really didn't like her tone. I was told by everyone at Guantánamo, even the Red Cross, that I had no choice but to leave to Serbia. They told me that if I refused, they would force me to go. There was nothing I could do to stop the relocation. If I didn't accept their offer, I was told I wouldn't get another and that I could spend the rest of my life in Guantánamo.

IN THE WEEKS before I left for Serbia, I said goodbye to Guantánamo. I walked the rec yard and the blocks and said goodbye to the cats and the iguanas and the banana rats. I said goodbye to my friend the sea and asked him to look after my brothers who stayed behind. I said goodbye to the guard towers, to Camp Echo, to Camp VI, and to Camp Delta and Camp X-Ray, grown over with weeds. I saw names and numbers scratched into walls, into showers, into doors, and I remembered those brothers. When I looked up and saw stains on the ceiling from splashing, or a broken window, I would remember exactly when that had happened. Everywhere I turned, I saw ghosts from my past giving me stories to tell.

My last night in Camp V, I was allowed to spend time with my brothers in the rec yard. These brothers had helped me through my hardest times here, but no one could help me with my situation now. It was hard leaving, but harder knowing that they would stay behind. I loved them all and wished we all could leave together. When it was time for me to leave the rec yard, we hugged and prayed for each other. As I was escorted away, my brothers sang for me one last time. They sang the song we sang to each other in Camp Delta when we were taken away to interrogation.

Go with peace, go with peace, may Allah grant you ever more peace and ever more safety. Go with peace, go with peace.

I was shipped out of Guantánamo in the same way I was shipped in: against my will, gagged, blindfolded, hooded, earmuffed, and shackled. I was loaded into the cold body of a military transport plane, chained to my chair, and flown halfway around the world to a scary place I didn't know. But that's another story, for another time.

Guantánamo, 2015

Acknowledgments

الحمدلله رب العالمين والصلاة والسلام على نبينا محمد صلى الله عليه وسلم.

All thanks and praises to Allah most of all. Without Allah's help, I would not be able to do any of this.

To my father and mother, sisters, brothers, and my entire family; I miss you so much and hope to be reunited with you one day. To my tribe and my people in Yemen, I love you all. May Allah make our lovely Yemen happy again.

To my sisters—Yumna, Huda, and Irfaanah Desai—our mother, Hafsah Mousa (Desai), our father, Nazir Desai, and the Desai family for your kindness and support.

To Beth D. Jacob, my dedicated and tireless lawyer, and to her children, Anna, Miriam, and Jeffrey Fogel, for their support and friendship.

To my good friend and first public defender Andy Hart, and to his parents, Aunt Donna and Philip Hart, for their continuing support. I miss my conversations with Andy. You are my family in the United States.

To all the lawyers who represented me and other Guantánamo prisoners, and especially to Annie Hawkins, Alka Pradhan, Ramzi

Kassem, Cori Crider, Tasnim Motala, Pardiss Kebriaei, and Shelby Sullivan-Bennis.

To the public defenders Carlos Warner, Claire Cahoon, Cathi Adinaro.

To my Guantánamo brothers without whose brotherhood, friendship, and support I would never have survived: Omar Khalifah, Bisher al-Rawi, Mohamedou Ould Slahi, Adana Farhan, Sabri al Qurashi, Fayeze Alkandary, Fouzi al Awda, Sami al-Hajj, Hisham Sliti (Hamzah al Batal), Othman al Shamrani, Boumediene Lakhdar, Abudlrahman Alghamdi, Tarek Dergoul, and Moazzam Begg for everything he has done.

To the brothers who remain detained without charges at the time of publication: our father, teacher, and mentor Saifullah Paracha, Moath al Alwi, Khalid Qasim, Suhail al Sharabi, Sharqawi, and to all the others. May Allah hasten your release.

And to the brothers who died at Guantánamo: Waddah Al Hanashi, Yasser Talal Al Zahrani, Mana'a Shaman Turki al-Habardi Al-Utaybi, Ali Abdullah Ahmed, Abdul Rahman al-Amri, Adnan Farhan Abd Al Latif, Awal Gul, Abul Razzaq Hekmati, and Hajji Nassim (Inayatullah).

To the guards, doctors, nurses, camp staff, and interpreters who saw us and treated us as human beings. To Steve Wood and Brandon Neely and other guards who have spoken out about Guantánamo. To all the teachers, especially Charlie, Nader, and Zaid, who believed in the power of education. A big thank-you to the art teacher, Adam, who helped bring a golden age to Guantánamo. And to Captain James Yee, who treated us with dignity and humanity.

Thank you to CAGE and Amnesty International for your advocacy and support. I wish to also thank Seton Hall Law School for their incredible research, and the University of California at Davis Center for the Study of Human Rights in the Americas for their Guantánamo Testimonials Project.

To my friends Enis Salihović, Stevan Tatalović, Luka Latinović, and my lawyer Petar Grozdanović for their support during my years in Serbia. And many thanks to the kind heart of Dr. Boris Prokić.

To the dean of the School of Engineering Management, Dr. Vladimir Tomašević, and all the professors and staff.

Many thanks to my brother and attorney in South Africa, Feroze Ahmed Boda, and to my friends Tahira Amatuallah and Sunny Collins. And to my intellectual property attorneys in New York, Jonathan Reichman and Jessica Cohen-Nowak.

To my friends and mentors: Ramsey Nasser, Alex Qin, Rose Parfitt, Dina Zaman, J. R. Biersmith, and Ana Djordjevic. Special thanks to Alexandra Moore and Ben Moore and their family for their continuing support and friendship.

To Sarah Geis, a good friend and generous soul who brought life to my stories for CBC and BBC Radio, and nurtured my creativity. To the radio producers who worked with Sarah: Cristal Duhaime and Mira Burt-Wintonick at CBC's *Love Me*, and Alan Hall at Falling Tree Productions, for their amazing work on the *Art of Now*. I also wish to thank Lilly Sullivan at *This American Life*, and Allia McCracken Jarre, Maha Hilal, and Latif Nasser.

To the journalists who have covered my life after Guantánamo: James Jacoby, Arun Shankar Rath, Jessica Schulberg, and Jeremy Gould. And a special thank-you to Valerie Hopkins.

And to those who shed light on Guantánamo: Carol Rosenberg, Charlie Savage, Yvonne Ridley, Scott Horton, Sebastian Köthe, Arnaud Mafille, Fatima Hamroni, Naza Amatulrazq, Jenifer Fenton, Natalia Rivera Scott, Mark Fallon, and Andy Worthington for his invaluable coverage and support.

On behalf of all my brothers, I wish to thank everyone who has worked and continues to work on behalf of Guantánamo prisoners. Thank you all from our hearts.

To Professor Erin Thompson for her dedication to bringing the Art from Guantánamo Bay exhibition to the world, and for editing my early writing.

To Sarah Mirk, Kane Lynch, Cora Currier, and the editors at *The Nib*.

To the Margolis family: Dian, Harry, and Philip. And to the late Richard J. Margolis for being an inspiration. And to Deb Bouton for believing in my work.

To the team at the Episodic: Pilot to Series Lab, for believing in our project, and particularly to Jennifer Goyne Blake for her friendship and support. And to all the fellows who welcomed and inspired me.

To Dara Kell, for her documentary short on *Art from Guantánamo Bay* and for introducing me to Antonio Aiello.

To my agent, Julia Eagleton, who believed in my book from the very beginning.

To my editor, Sam Raim, for his patience, unwavering support, and friendship, and to the entire team at Hachette for making this happen.

To Anita Merk and her team at Flyleaf Creative, for creating the book's maps.

To my friend and partner Antonio Aiello, for his patience, brotherhood, and dedication to telling my story and the story of Guantánamo. Thank you, Alison, Hazel, and Henry, for taking me into your family and putting up with our hundreds of hours of Skype calls, phone calls, and texting over so many years. I wish to share a meal with you all one day in person.

To the iguanas, especially to Princess, cats, banana rats, hummingbirds, our dear friend the sea, and even the pesky, noisy woodpeckers: I wish to thank you for your companionship and for bringing light into our lives in such a dark place as Guantánamo.

And finally, to 441, who fought so hard for my survival.

الحمدلله رب العالمين

ANTONIO AIELLO is a writer, editor, and storyteller. For many years, he was the content and editorial director of PEN America. Most recently, he was a Sundance Institute fellow in the Episodic TV Lab. He lives in Montclair, New Jersey, with his wife and children.